John Firth is 47 and lives in Wakefield. He is married to Sharon and has two sons, Ashley, aged eighteen and Luke, aged seven.

John had a glittering career in the glamorous world of cardboard packaging, where he was a Sales Manager for over ten years. When his son Luke was diagnosed with Autism, he resigned his position to give the care and support that their son desperately needed.

He was not the sort of person to sit around doing nothing however, so he started up a plumbing business that is now flourishing.

What precious spare time that he has is taken up by writing and obviously following Sheffield Wednesday, which is a huge passion in his life. He also has a pilots license and he is a part owner in a small aircraft based near York and is writing his second book.

I
HATE
FOOTBALL

JOHN FIRTH

peakpublish

Peakpublish
An imprint of Peak Platform
Hassop Station
Bakewell
Derbyshire
DE45 1NW

First published by Peakpublish 2009

Printed in England

A CIP catalogue record for this book is available from the
British Library

ISBN: 978-1-907219-02-3
www.peakpublish.com

Dedication

This book is dedicated to my family
who I love so much.

It is for my wonderful wife,
who accepts even though she
doesn't understand.

It is for all Wednesday supporters
that truly appreciate what
suffering means,
but most of all it is for
my brothers
with whom I have shared
the total extremes
of despair and
complete and utter joy.

Acknowledgements and Thanks

A very big thank you to everyone
involved in this project,
particularly to Sheffield Newspapers,
Sheffield Wednesday and Steve Ellis
for kindly allowing me permission to
reproduce their images.
Thanks also to Alan for always being there
through thick and thin,
Ian for creativity and patience.
All at Peak Publish for believing in me.
Robert for all the good times,
Scott and Ethan in the rain!
Lee and Nick for giving the club back
to the fans when all seemed lost.
Billy Bremner and Dave Mackay
for saving the day.
Ian Orange and Chris Coley for the cover design.

INDEX

Foreword

I hate football. I can't tell you how sodding pissed off I am. I have wasted hours travelling to this and for what? I have spent my hard earned money coming to a game that I couldn't really afford to go to and am rewarded by this shambolic performance. My sad excuse for a team are losing again, the minutes are quickly slipping by and I am wondering why I bother. Why do I put myself through this? What is the point of it? Yet, you get sucked into it. You are told that it is in your blood, a passion like no other. You've got to be joking. Where is the passion in this! I'm freezing cold. I'm soaked to the skin and been herded into a cattle pen along with another 2,000 or so sad souls. Some are stood complaining and being abusive, some defiantly singing in their delirium, but mostly quiet like me.

Lost in their own thoughts. Surveying their lives.

My thoughts have moved away from the match, because it is pretty damn dull. Instead I'm thinking that I hate my job.

God, is this what life is really about? Working in a job that you don't like all week, just to stand out in the cold and wet, treated like a criminal and feeling miserable......but then I am rudely jolted away from my thoughts by a crack to the head. A can of cola whacks me on the back of the head. Bemused, I look round and see someone apologising. There had been some nasty banter between a group of fans to my right and a guy just in front of me. The guy in front had been mouthing off about how crap we are all afternoon and the group to the right didn't like it.

The can was aimed at the moaner but instead it hit me. People all around are now getting pissed off and you could sense that a fight between groups of fellow supporters was brewing............but then......... YEEEEEEEEEEEESSSSS! Suddenly my world is turned on its head! Everything in life is suddenly fantastic. I am screaming, laughing, jumping for joy, and hugging a total stranger next to me. My brother jumps on top of me squeezing the life out of me and screaming in my ear.

What the hell has happened to turn my view of the world so radically in an instant?

A late, late goal at QPR to earn a draw.

As only a real football supporter can ever understand. The simple act of kicking a ball between two sticks can drastically change your view of everything in the world.

The group of lads mouthing off at each other earlier are suddenly embracing and apologising and I get a kiss on the head and another apology from the guy who threw the can. We are all singing as loud as we possibly can. Goading our rivals in the next stand. Calling our team the best in the world! Ridiculous isn't it. Grown men singing ridiculous songs with atrocious 'lyrics', but it's also just about the finest feeling in the world.

My team is Sheffield Wednesday. It could be anyone, but it isn't. There is only one team in the world for me. Sometimes I wish it wasn't. Sometimes I curse that I support a club that is generally mediocre and drive me to distraction. They have totally ruined so many weekends for me that I feel as though I should hate them. Sometimes we have highs, but mostly its lows, lows and more lows. Supporting Wednesday isn't easy. In fact, it is very bloody difficult and when the addiction gets inside you it is like a prison sentence. Something that you can't get out of. You are a lifer and you have to endure it, every bloody minute of it. There are good days, there are amazing days, but mostly it's heartache and pain. Something inside you commits and from then you are lost. You become irrational, you prioritise your life in ridiculous ways. I once missed one of my best friends wedding day. Why? Because Wednesday were at home and when it came to the crunch, I couldn't miss the stupid game. That decision cost me his friendship (quite rightly. Oh and of course we lost that day too) but it isn't in isolation. I have turned down jobs because it meant I may have to miss a game or two as well as upsetting friends and family many times, all because of Wednesday.

So what is it about this bloody game that gets under your skin and makes you behave so irrationally? I mean it isn't as if you know you will have a good time going to the game. Supporting an under achieving team, as I do, usually means that I am leaving the ground absolutely pissed off and having spent £40 to £50 for the privilege.

Yet there is something that gets to you, that brings you back, week after week.

I love going to the match, absolutely love it. There is an incredible feeling about people from all walks of life coming together on a Saturday afternoon for the love of the club. The anticipation as you drive down the motorway, spotting fellow supporters or rivals. Scarves proudly flying from windows.

Then, as you get nearer the tingling buzz of expectancy starts as you hear the distant noise of the crowd already in the ground. The nearer you get the more frustrating it is. We all love the big crowds, but there is also a certain resentment at the part timers who are suddenly causing the queues at the turnstiles. At this stage you just want to be in the ground. Your nerves are tingling and for a big match, such as a local derby, your stomach will be doing somersaults. Of course, the closer you get, the more densely packed the crowd becomes and in the confines of the concourse under the stands, progress becomes torturously laboured. But all the hustling and jostling of the packed crowd only builds up to the glorious feeling of suddenly walking into the wide open spaces of the stands. Your senses are instantly hit by the change from near claustrophobia to agoraphobia in a few short steps and then your senses are bombarded with new sounds, colours and smells as the beauty of the arena reveals itself before you.

You are home.

It is hard to explain, but the feeling of entering the stadium gives you a lovely warm feeling of being home and belonging. These are my people, this is my club. This is my home.

There is nothing quite like that feeling of scoring and winning and the enormous buzz and adrenalin that you get when things are good.

The love of the club does incredible things. It creates friendships, it creates hatred. It disrupts lives and it can destroy relationships. It conjures up the deepest, most passionate love and at the same time complete and utter desperation, anger and sadness. It creates feelings that outsiders find incomprehensible, yet fellow fans share and understand completely. It brings people together. It let's people be part of one, huge family and unites people through one true common bond.

Yes, they drive you crazy, yes they let you down. They fill you with rage, frustration, anger, desperation and cursed with the worst luck of any football team in the world, but they are my club. I can't help it. I'm stuck with it.

I am fiercely proud of Wednesday. It is part of my identity. It is part of who I am.

Football has changed such a lot over my life of watching Wednesday and I can't say that it has changed for the better to be honest. It is now about money. The higher you go the more money you get and the greedier the clubs and players get. The so called top clubs want a monopoly on it. In 2008 there are now four clubs that dominate English football. Manchester United, Chelsea, Arsenal and Liverpool and they will do all they can to stay there and stop anyone else getting close. Their players are virtually all foreign mercenaries, who kiss the badge when they score (do you think fans are that stupid that they believe that?) and then bugger off to the highest payer. The so called Promised Land is now full of these mercenaries whose interest in money comes before football.

A few years ago I sat down to watch the FA Cup final between Arsenal and Chelsea. It used to be a family tradition to watch the FA cup final and I can remember some amazing moments. Sunderland 1 L**ds 0 in 1973, Arsenal 2 Liverpool 1 in 1971, Man United 2 Arsenal 3 in 1979.

I even remember bits of commentary. Who can ever forget, "Keegan two, Heighway one, Liverpool three, Newcastle none."

But now it's all changed. I sat down to watch the Chelsea v Arsenal cup final in 2002, until they read the teams out and I think there were only two or three British players playing. I turned it off at that point. Don't get me wrong, I'm not xenophobic. I love to see the skills of foreign players, the different techniques and styles they have and my own club has had some amazing oversees players too. Di Canio and Carbone being the two greats that spring to mind.

But the FA Cup Final has always been about tradition and history and somehow, it has now lost that magic. I just don't like the way that money has divided the game nowadays, but I doubt that it will change. If anything it will get worse. The media is so obsessed about the 'big four' it seems the rest aren't significant anymore. Getting to the promised land of the Premiership and the £60 million it brings is all that matters. But there is still such a lot of passion and energy in the lower leagues that simply gets ignored now.

Everything that is wrong in the game today, captured in a simple poster. I am sure TV would love a Super Premiership of these four clubs, where they play each other every week. How exciting would that be!
Maybe they could build new stadiums in somewhere nice like Tahiti, so that the obscenely overpaid players could live in a better climate and maybe somebody would hopefully pull the plug on them and leave them in isolation, on the other side of the world for ever, so we could go back to proper football again. Bitter me? Nah!

I recently watched a TV programme called 'Footballs gone soft.' In a lot of ways it inspired me to write this book, as it made me realise how badly football has changed. The game is now played in sterile stadiums by obscenely overpaid pansies and it made me nostalgic to see how the game was in the 1970's. I feel sorry for youngsters watching the game now, as they will never experience the game in its heyday, with supporters mixed in together, pushing and swaying and a REAL atmosphere, played in front of honest and skilful players.

I also watched part of the Champions League final ("Champions" league, that's a laugh) in 2007 between Liverpool and AC Milan. Well I watched the last 10 minutes or so, I can't say that I found it that appealing to be honest. The first thing I saw when I switched it on, was a Milan player rolling around in agony following an innocuous challenge. The ref told him to get off, so he tried, but again went down saying it was so painful that he couldn't walk the 5 yards to the touchline. Good for the ref, he had none of it and told him to get off. He did so, hobbling terribly, only to reach the touchline and 'miraculously' recover and urgently signal to the ref that he was OK to come on.

Sadly I have noticed that this type of cheating (for that is what it is) is now commonplace. For some reason the last few seasons has seen a huge increase in the play acting in the domestic game and it is now the English players that are doing it as much as any foreign import.

I mean what is it with footballers now? These are young men in the prime of their life. Professional athletes, who do nothing except work at improving their strength, agility and stamina, yet drop to the floor like a bleeding pansy if touched.

I've seen the likes of Frank Lampard, a hard battling midfielder, go down like a big girly puff, rolling around in apparent agony under a bit of a push.

I don't particularly like Rugby, but you compare those players to footballers and it's totally embarrassing. Rugby players will absolutely batter each other, punching each other in the face, several times (and these are big guys), yet they just get on with it.

Breathe on a modern footballer and they are rolling around in agony.

Can you imagine what the likes of Dave Mackay or Billy Bremner, real honest tough players from the '60's would make of this weak play acting.

There is a famous photograph of Mackay grabbing Bremner by the throat during a match, which so sums up the character of the game from those days. I originally included it in the first version of the book but the Mirror group, who own the picture, wanted a huge sum of money to let me reproduce it here, so sadly I had to take it out. Fortunately big Dave Mackay and little Billy Bremner were really keen to help out and volunteered to recreate the shot.

"Tie yer own boot laces ya wee ginga baser."
"Get orff ma shet or al kick ya knackers off fatty."
Thousands of man hours were spent tracking down the original crowd in the background too, but sadly only Ronnie Cocksparra and his dog 'Knobber' turned up on the day. Tottenham were also asked if we could use White Hart Lane for an hour but I was told, "not to be bladdy stupid."

Players are openly conning referees and sadly the refs are either too stupid or powerless to stop them doing it.

Guys come on! Do you realise how pathetic you look!

And, one more thing. What the hell is all this dancing about after scoring a goal? What is going off there? Players can't be taking it too serious if in the moment of glory of scoring a winning goal, they suddenly all start a choreographed dance routine. For God's sake! Fans want to see passion, not Pans People. I remember Bremner scoring for L**ds many years ago in a game at Wolves and he went absolutely crazy. Screaming and shaking his fists in front of the crowd. He was so totally delighted he simply couldn't control his emotions. Compare that to 6 players standing in a line doing a breakdance routine or pretending to rock a baby to sleep, that you would get now. What is wrong with these people? What a set of bloody pansies.

Act like men for God's sake.

Any way, that's enough of me on my soapbox. I could write a whole bloody book on what's wrong with the game, but that's not what this is about.

I have thought about committing to writing some of the adventures that we have had supporting Wednesday for some time and as the game continues to change, I realised it was about time I did so.

I need to say here, that everything in this book actually happened and although I am sure that the various characters involved, will have a slightly different take on things, this is how I remember it all.

If you don't like it, write your own book.

Football has changed so much since I have been watching it and I wanted to try and capture what is was like when I first got the bug and some of the wacky things that happen when you get the fusion of young male adults, the passion of football and a large quantity of alcohol all thrown in and mixed together.

CHAPTER 1

Being Bitten

One of my earliest memories of football was from that amazing year 1966 (and no it wasn't the obvious one you are all thinking of). My first memory was the FA Cup Final. Sheffield Wednesday v Everton and at the time it didn't mean anything to me in the slightest. I know my Dad and my eldest brother got tickets for the game and went, but I can't say I was interested. The only thing I remember were that the streets were totally deserted and I was allowed to play outside on my own. I asked to be called in at the end when the winners were given the cup (for some reason) and when I went in I can remember my Mum being upset and being puzzled as to why. Of course this is Wednesday that we are talking about, so it shouldn't be any surprise whatsoever to know that they were 2-0 up and gloriously went on to lose 3-2.

For the next few years my interest in football grew and like most boys would play continuously on the road with a ball and I was taken to games, to see both Wednesday and Sheffield United, but it was always Wednesday that appealed. Having two older brothers that followed Wednesday as well was inevitably a huge influence and so it became that I was cast in blue and white.

My parents were Wednesdayites, before me, and even postponed their wedding as it coincided with a match (which Wednesday duly lost 7-2, so I'm told). I was taken to football matches a lot, probably because I pestered to go, but if I'm honest I can't say I was that bothered when I got there and was asking how long there was to go before we could go home, after about half an hour.

I was fortunate though to be taken to see Wednesday play the great, all conquering Manchester United side in 1968. United had become the first English club to win the European Cup and had a side that boasted such legends as George Best, Dennis Law and Bobby Charlton so a huge 51,000 turned out to see how Wednesday would fare. I can remember it being 2-2 within 20 minutes, before Man United then opened up a 4-2 lead and you thought they would run away with it. Amazingly, Wednesday scored a goal just before half time, to end the period at an incomprehensible 4-3. The second half started in a similar vein and it was soon 4-4. Wednesday then went on to get a fifth and go on to topple the European champions 5-4. I can remember being sat on the terrace of the South Stand and it seemed as though the whole ground was singing "We want six! We want six!"

I was sat next to my Dad, who was always very vocal at football matches and would wait for a lull in the noise of the crowd before shouting some witty and derogatory comment (Clearly this was where my brothers and I got it from in later football matches). But other than being lucky enough to be present at probably the best game that Hillsborough is ever likely to see, what I do remember is the total joy of people around me. My Dad singing and beaming all because of a football match.

The seeds were being planted......

Hillsborough was seen as a magnificent stadium in those days and hosted World Cup games and FA cup semi finals, every year. Leppings Lane is seen here for the 1972 FA cup semi final between Sunderland and Arsenal. These were the only occasions that you would see it full during the dark days of the 1970's

I was lucky that I had parents that loved football. In February 1972, Wednesday hosted Santos of Brazil in a friendly game. The great Pele and Carlos Alberto were due to play and it was a game everyone wanted to see. Bizarrely, the kick off time was 2.30 on a Wednesday afternoon, which meant it was school time.(I think this was due to ongoing power strikes, but can't say for sure). I can remember all the kids talking about it and the rumour was that school would be closed for the afternoon, so people could see Pele. My parents wrote to school, along with quite a few others, asking for young John to be excused school for the afternoon, but the resounding reply to all was an emphatic NO. It was deemed inappropriate for children to miss school for a football match and warning parents that there would be repercussions should children miss school.

All of my friends were at school that day.

I went to the match and saw Pele (Wednesday lost 2-0 for the record.)

The great Pele at Hillsborough, being treated with the utmost respect from Wednesday players, Dave Clements and Peter Rodrigues. Clements is just about to slam Pele's head into the desk as he innocently signs autographs. How the great man laughed about it after!

I am embarrassed to say that I had a small flirtation with Liverpool in the late 1960's and early 1970's (which is ironic as they are one of the clubs that I seriously hate now) and can remember them beating Everton in the 1971 FA Cup semi final 2-1 and being overwhelmed in disbelief and crying for joy because they had got to the final. The football bug was getting under my skin.

It was round this time though that I was starting to grow up in football terms. I started to actually support my team, rather than a team that was successful. I think that it is OK for kids to support the successful teams but there comes a time when you have to support your REAL team. This is mostly your local team, or team supported by your family, but what I really can't abide and I think most real fans will agree with me here, are the glory hunters. I find it amazing that adults support the likes of Man Utd and Liverpool. I see grown men with a Liverpool top on walking in places such as Wakefield and Lincoln and I just think, "you absolute w*nker." What the hell is wrong with these people!! Granted there will be some people that genuinely do follow them because they are actually from Liverpool, but most are just glory hunters who follow them because they win things. Grow up you tossers!

As if proof were needed you now see people with Chelsea shirts! You would never see a Chelsea shirt a few years ago in the North of England but hey presto, Abramovic comes along with his millions, buys a few trophies and miraculously they appear!

Even more bizarre is seeing people in LA Galaxy shirts! What the hell is that about? I swear I saw a guy in his late 20's in a Galaxy shirt walking round Ikea recently! Just because David Beckham has signed for them. No one had even heard of them last year. What is wrong with people?

If a club like Macclesfield suddenly had millions and millions thrown at them and went on to win the title and European glory, you know what, there would be loads of people who would suddenly appear in Silkmen shirts....."Oh yes, I've always followed Mac...no, I know I have no connections with Macclesfield, but I have always followed them..."

Yeah, whatever.

Anyway rant over. That's human nature I guess, but just for the record if any glory hunters ever read this... All REAL football fans absolutely despise you!!

From the highs of 1966, my club started its wondrous slide down the league and curiously the further they slid the more I got hooked.

5

Wednesday were relegated from the First Division in 1970 in a style that sadly befits Wednesday. They needed to beat mid table Manchester City at home on the last match of the season. It was a night game that had been re-arranged after an earlier postponement. Sunderland were already relegated and Crystal Palace hung on perilously, having finished all their fixtures and two points better off than Wednesday. All we had to do was win the last game and we would survive on goal average. (Although this scenario would have been wholly avoidable had the team picked up more than the one point from the previous five games)

Manager Danny Williams asked for "One last supreme effort tonight". He told the fans that if you give us your support "The boys will do the rest." The story goes that Man City did just about everything in their power to give Wednesday the game but we were unable to take the chance and a solo performance by City player Ian Bowyer condemned Wednesday to defeat, relegation and a bitter slide down the leagues.

Perversely enough it was at this point that I became a lot more interested in football. My first real season was 1972 - 1973 when there was a real buzz about the place. Our hated rivals Sheffield United, or the 'pigs', as they are known to Wednesdayites, were in their golden period having being promoted to the First Division, the season following Wednesdays relegation and it was important locally to get back to where we belonged.

The first two seasons in Division 2 were very disappointing to say the least, finishing in the bottom half on both occasions, the latter being another relegation scrap. But as I became more hooked, I grew to idolise players like Brian Joicey, Mick Prendergast and Tommy Craig. They seemed like world beaters to me and I couldn't understand how we didn't win the league every year.

*Tommy Craig bangs in a 75th minute penalty in a 1-0 win
against Preston North End in 1972*

But for the 1972 -73 season there was a new optimism. Advertising leaflets were sent out asking for support as this was the season of promotion. Back to the first division where we belonged.

The soft toy Owl was enough to get the crowds flocking to Hillsborough. Marketing at it's finest.

The season started well and the return of Peter Swan from his 8 year ban and the elegant Peter Eustace to midfield, coupled with the wonderful new signing Willie Henderson from Glasgow Rangers gave a surge of optimism.

The first game was a lovely hot sunny day at home to Fulham and we won 3 - 0. It continued in similar fashion and all the 'hype' seemed true. I was totally onboard by now and attended every home match. It became my real passion.

David Sunley heads home a very late winner against Portsmouth in 1972 despite a very valiant attempt by the defender at the far post, whereas the defender at the near post can't be arsed to get up. He was probably feigning injury. Ha Ha Ha 2-1, loser.

My whole world revolved around Sheffield Wednesday and Saturday afternoons, but I hadn't experienced an away match yet and this is where it all changes.

I had been pestering my parents for some time to go to an away match, so when the reasonably close fixture of Preston came up in October, with Wednesday flying high in the league, the pressure to go intensified. When my brother promised them that I would be well looked after and that we would go on an official coach, so I would be safe, they said they would think about it. I could hardly sleep on Friday night wondering what the verdict would be. When I did wake it was straight into their room to see what they would say. Eventually I was told, 'Yes' along with several provisos, but yes was all I needed to hear.

9

There was me, my two brothers and my eldest brother's girlfriend. We got the coach from the city centre and off we went, full of excitement.

What happened on our arrival in Preston was absolutely nothing like what I expected, though. We pulled into Deepdale and ours was the very first coach from Sheffield to arrive. In those days there was no organisation or police escort. You simply took your chances and being the first coach there was not good.

My first visit to an away ground obviously needed a welcoming committee and that's what I got. Within 30 seconds of stopping, the coach was attacked by Preston fans. Fortunately for us we were virtually the last to get off, so were still on the coach as the trouble started. The driver closed the door and drove off with us still on board. The rest were left behind for a kicking or a practice at being a future Linford Christie. When we stopped later the front of the coach was smashed and the headlights put through, but at least we escaped. Being 11 years old I was terrified and not sure I liked this away match lark. We made ourselves 'invisible' for the next hour or so as we walked round Preston before cautiously starting to walk towards the ground again. We came to a park and I saw an amazing sight. It was honestly like something out of a film. Coming over the small hill was a mass of people. We hesitated for a while, but then heard the familiar roar of Wednesday fans.

It was like seeing the cavalry.

The trains had arrived and swollen the number of visiting fans enormously. We pulled our scarves out and ran to join up with this invading army of several thousand Wednesdayites and the rush was amazing. As an impressionable youngster the feeling of suddenly being part of this invading tribe was immense. Thousands of people all committed to the cause, singing and clapping in unison was something to behold and embrace. The violence was scary but it was also perversely exciting and gave the experience an edge. Being part of this victorious army was immense and the sheer noise that boomed within that old wooden kop was awesome. The feeling of brotherhood and camaraderie was overwhelming and I am convinced that it was this point more than any other that my addiction was complete.

There was some trouble, but the sheer weight of numbers from Sheffield, meant the outcome was inevitable. Everyone went on the Preston home end. It was a large timber built standing area in those days and it seemed to shake to the noise of the conquering army. We heard that Preston tried to defend their territory but got chased off onto the visiting end. By the time we emerged onto the terrace it was a mass of Wednesdayites. The feeling is hard to explain, but it was amazing being part of this travelling, conquering army.

In reality there may have been only 3 or 4,000 visiting fans and were still outnumbered out of the attendance of 15,600, but we had taken their end and it felt good.

Like all battles there was more to come as pockets of resistance were 'mopped up' and counter attacks were dealt with. There were even further probing attacks deeper into their territory as the afternoon unfolded, but by the time the teams entered the field (Wednesday in an all tangerine kit that day) the borders had been drawn and the hostility was left for the pitch. Despite Wednesdays lofty position that day, I can remember them struggling to make any headway and being a goal down. The equaliser came from the penalty spot in front of the Wednesday fans and coolly converted by Peter Eustace. I can't remember seeing the ball hit the net from the spot kick, but I knew we had scored from the reaction of everyone around me. I was obviously familiar in how to celebrate a goal, as I'd been to many matches before, but an away goal always seems more special. I can remember being picked up by a total stranger and thrown around and held up like a trophy. The game finished 1-1 and we were still joint top of the table with Burnley, but something special had happened to me. I was now officially diagnosed with having the disease that is known as "Wednesdayiteis" and the blood in my veins became blue and white.

I also discovered that I didn't have two brothers after all. I had several thousand. I was accepted for being Wednesday and part of a huge family.

I belonged.

*My first away goal. Peter Eustace
scores at Preston.*

The march to promotion started to falter the following week, when a young Leighton James tore Wednesday apart at Hillsborough.

As is usual for Wednesday, it seems, we were robbed of key players Tommy Craig, Willie Henderson, Peter Rodrigues and striker Mick Prendergast through injury and in front of 30,200 fans and the BBC Match of the day cameras (which was unusual for a Second Division game) Wednesday lost 1-0. I think the team realised they weren't good enough after that game and so the sorry slide set in.

To me the damage was a lot deeper. I had been bitten and the scars will last a lifetime. It was now a matter of having to go to every home match, without fail. Even when the entrance fee for the Kop went up from 20p to 25p (and programmes cost 7p!) I still managed to scrape the extra 5p together for the game!

*Lulu was rumoured to be a l**ds supporter and there were claims that
her name actually comes from the l**ds initials (twice). In reality Lulu
was a die hard Wednesdayite, who liked nothing more than pouring a
cup of tea for the lads after a win. She is seen here celebrating with
'Wee' Willie Henderson and Tommy Craig. Derek Dooley, John
Holsgrove, Peter Grummitt and a rather lust crazed Peter Eustace look
on. Lulu actually started the craze of wearing replica shirts at matches,
as seen here. This was after a league Cup round 2 match against Bolton
in 1972. She should have been performing at the London Palladium that
night, but cancelled using the excuse of a throat infection, so she could
be at the game*

We still finished well up the league that season but the belief that a
promotion push was possible was lost and the inevitable decline was in
place. Far from building on the good season we had, the club entered
back into a struggle and the following season saw the team again going
into the last game of the season needing to win to stay up. This time the
plight was even more horrendous, as failure to win would see us slip
into the lowly third division for the first time in the clubs proud and long
history.

There wasn't a great deal of optimism before the crucial game, at
home to Bolton, as the team had been turned over by a thumping 8 – 0
margin at Middlesborough the week before. However, part of being a

football supporter, is having a totally unreasonable level of optimism. For some bizarre reason despite everything that you know, there is something deep inside you that tells you it is still possible. It is an odd thing as well, because, it is almost as if you daren't think good things too much, for fear that you will be found out and the exact opposite of what you wish, will happen.

I think being a Wednesdayite has taught us now, that if anything can go wrong it will. We specialise in cocking things up. Injury crisis are a speciality at Hillsborough and I don't mean just having a few players out. Even now we still seem to be cursed with injury plague. In the 2006-07 season, we had a spell where 13 first team players were unavailable for one reason or another. It makes you wonder why you bother with ridiculous superstitions, yet certain laws have to be adhered to, for fear of disturbing "The Cosmos."

I'm sure that all football supporters have similar ridiculous superstitions, with 'lucky underpants' rituals that they go through, to bring their club good luck and we are no different.

Melv was the creator of "The Cosmos" and we all believed it, me more than anyone.

I have two older brothers and Melv was a friend of my eldest brother, initially. As a passionate and devout follower of the Blue and White faith, we came to know and love Melv as the fourth brother. He was wise, hard, and generous to a fault and a great character. He taught us loads about Wednesday and life and had a great taste in music, which had a huge influence on us all. To a young naive lad like me, he was inspirational and so when he spoke of 'The Cosmos', I believed him. One of the great parts of The Cosmos was a pair of lucky gloves he had. If he wore the gloves Wednesday won. If he didn't we would lose. Simple as that. The odd thing is, it was true.

The gloves became a sacred and holy symbol of The Cosmos. I can remember one game he forgot the gloves and I was horrified. I couldn't believe that he could be so irresponsible and worse was that he wouldn't turn round and go home to fetch them. Inevitably we lost that day.

I can imagine the scene in the dressing room as the news filtered through. The then manager Steve Burtenshaw would have been giving a final team talk before the players took to the pitch, when his assistant burst into the room. "Boss, Boss........Melvs forgot the gloves!........" You can hear the collective sigh of the team ...   "Boll*cks! We're done for lads..." and no matter how much the manager tried to convince the team it was just a pair of gloves, everyone knew that The Cosmos was out of balance and defeat was inevitable.

For the Bolton game, Melv must have had the gloves, for that Saturday afternoon turned out to be one of highs of a dismal decade. A bumper 24,000 crowd turned up to see the last rites performed and all seemed to be going to the sorry plan, as the spectre of relegation stalked closer. That is until with only six minutes remaining, Ken Knighton poked a scrambled goal in, to wild, ecstatic scenes, reminiscent of a cup final winner. I can remember it being the best feeling in the world. The whole place went absolutely ballistic. Grown men hugged each other and wept with joy at the incredible thing that happened. The remaining minutes were a bizarre mixture of elation and ecstatic singing as the ground bounced with joy, but, interspersed with the dreaded fear that we wouldn't hold on for the remaining minutes, every time that Bolton attacked.

Fortunately, we did see out those last minutes and a triumphant invasion of the pitch ensued, at the final whistle.

This was as close to success as I had ever known and boy did it feel good. Surely this was the turning point now and the club would learn from its mistakes. The club made statements to the press that it would never happen again.

See!

But no. It was merely putting off the inevitable and the following season saw the club finally succumb to the depths of Division Three with barely a whimper.

It was really tough being a Wednesdayite around that time. United were doing well and at school there weren't many kids who stuck firm and kept the faith. Even the ones who did were a bit geeky (I probably fitted into this category myself thinking about it) and the club became the butt of comedian jokes. Crowds were unsurprisingly well down. Starkly averaging the 12-13,000 mark, but there was something inside me that always made me stay true. I can't say why. I guess that I have a stubborn side to me when it is something I feel strongly about or maybe it is that I like to be individual rather than following what everyone else does. Either way, I was still proud of being cursed with Wednesdayism and would argue with anyone at school as to why Wednesday were better than United (a pretty difficult thing to do given their plight.) I guess it is part of my identity. It is what I am. I am Wednesday.

The relegation season of 1974 – 75 was largely forgettable, but even then there were some things that will live in the memory. I can remember clearly a 3 – 0 home win over York City in November, which will also be remembered for a streaker. Not the nice young shapely female type, but a rather old and flabby bloke, who I can only presume did it for his own sexual gratification. He looked every inch an accountant (it was a cold November day though, so there weren't many inches on show) on the verge of retirement and I wonder what he said to his wife when he got home. It was even televised on YTV's "Sunday Soccer" programme and in those days streakers were given screen time, unlike now when they refuse to show them.

"Albert, is that you with no clothes on in front of 12,495 football fans?"

"…errr….. No Ethyl, you must be mistaken.

But they certainly look like your shoes and socks."

"Excuse me Ref. have you seen my carpet slippers?"

That season was also famous for setting an extraordinary record of going nine games without scoring a goal. Every one knew that relegation was a done deal, yet the wild celebrations when Wednesday finally scored were unbelievable. I can still remember it vividly. It was a warm day in April and the final home game of a dismal season was against Oxford. As usual we were 1 - 0 down (we lost a lot of games 1 - 0 for some reason that season) with time slipping away, when David Sunley did a bizarre thing for a Wednesday striker. He scored! It wasn't a good goal particularly, but a goal it certainly was and it was celebrated with only a joy that the most oppressed people could ever understand. It was one of only two goals that the team scored from its last 17 games (Yes, that is right. Two bloody goals in seventeen chuffing games!) and a meagre sum of 21 points saw the team deservedly slide into Division 3.

Being lucky enough to see the 5 – 4 victory over Manchester United, I can also say that I saw one of Hillsborough's other most amazing matches, which was also against Man. United. United had been relegated from the First Division (as it was before the pompously re-named 'Premiership') and their stay in the Second Division was to be brief indeed. They were already six points clear of second place after only 20 games played (two points for a win in those days, remember kids) and Wednesday were but one point off the bottom, so it was with some expectation of a hammering that we attended.

Crowds were around 11-12,000 by now for home games, but the crowd that day was 35,067, swollen by a huge following from Manchester.

There was a lot of pride in holding your own Kop from visiting supporters and in all the years that I have been at Hillsborough, I can only remember losing it on two occasions. This game against Man U and then against Aston Villa, ironically enough in the same season, when they needed a win to secure promotion, against a sad Wednesday side, long since relegated.

It was almost a done deal as the police had effectively assigned the Kop to Man United's huge following and there wasn't much if any fighting, to "take" the kop. In my first away game at Preston, the sheer weight of numbers ensured victory, yet there was still some serious brawling undertaken to allow the numbers to claim the territory. In the case of Man United, it was simply the flood of numbers that won the day. United had a particularly bad reputation in those days as being one of the nastiest set of fans around. My eldest brother was at the game and when asked directions to Hillsborough by some United fans, took them to the ground (they were walking). On arrival at the ground, he was thanked by a flurry of punches for his trouble. Nice.

Wednesday also had quite a reputation and a group of Wednesdayites that day decided that they wouldn't go down without a fight. A mob of several hundred had gathered together and steadfastly refused to move off the Kop. The fighting went on and off for a large part of the game, with the massively outnumbered Owls being attacked and maneuvered around the Kop. From our vantage point in the North Stand, we had a clear view of the constant battle and at times it was difficult to know which to watch, the game or the brawl! As the second half continued, the fighting intensified and the Wednesday fans were pushed towards the bottom of the Kop, but still battled furiously to hold their ground. It got to the stage where the police brought horses in and actually on to the Kop, (in a scene reminiscent of the famous White Horse Cup Final - for different reasons) to try and quell the fighting. The game amazingly continued while the battle reached a peak, with the police eventually creating a successful cordon between the warring factions for the duration of the match.

18

Stop fighting you boys!

The game itself was equally intense and although we didn't witness the silky skills of Best, Charlton et al it was still amazing. Wednesday went 1-0 down, but then surprisingly hit back with a goal from Sunley, followed by Colin Harvey and Bernard Shaw both hitting absolute screamers to put Wednesday into a half time lead of 3-1. I can remember at the interval the tannoy system playing "It's Magic" by a group called Pilot and Magic it certainly was.

Wednesday were punching way above their weight (on and off the pitch).

United inevitably pulled back and levelled at 3-3, in the second half, only for Wednesday to then go 4-3 up, by a scrambled David Sunley goal.

Eventually Man United got a fourth and the game swung precariously either way, before honours finished even at 4 - 4.

An amazing game.

Of course the scale of this fracas, was sufficient to be the front page story of Mondays local paper. Sixty fans were injured and over one hundred arrests made. Man United coaches were even shot with an air pistol on their way through Oughtibridge.

Now that's what I call Anarchy.

Of course everybody connected with the game denied any responsibility. The local press must have been thrilled with it though. Note that the second biggest story that day was the tragic death of a chubb in the River Don. An autopsy showed that it had choked on a sweety wrapper. Is that what they would have called a slow news day?

From that point on it was all downhill and amazingly after scoring four goals in that game, the team found it impossible to score again. They did it the following week in a 1-1 draw with Oldham on the 14th December, but incredibly would only score one more goal at home for the rest of the season (against Oxford) and as previously stated, only two during the whole of 1975 until the season ended.

It takes a lot of guts to follow a team through that.

The local newspaper even started up a campaign, "Save our Owls," to try and drum up support to help keep the club out of the clutches of Division Three, but it was a miracle, not publicity that was needed.

Trouble at matches in those days was very different to today. It was far more commonplace, in fact there would be fighting up and down the country every week. It didn't even register a mention in the press because it was so frequent. It wasn't worth reporting unless it was on such a large scale.

I can remember almost a year to the day before the 4-4 Manchester United game, Wednesday were at home to the would be run away champions, Middlesbrough. They had an awesome team that season, with Graeme Souness, John Craggs, Stewart Boam and a certain Jack Charlton as their manager. They were a real powerhouse of a team and swamped virtually everyone. They brought a large following with them and as was the custom in those days, came on to the Kop end. There was fighting throughout the first half as the battle raged, before the Teesiders fled across the pitch, making a run to the relative safety of Leppings Lane end. In the local Sheffield 'Star' paper on the Monday there was a picture of the fleeing Middlesbrough fans, with a banner almost taunting the fact that they were chased off. It was seen as a victory rather than the scandal that it would be today.

Boro' fans sound retreat after terrace incidents

ON the run . . . Middlesbrough fans take to the pitch on Saturday after trouble on the Kop as they head for the Lepp ings Lane end.

Run Boro' Run! The comment underneath the picture reads "On the run! Middlesborough fans flee across the pitch after the EBRA gave 'em a right good kicking. Who are ya! Who are ya!"

I can also remember the simple stupidity of trying to take the Kop sometimes as well. We played Millwall at home one season in the early 1970's and in those days we would take two bus trips across the city to get to Hillsborough. I can remember there being about half a dozen Millwall fans on the bus from the city centre to the ground, absolutely pissed off their heads passing a bottle of Whiskey round, which rather curiously they called Vinegar. These guys weren't the archetypal hooligans of the day though. They were grown men in their forties. As was common practice in those days, the Kop from 2 o'clock onwards was mostly Kids and families, so it wasn't unusual for visiting fans to get on the Kop early without much resistance. Us kids would run away and leave them to hold the centre ground. The problem came for the visitors when it got towards three o'clock and the pubs emptied of the real Wednesday hoolies and they came onto the Kop to re-take their territory. Quite often, the fight would be brief as a mob assembled and simply chased the visitors off. The same situation arose for Millwall that day, in that about 50 or 60 Millwall fans had chased the Kids off (me included) and none of us were going to attempt to challenge them.

At about 10 to 3 however, the big lads arrived and charged the visitors. In fairness to Millwall that day, they did fight back but their cause was pretty hopeless and they got pushed further back. Anyone who remembers the old Wednesday Kop in those days, will know it was an odd shape, with a hump set off centre, as you looked at it from the pitch.

The Millwall fans kept retreating, slowly being pushed up and up towards the back of the Kop. Although the Wednesday fans advanced, by always keeping the higher ground meant that Millwall could stave off any serious beatings. This could only last for so long though and inevitably they reached the summit. They battled hard for a while, but, with suddenly nowhere to go, the front line reached equal heights. From this point on the outcome was inevitable and the visitors took a beating as they fled every man for himself, much to the cheers around the ground. It is a high Kop at Hillsborough and it must have seemed a hell of a long way down for the Londoners that day, as they succumbed to a flurry of fists and boots. As the last stragglers fled onto the pitch, I can still remember one of the drunken old guys from the bus, hopelessly trying to vault the wall and not getting remotely close to getting over it. He took a few more kicks before being physically thrown over the wall and onto the pitch. He got up and staggered unsteadily back to the away end, making the odd gesture to the home end. He wasn't arrested or anything, he was simply allowed to make his way to the Leppings Lane end and I'm sure he didn't complain about the beating he and the others took. It was simply part and parcel of the game and probably what they enjoyed.

*This picture was from 1979 and shows the famous
hump shape of the Kop*

Going on the home end, at away games, was just something that you did and Wednesday were no different. My two elder brothers went to an away game at Norwich (before I was allowed to go, thankfully!) and I am told that there were about 100 of them. Some pretty big lads too (not my brothers though!) and after a few pints made their way onto the home end. Like a covert operation, they split up to avoid detection and then met up and went straight into the middle of the Norwich Kop. Once positioned, they let out a cry of "The Wednesday!" and then waited for the boots to fly. All the youngsters beat a hasty retreat, as they knew trouble was starting, but the older Norwich lads simply piled in. Ridiculous odds 100 against a few thousand and sure enough they were chased off under a flurry of fists and kicks, but that was the way it was. I found it amazing when I was told this, because it just seemed so stupid, but of course it did further glamorise the whole away day experience and make me want to go even more.

The fighting in those days was so different to now. Visiting fans would nearly always attack the home supporters Kop, or at least have a go and the fact that Wednesday were a big city club meant that despite their lowly status, they still had a large hard core following, particularly at away games (even though the average home attendances were plummeting). As a result they would nearly always attack the home Kop and on a lot of occasions take the territory. This was indeed a huge victory and deeply embarrassing for the conquered home team

23

It was very territorial and very tribal. It was about having a go. Regardless of the odds, it was just the way it was. Yes, sometimes it could be ferocious and yes, sometimes people would get hurt, but generally it was a few fisticuffs and nothing like the mentality that we have nowadays where people are kicked senseless, be it football or on a Friday night in town.

Sadly, that sense of not needing to take it too far has been lost.

While on the subject of "Aggro," can I make it clear that I am very much against violence, in any shape or form. I find it sad and sickening to see the mindless acts of violence that go on in our society and worry about the future of mankind, when in the 21st Century we still haven't worked out how to all get along. Every day on the news, we hear of some organisation blowing innocent people up in the name of some cause or other, or someone being murdered over some form of altercation. I think generally that mankind is a violent species, or at least has a percentage of violent offenders and that these acts will always go on.

Having said that, this is not about football violence, like a lot of books that have been written recently. It is about the things that have happened to us, whilst watching football and like it or not, violence at football, particularly in the 70's and 80's was always present.

As much as I dislike the fighting, it did give you a weird sort of edge. Sort of an adrenalin rush. Like doing a parachute jump or a bungee jump, there is a threat of danger. The thrill comes from avoiding the danger and laughing afterwards when you came out safely the other side. The same "buzz" came from avoiding the trouble, but its constant presence made you on edge. I can honestly say that none of us have ever sought out trouble, or joined in when it has happened. We have been in the middle of it a few times, when it has kicked off around us, but being a set of girly puffs, have always made a hasty retreat.

It is an odd thing when you are witness to it from a safe distance though. You obviously want your own fans to come out on top and there is a sense of admiration for them. Likewise when they are on the receiving end there is an anger and a wish to help (even if it only remains a wish).

I can remember an FA Cup Quarter Final game away to Burnley in 1983, which obviously generated a lot of interest and a huge following from Sheffield. Wednesday had sold out their allocation very quickly and we were put on a standing terrace which was split partly along the length of the pitch, to segregate home and away fans. I always used to

24

like these set ups as the atmosphere was always terrific, from having both sets of supporters under the same roof.

As was expected there were a lot of Wednesday fans that didn't have tickets, so went on the home end rather than missing such a big game. They had massed in the standing area behind the goal to our left and it was clear that it would become a problem. By 1983 most clubs had erected fences to stop supporters getting on to the pitch and Burnley was no exception. The police decided that the best move was to get the Wednesday supporters off the home end and put them into an already ridiculously crowded away end (in those days there was no thought whatsoever about the comfort, or even safety, of football supporters, you were treated like cattle, so squeezing more in to a full pen wasn't an issue) There were probably about a thousand Wednesdayites on the opposite end and all started to go well as they opened a gate in the fence to start to let the visitors out on to the perimeter of the pitch. It was obvious what was going to happen next, to everyone (except the police) and sure enough when there was only a handful of Wednesdayites left, the Burnley fans attacked them and the poor lads left got a hiding. The outrage amongst us watching from the away section was enormous and it became close to becoming an all out riot. For once the fences actually served a purpose and contained the angry mob that was baying for revenge.

The atmosphere was very hostile, but electric, as the match started and in the very first minute Burnley were awarded a harsh penalty, which only incensed the visitors further. Fortunately it was saved and early in the game Wednesday took the lead (ironically enough at the end where the trouble had been), which changed the mood. The game finished 1-1 and a replay followed which Wednesday won emphatically 5-0 (one of my all time Hillsborough highs), but the reprisals continued and there were lots of stories around about how Burnley fans were ambushed before the replayed game, as an act of revenge.

There is a definite bonding with fellow fans, even though, if you stripped away the colours and the allegiance, you would probably have absolutely nothing in common with these people. In fact in a lot of cases, you would want absolutely nothing to do with them.

In the early 1970's the fashion was to wear scarves tied to your wrists or have them hanging down your leg, tied to your belt round your waist. It became the rage then to steal scarves from opposition fans and a badge of honour amongst teenagers, particularly, to show the scarves you had stolen. I was always incredibly proud to show my colours and would set off from home, which was the opposite side of the city to Hillsborough, decked out in my scarves, wanting the whole world to know I was a Wednesdayite and on my way to the match. It was a great feeling as you got near the ground and joined the buzz of the crowd.

Walking along Penistone Road you would always hear the familiar cry of "Hot pies inside!!" from a guy who had a shop that surprisingly sold hot pies. It is weird, but that phrase brings back so many memories. Everyone would join in shouting "Hot pies inside!!" as they walked past the shop. A daft little memory, yet it makes me smile just thinking about it.

By now woolly scarves were seen as old fashioned and 'silk' scarves were all the rage. Where I lived, all the young lads on our road were Wednesdayites and we would go to games together, kitted out in our scarves. We always went on the Kop and took up the same position for every game. Of course, in those days, it was before all seater stadia, so it was standing only on the ends behind the goals at Hillsborough, and we would position ourselves about half way up the East Bank, in the middle. At the time the ground boasted a "state of the art" electronic scoreboard, which when you look at pictures of it know, was like comparing the brick like mobile phones of the 1980's against today's slim line versions.

A huge black box, that could convey the time and score or any other messages necessary. It makes me laugh now seeing old programmes praising this wondrous technology and showing pictures of it, with press quotes lauding this wondrous technology.

At the time it was impressive, but as time passed and the club became unable to service it, for whatever reason, the scoreboard became more and more erratic. Half time became great fun, trying to translate the latest scores! Some were legible, but mostly it was total guess work as to what the hell the scoreboard was trying to say. Scores like NOZNUGOYL 2 FIGDAPPN 0 were not uncommon (that as Nottingham Forest 2 Ipswich 0, in case you didn't spot it).

As a result most people reverted back to the manual scoreboard along the side of the North Stand, to find out the real score.

This was a series of letters that hung on the side of the wall and when a score became known, the scoreboard man would pick up the appropriate numbers for the scores and walk along the scoreboard to hang the numbers up under the appropriate letter to show the current score, which corresponded to the fixtures that were printed in the programme. Of course you needed to buy a programme to be able to know who the teams were, when it was shown that in match B the score was 2-0 for instance.

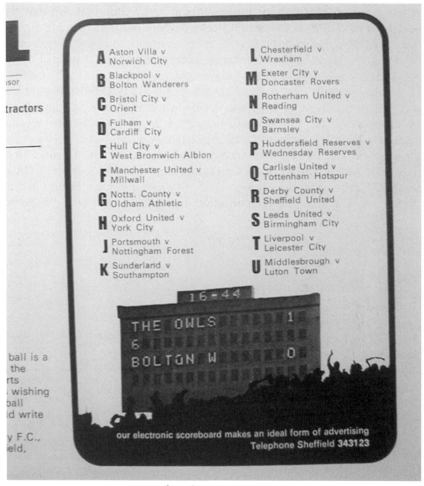

....as seen here!

The other score that people looked out for was of course our hated rivals, Sheffield United and it became apparent that United's score was nearly always the last one on the board. As a result when the scoreboard man got news of a goal, it was quite a way for him to walk to register the score, for say letter T. At this point most people would virtually stop watching the game to see where the scoreboard man would stop. It caused great fun and anticipation, waiting for the score and if it signalled United were losing, it would be accompanied by a great cheer. After a while Mr. Scoreboard, obviously enjoying his moment of attention, would tease the waiting crowd and would make a great play out of walking particularly slowly or hesitating at an earlier letter, as if he was going to put up another score, before deciding that it wasn't that one and move slowly on again, heightening the anticipation. Sometimes, he would hide the score behind his back, so you couldn't pre guess. I can even remember one time when United were already 2-0 down and he brought another 2 out. This brought a huge groan as the crowd anticipated that United had scored two quick goals and were now in fact drawing, only at the last second to brandish a hidden "3" to show that they were in fact now losing 3-0. This brought a huge cheer and a little wave from Mr.Scoreboard.

This picture shows Wednesdays fourth goal in the 4-0 victory over Luton Town in 1972, a wonderful chipped goal by Peter Eustace (out of picture). Letter 'N' clearly showing a satisfying 5-0 lead to Liverpool against United after 60 minutes. What a good set of results that day!

Nowadays we have a super new electronic scoreboard (which works) that shows the latest scores at half time and full time. Every now and again at Hillsborough a flashing "SCOREFLASH" message will appear

28

during the course of a game. This is obviously to attract people's attention, prior to quickly showing the latest scores at other games. This then became followed by a "SSSSHHHHHHHHHH" sign that signified United's score was next up and almost certainly that they were losing. As a result everyone was now conditioned to expect to see Uniteds score following the 'SSSSSSHHHHH' and that they were losing. It was rather amusing then that at one game last season the scoreboard flashed up 'SCOREFLASH' followed by 'SSSSHHHHHHHH'. A buzz went around the ground as the eagerly anticipated 'United losing' result was surely about to follow the long and dramatic pause. Instead ' Berwick 1 Cowdenbeath 0' was flashed up, to be instantly replaced by Coventry 2 Sheffield United 0, much to the amusement of everyone there and I wondered if Mr Scoreboard was looking down from above and smiling

In the 1970's the bigger lads tended to congregate about 3/4 of the way up the Kop, so by standing just in front of them, it was a good place to get the atmosphere, but still be able to see the game. As a young teenager, still lacking the height to see beyond the person in front of you, it was also quite a perilous place to stand as well. The very nature of standing on a steep banking of steps, naturally meant that as people stood on their tiptoes to be able to see an exciting moment during the game, there would be a tendancy for people to push forward. This wonderful phenomenon is a crowd surge and even at the poorly attended games that Wednesday endured in the 1970's, the tendency was still to congregate together in the middle. As a result surges were common place and at games with a large attendance were highly frequent. To help control this, grounds had crash barriers erected on the terraces which would break up the crowd surges and prevent major serious accidents happening.

This was fine unless you were stood directly in front of a crash barrier. They were great to lean on before the game started, but heaven help you if you were in front of one following a major surge. Like a giant wave crashing down on you, you were helpless to resist the flood of bodies pushing you down. It was agony having the weight of dozens of grown men squashed down on the barrier and your stomach taking the brunt of it. You would feel like your guts were about to be pushed out of your mouth and it was impossible to breath again, until the surge had receded.

In the mayhem that ensued following a goal, you were bound to be pushed dozens of feet forward by the weight of people dancing around and losing their balance on the steps. To be honest it was part of the fun and we would exchange stories of how far down the Kop we ended.

At one particular game in the early 1970's I can remember Wednesday scoring and after jumping up, being pushed bodily downwards by the following surge. At the time I was surprised by how far down the Kop I was being washed, until it came to a very abrupt end as I lost my footing and went headfirst into a crash barrier and it all went black.

The next thing that I knew was coming round by the side of the pitch. Fortunately for me, someone had spotted me, unconscious and bleeding on his shoes. I had been carried down to the front and being attended to by the St. Johns Ambulance men. I was taken away, to a treatment room under the North Stand but fortunately didn't need any more treatment other than a ridiculously large plaster, to cover the cricket ball sized bump growing on my head.

Looking back I am surprised that a major blow to the head was treated with a plaster. I'm sure nowadays it would be an overnight stay in hospital, but I was glad to get back on the Kop anyway and see the rest of the game. As I walked back along the touchline I can remember Jackie Sinclair, who played on the wing for Wednesday, asking me if I was alright as he went to take a throw in and I felt elated.

I made my way back to my mates on the Kop, who had no idea what had happened to me or where I had gone, following the goal. All I can remember was feeling decidedly groggy and wanting to throw up. I was glad when the game finished and went home, but then had the pleasure of explaining to my parents why I had a plaster the size of a handkerchief on my head.

Despite the way fellow fans had helped me then and my feelings of this wonderful brotherhood, of course it wasn't really like that. There are good and bad in all walks of society and Wednesday were no different.

I was at a home match later that season, when after the game had finished, a young lad, similar age to me, tried to hit me and steal a scarf from round my waist. Fortunately for me, the punch missed, the scarf jammed in my belt loop and he scarpered, but I was stunned that a fellow Wednesdayite, would do such a thing.

I guess I learned a lesson that day, that this band of brothers were maybe not so holy after all.

I never took part in the scarf stealing ritual, as, one, I was too scared and, two, you never really saw any away colours at Hillsborough and I was still waiting to go to my first away match at that time. Wearing colours was not something that you did at away matches, unless you had the safety in numbers. It was always wise to hide your scarves, etc until you were safe. You would be attacked for simply wearing colours in those days. That was reason enough and it was understood by all, that those were the rules.

You would also be asked the time probably a dozen times on the way to and after a game. This was a simple trick to try and catch opposition fans out, as there accent would potentially give them away and lead to a quick punch to the head. Nobody wore the club replica shirt at games either. That was something that started to happen in the 1980's. Around this same time, it also started to change that you wouldn't be attacked for wearing opposition colours also. The violence has changed from being very widespread, but not as severe, to highly infrequent, but more vicious. You hear about how gangs of hardcore hooligans will now arrange to meet up, usually well away from the ground, to fight it out. I personally think this is better. If they are mad enough to want to do it, let them get on with it, as long as innocent people don't get dragged into it. There have been lots of these incidents happened between the two Sheffield clubs lunatic element, Wednesdays OCS (Owls Crime Squad) and United's BBC (Blades Business Crew) usually resulting in some extraordinary violence and horrific injuries.

You don't get attacked now unless you do something to provoke it or are just plain unlucky. I can't honestly remember the last time I saw any trouble at Hillsborough. I mean literally years and years (with the sole exception of when Wednesday play United, which is particularly nasty and guaranteed to have trouble, but more of that later).

CHAPTER 2

The Dark Days

Of Course when relegation to the Third Division happened in 1975, it was widely accepted that there would be an instant triumphant return, but it wasn't to be. Five long sad seasons followed, but it wasn't all doom and gloom, there was some magical highlights (if you can call avoiding relegation to the 4th Division on the last game of the season a highlight)

The football bug had become a religion to me now and it was inconceivable that I would miss a home game and as I grew older I would get to as many away games as I could. The fact that my eldest brother had a car and our new friend Melv also had a car, meant that away games were more accessible, although it was still mostly restricted to local games.

The first season in the Third division was a total disaster. It started away to Southend United. I wasn't allowed to go, but my brothers did. Despite relegation, there was a huge following from Wednesday and all the bars along the sea front were packed with Wednesdayites and obviously there was a lot of trouble and various bars suffered.

The pub that my brothers were in had a band playing live and apparently were made to play "Hi Ho Silver Lining" continuously. Every time they tried another song they were booed and had things thrown at them until they played Hi Ho Silver Lining (to which the rowdy throng sang along, Hi Ho Sheffield Wednesday). It later ended in tears though with a table being thrown through a window. Needless to say, Wednesday later lost the game 2-1 and all the pre season optimism vanished.

The season was awful and as only two seasons before, we went into the last game of the season knowing that only a victory would prevent relegation, but this time to the unthinkable depths of the basement that is the Fourth Division.

The rest of the league had finished and Wednesday were languishing in the bottom four, as the Owls took on the same opening day opponents, Southend, on a Thursday night (The fixture being re-arranged following an earlier postponement because an FA Cup semi final was played at Hillsborough on the day the earlier fixture was scheduled)

In a winner takes all match, in front of 25,000 fans, Southend were in a similar predicament and needed to win to stay up, so defeat for either side meant certain relegation.

Wednesday were fortunate to be at home, as their home form was particularly good at the end of the season, taking 15 points from a possible 16 in their last 8 games. Indeed it was this sudden found form at the end that was to be their salvation. A run that won them 7 points from a maximum 10 in their last 5 games, including a vital away point at promotion chasing Brighton and Hove Albion on the preceding Saturday.

Unlike the Bolton game two years before, this was not as fraught and Wednesday went into a 2-0 lead, with goals from Mick Prendergast and Eric Potts. Southend did pull a goal back to make for a scary last few minutes, but the escape was complete.

Prendo scores the second goal against Southend United

As joyous as it was at the time, looking back, it didn't have the same magic as the Bolton win and to be honest I can't remember the goals at all now, whereas Ken Knighton's winner is still etched in my mental photo album.

Yet this win, was probably more significant, because at long last, this was the very bottom of the fall. Like turning a giant tanker round, it takes time to finally see any deviation from course and although widely berated as being part of the dark days, I believe that the then manager Len Ashurst had started to turn the ship.

Manager Len Ashurst, with a hairstyle heavily influenced by Dr. Spock from Star Trek. Sadly his brave attempt to set a new trend by growing his sideburns into his eyebrows never caught on. He is seen here with player of the season for 1975, Eric Potts and on the left chairman Bert McGee. There is a lovely line in the programme from which this picture is taken, saying that Eric Potts is now in business painting and decorating and giving his phone number, should anyone wish to contact him! How the times have changed. I can't see them printing David Beckham's home phone number in the programme. Let's hope Eric wasn't responsible for the decorating in this picture.
(nice jacket though, Eric)

Ashurst brought with him a real tough sergeant major type assistant, in Tony Toms, and an amount of fitness and backbone was instilled into the team. They still lacked that quality, but signs were there, that this was also being added.

A young Chris Turner established himself as a regular keeper in the 1976 -77 season, together with solid fullbacks, Richie Walden and Dave Rushbury, Jeff Johnson in midfield and the emergence of a certain Rodger Wylde.

A striker who actually scored goals on a regular basis, netting over the 'famous' 20 goals, in his first full season.

Trainer Tony Toms
I can't see today's prima donnas taking too well to this guy. I met
Tony in 2009 and he is amazingly even bigger and fitter now despite
probably being in his sixties. Tony had a big impact at SWFC and went
on to be a body guard for the likes of Madonna and Lionel Ritchie.

Things were looking up and I was just crossing that threshold of becoming an adult and enjoying a whole new world of fun and in the next 20 years Wednesday would provide me with some marvellous memories. There were still a few years to go before I would get any sense of success, but I was loving life and loving watching Wednesday.

I had moved to the North Stand for watching home games, which offered a much better view of the match. The Kop is fine, when attacking that end, but when the game is being played at the opposite end, you have a pretty poor view of what is actually happening. We generally would sit somewhere near the 18 yard box at the end Wednesday were attacking and then move to the opposite end for the second half. Attendances were very low during these dark days, so finding empty seats was never a problem. In fact we all could have laid down, if we wanted.

At this time, our "mob" was down to three. Me, Melv and my brother Mark. My Kop mates still went on the Kop and my eldest brother, Graham, played rather than watched on most Saturdays. At that awkward age of mid teens, I was in a position where my spending usually exceeded my income, as I was still reliant on pocket money, so finding the extra 20p to go on the North Stand was difficult. Mark and Melv wouldn't consider going on the Kop, so it was usually Melv that would make up the difference for me (to which I am still grateful) and which made me get a part time job, so I could finance myself.

I love this picture. It captures the total magic of that moment when the ball hits the net and the crowd and players rise as one to celebrate. This one was scored by David Herbert in a 4-0 win over Grimsby Town in 1975

It is a wondrous time, as you reach adulthood. Your whole perspective of life changes. I can remember being taken to the, "Crazy Daisy" on the corner of Yorke Street and High Street, one night after a match just before my 15th birthday. The Crazy Daisy was THE place to be in those days and I was really excited at the prospect of going. It was also a bit scary at the time, as an adolescent, because I was sure to get found out that I was so young and would be embarrassingly ejected. Melv and Graham, knew the guys on the door though and they turned a blind eye while I was sneaked inside. I was blown away by what I experienced when inside though. Roxy Music were playing constantly that night and the room was full of gorgeous women, gyrating away to Brian Ferry and there was such an amazing buzz about the place. I was hooked!

Music, football, women and beer. Oh Yes!

Going to the pub before a game is part of the ritual, but at 15 I found it both exciting and nerve wracking, wondering if you will be allowed in or not. I was lucky that the music scene around this time was exploding with vibrant new sounds. I always loved music and grew up on rock music. Melv was our musical guru and would pick us up from home on match days and play us the latest stuff on his 8 track stereo. He had a green Ford Capri in those days which had a horn that sounded like a breakout alarm at Borstal (or at least how I'd imagine a breakout alarm at Borstal would sound!)

I would have that exciting anticipation from waking up on a match day, which would grow the nearer it got to pick up time. Eventually that horn would sound and off we would go. The stereo would already be cranked up and we would be briefed on the particular artist playing. Melv would spend hours scouring music shops and using his contacts to find the latest hot band. He had a particular like for American music and we learnt about a young Bruce Springsteen or Tom Petty or Bob Seger or Rickie Lee Jones. We grew to love these musicians and their songs became the soundtrack to our lives. It is wonderful that music can spark so many memories of events long gone, just by listening to a certain song. I recently heard the track "I'm in love with a German film star" by The Passions. I had not heard it for years and years, yet the first few notes transported me back to 1981 and dancing away in The Limit on a Friday night. The feeling was so real that I felt I could "grab" the memory, it was so strong. I could even see Tim and Steve dancing with me and three girls from all that time ago. It was amazing that this one minute of my life from twenty odd years ago had been stored dormant at the back of my brain, waiting for the stimulus of that song to dramatically bring it hurtling back. The colours, sounds, sights and even smells seemed to be brought back to life from nowhere.

In the UK the music scene was probably as exciting as it has ever been, with the punk explosion of 1977. I loved it from the first time I heard "God Save the Queen" by the Sex Pistols. I loved all the raw energy of The Jam, The Stranglers, The Clash etc and saw pretty much all of them live, bar for the Pistols. I never quite went as far as sticking safety pins through my nose, but wore a ripped up shirt with 'Chaos' scrawled across it and pogo'd till I dropped at gigs. The energy at these concerts was absolutely electric. Being part of a mass of bodies, all bouncing in unison to the raw, powerful music with everyone singing along was just amazing and we all got such a buzz from it.

My life revolved around watching Wednesday and live bands. I would go to a club called "Improvision" on Sunday and "The Limit" on a Friday with my mates. The music scene in Sheffield was fantastic around this time, as it went from punk to new wave and then new romantics and you really felt like you were part of something. A change, something new. It also helped that Sheffield was such a buzzing place musically and there were loads of great bands about such as Heaven 17, Human League and ABC.

I was always heavily influenced musically by my two older brothers and love the way that music can make you feel so many things. I can remember from a very early age falling "in love" with girls and that music from around that time can bring back such fantastic memories.

It is hard to explain this, but I think you are "into" music or you aren't. For the vast majority of people, music is just something that is on the radio and you sort of like certain songs. But, to others music is so much more and can raise incredible feelings of highs and pain and sorrow and frustration. If you are "into" music it can touch you so deeply. Sadly the majority of the population are influenced by the commercial candy floss music that is played on the radio. This is such a pity as there is so much fantastic stuff being made that simply goes unrecognised.

Most people are happy to put up with "la la la la oooh baby, I love you" and have no idea how much intelligent music there is out there. If you compare it to reading the 'charts' are like reading 'Janet and John' or 'The famous five.'

Open up your minds people and listen to Tolstoy, John Grisham or Jean-Paul Sartre!

Nowadays in the age of the internet, communication is easy and "discovering" new bands is a lot more accessible. Before the internet it was very different though and there was almost an underground movement, a secret society that passed on great bands and great albums around by word of mouth. It was like being in on a great secret and there was always a lot of kudos about 'discovering' a great band and passing them on to fellow members of the musical brotherhood. Sadly to me, it is when bands break into the public domain that they go downhill.

Understandably it is hard to resist the urge to sell to the mass public and inevitably the great music that got them there in the first place, is sacrificed. I have sadly seen it happen so many times.

I was always into music in a big way and to me that period of punk/ new wave/ new romantics was as good as it will ever get. There was so much originality and new sounds. Music was evolving all the time and I loved it.

I can remember once bumping into Phil Oakey and the girls from Human League the week that "Don't you want me" went to Number one in the charts. I was walking along Chapel Walk in Sheffield city centre with my girlfriend. She knew Susan and Joanne as she went to school with them so they were chatting about what was happening to them etc. while I made small talk with Phil Oakey. He didn't like football so we quickly ran out of things to talk about but it was weird as everyone was stopping and saying, "Ooooh look. Human League and John Firth."

Life was really good and I was lucky to have been at that age at such a wonderful time and with such really good friends to be able to do so much.

Talking about music reminded me of a funny incident when we went to see Nils Lofgren in Sheffield, once. The show had finished and we stayed for enough extra beers to ensure that all the buses had stopped running and we didn't have enough money for a taxi home. Fortunately my mate, Robert, had the brainwave of stealing Nils Lofgren's tour bus. It was conveniently parked up a side street and seemed to be left unattended, with the added bonus of the keys being in the ignition. He jumped into the driver's seat and started it up, until a sleepy crew member in the back of the coach was alerted to the engine starting and our giggling. A "Hey maaaan, what do you think you are doing you crazy dude," was enough to persuade us to leave Nils with his tour bus where it was. Apparently the crew member would have offered us drugs and groupies to not steal the tour bus, but we were too pissed to negotiate and left empty handed.

There was a definite split from my footy mates and my social mates though, as nearly all the lads I went out with on a Friday night were Unitedites. Generally we didn't talk that much about football when we were out, at least not in a rivals slagging off way. We sort of accepted each others allegiances and left it at that. There was always a bit of banter of course, but nothing hostile. I loved going out with the lads on a Friday, as much as I did going to the match. My Friday night career probably lasted about fifteen years and we had an absolutely fantastic

40

set of lads. There was probably about ten of us that would religiously be out. We had a real bond and were like a family. I can't remember anyone ever having crossed words, we just all got on so well and looked out for each other. The whole buzz about Friday nights was great, the beer, the music, the scantily clad women but most of all the camaraderie of a close bunch of mates. We always had such a great laugh. In the Eighties the main pub runs were in the very City centre and although our route slowly changed over the years, we largely did the same pubs in the same order. This meant that even if you were late and had to meet everyone in town, you could work out at any one time where everyone else was with some accuracy. I don't even know if pubs like the Blue Bell, Golden Ball, Dove and Rainbow, Museum or Stonehouse even exist anymore. The Stonehouse was a great pub in the Eighties and had a courtyard that I thought for ages was actually outside. It took me some time to find out that the roof was cleverly designed to make it look like the night sky. It was normally late into the evening though when we were there, so I wasn't usually at my best by then.

The Stonehouse was the scene of one of the wildest fights that I have ever seen one night. We were there about ten o'clock-ish as usual and had bumped into a ridiculously large stag night from Intake that was also on the town. (Stag nights in those days were nearly always just a night on the town. Grooms to be nowadays don't realise how lucky they are that someone invented Stag weekends abroad). For some reason some of the bouncers there started trouble with some of the Intake lads, not realising that over half the pub was made up of the Stag party. It absolutely exploded and was just like a brawl from a wild west movie, with tables and chairs flying everywhere! It was absolutely manic.

The Stonehouse bouncers took a bit of a pasting and I gather that bouncers from other pubs were called in from nearby to try and help out.

We were never into fighting, so just kept out of the way, although we did join in with throwing a few chairs in the air, just to add to the effect.

It would have been rude not to.

We would sometimes go onto a nightclub from the pubs, although I can't say that we were regular club devotees. My fave was the Limit on West Street, which was very small, with a low ceiling and created a great atmosphere. This place was a lot more about the music and was more cutting than the other mainstream clubs in Sheffield, such as Josephines or Romeo and Juliets (we tended to go to these more for stag nights or special events, as the music was more commercial). The post punk / new wave movement had been taken over by the electronic/ new romantic era which I also loved. The music was more atmospheric, almost haunting, but with a heavy beat and after a night of drinking a lot of people went there to be absorbed by the music. It was wonderful. So many people all with the same taste in music, dancing and singing, lost in the sounds that filled your head. The atmosphere was amazing. Loads of people happy on the alcohol, totally lost in the music. We didn't need drugs to get high (not that drugs were really used or available anyway) the beer and the wonderful music were more than enough.

A lot of the bands being played then went on to become huge, but at the time the early Ultravox, U2, Joy Division, New Order etc etc was radical and completely different to anything done before.

God I loved that time.

I would give almost anything to go back in time and have a Friday night out from 1981/82.

Slowly our numbers deteriorated after about six or seven years and we got down to a hardcore of four or five that still went out regularly. The bond between us was even stronger and that smaller group still continued going for quite a number of years. It was still absolutely fantastic though and we always had such a good time. I genuinely loved those guys.

Of course age eventually catches up with you and soon I found myself missing the odd night and before I knew it. I too had stopped. You don't think it will ever happen, but time always wins. Fashion, music, locations all change and you become aware of not being part of the crowd anymore but rather looking in. I never wanted to become one of those middle aged blokes that goes out on a Friday thinking he can still pull and so I retired from the Friday night scene gracefully.

I don't even miss it now. I have no longing to be there at all. I am happy that I did it and had such a good run and have such brilliant memories, but time has won my battle of youth.

CHAPTER 3

Turning the Tanker Around

I now had a season ticket for the North Stand, thanks to my parents. I was given the choice of going on holiday with them or I could have a season ticket. I think it took me 0.00023 seconds to decide.

The move to the North Stand brought an all together different perspective of the game. Not only was the view considerably better and the atmosphere more intense, but it also brought a whole new dimension to the game.... Linesman baiting!

We used to sit ourselves about 15 rows from the front, which meant that players and officials were easily in earshot of us. Crowds in the late 1970's were still around the 13,000 mark and although vociferous, you could still make your shouts known to the people on the pitch. Referees are always up and down the pitch, so are not an easy target. Linesmen however, have no choice but to patrol up and down the same touchline for 45 minutes.

There is no escape.

Most of the time, if they are having a reasonable game then you don't notice them. However, when they start to make mistakes, they are totally exposed to the wrath of the crowd. We soon discovered, more out of frustration than anything, that you can start to influence them during the course of the game. At the end of the day they are human beings and have the same weaknesses and frailties as us all and as far as I am aware, don't have any sort of training to deal with the mental pressures applied by a crowd. As a result you would find that there were certain linesmen that had a character that could be exploited. Of course all officials will claim this to be nonsense, but I have seen it happen.

I remember one game in particular, when the linesman at our end was having a nightmare of a game, getting decisions wrong and seemingly giving everything against Wednesday. Consequently, the crowd picked up on it and he started getting all sorts of abuse. The level of hostility that night was quite intense and we would wait for a lull in the noise of the crowd to be able to shout something derogatory at him. We usually looked the name of the linesman up in the programme to be able to personalise our comments (nothing abusive for the sake of abuse, but highly critical of his ability to see basic things and interpret the rules). You could see Mr Chadwick (for that was his name) wavering in his decisions, knowing that if he gave the decision against Wednesday, he would face another barrage of insults and abuse. We started to get 50/50 decisions suddenly going our way and just before half time, he let a potential offside decision go and we scored to level the game at 1-1. Despite this he still got booed off at half time. At the start of the second half, as he ran over to where we were sat, to take up his position for the re-start of the match, he must have been dreading the stick likely to come his way. Instead he was treated to mass reverse psychology and was surprisingly greeted with applause and singing his name. God's honest truth, he was chuckling and waved to the crowd. It was a good second half and he signalled for a penalty later on, in a 3-1 win. Now this linesman, I am sure would deny that he was influenced in any way whatsoever by the crowd and that he gave his decisions based on what he saw, but no one will convince me that he didn't succumb to the pressure of the crowd that night.

Of course everyone is different and so not all will be influenced in this way. One particular linesman, steadfastly refused to be swayed. In fact the more hostile the crowd became the more it seemed to sway him against us. The crowd were getting livid with this guy as he carried on giving virtually every decision against us, until he finally paid the penalty! It was a bitterly freezing cold night in February and just into the second half, gave an offside decision against Wednesday, that looked very much onside. It was too much for one guy in the crowd who had just bought his half time Bovril and he marched down the 4 or 5 rows to the very front and hurled the full cup at the linesman. It was a direct hit in the middle of his back. Now to anyone who has never enjoyed the pleasures of catering at football matches. It is the law that all food and beverages (with the exception of Wagon Wheels) are served at a temperature concurrent with a nuclear reactor. For the next five minutes the poor old linesman, carried on running the line with a vapour trail of steam trailing behind him in the cold night air, much to the delight of the unsympathetic crowd.

Of course its not just officials that can be targeted.

Ex manager Trevor Francis was also the victim of half time refreshments one night at Barnsley. He foolishly stood up out of the dugout for a short while just after half time following an incident that our dingle friends didn't like. The Barnsley fans that were stood on the terrace behind the dugout were incensed about something or other and Tricky Trev was an easy target. A hot pie (not sure if it was steak and onion or meat and potato now) was hurled at him, but fell short of its target. Unfortunately for Trev, it landed on the dugout roof and splattered, spraying its contents over the back of his head and shoulders. Mmmmmmm I bet he smelled delicious in the second half.

Anyone in football should know better than letting themselves be a target after half time.

Not many officials are swayed by the crowd, but of course it was always worth having a go. Whatever we could do to help our team win, we would happily do. It can have exactly the opposite effect as well. It seems that some referees, will go even more against you, the more abuse they take. I think that when Wednesday had a second spell in the Third Division (or First Division, as it is now known …….what a bloody nonsense!) in the early 2000's, that most referees came with the attitude of not being influenced by a big crowd. A lot of them were used to officiating games before 3 or 4,000 so a 23,000 crowd was something to be wary of. I'm sure that some of them would be thrilled to be booed off by 23,000 irate fans, as it must mean that they had a good game, as they weren't influenced by the crowd.

Being totally pissed off with the officials is a fact of life as a football supporter and often it is not enough to simply shout abuse at them.

In the 1960's the tradition was to hurl cushions on to the pitch, to show displeasure. The club hired these little cushions for you to sit on, for a small fee, but when things went wrong, the cushions would come flying down out of the stands and on to the pitch. It was the most wonderful spectacle to see this torrent of cushions hurtling out of the stand. A visible protest of anger.

How bloody fantastic!

Sadly, it brought an end to the cushion hire business, as it was almost every week this would happen!

Nowadays, the ground would be closed and the club docked points, but then it was wonderful and anyone that saw the terrific spectacle of cushions raining down from the stands, will have a tinge of nostalgia, if not a tear in their eye, as they read this.

This is so beautiful!!

The cushions rain down following the sending off of 'Bronco' Layne. Curiously I can only ever remember the avalanche of cushions, coming from the more unruly North Stand, but what a wonderfully spectacular sight. One of those cushions surely must have hit the linesman but did he complain ? Linesmen were real men in those days

I am a huge critic of referees, although I will admit that they have a pretty thankless task and in reality it must be almost impossible to get all decisions right. What I do find hard to accept though, is the sheer ineptness or bloody mindedness of some referees. They seem to go out of their way to try and piss off the crowd. How is it that 20,000 people can all see an incident totally different to the one with a whistle.

When all those people shout, "handball," at exactly the same time, it is because we all see a handball! Do referees think we all come in to the ground for training practice for simultaneous appealing! Yet this one guy will always know best. He sees things that we all can't or knows that we are all shouting for decisions at exactly the same time to try and con him.

I would love to sit and watch a TV replay of a game the following day with a referee and ask him how on earth he came to make the decisions that he did.

Not necessary the big decisions, but the total inconsistency of the average minor decisions.

In this day and age, with the technology and money available, it is amazing that the biggest sport on the planet still refuses to use the help of modern technology and instead relies on just what one man in black decides to see.

Cricket does it, Rugby does it, American football does it.

Come on guys, it's time to wake up.

Of course, if you can't get to the officials, you could always try the opposition players. Anything to put them off their game would be worth a try. I can remember playing at Brighton in 1983 and they had Clive Walker, playing on the wing. He had some form of bad publicity many years before, but must have thought it well forgotten, when we played them at the Goldstone Ground. But, football fans have long memories, if you play for the opposition and within minutes of the start he was getting mercilessly heckled with shouts of 'queer' and other such abuse. He disappeared from the game after that and hardly strayed wide, near the travelling supporters for the rest of the game. A strong Wednesday side won the game 4-0.

It is also quite bizarre now to look back at the racist chanting that was totally commonplace in the 1970's. I don't honestly think that in those days fans realised it was racist. It was just a way of getting at an opposition player to put him off his game. If I remember rightly, the first black player to grace the blue and white was Tony Cunningham, who was signed from Barnsley for £ 100,000 in 1983 and loved by all Wednesdayites. I can remember going down to Fulham to see him making his debut on a Friday night (I don't know why it was a Friday night. I think Fulham played on a Friday for a while to get their crowds up). He scored in a 1-1 draw and can't remember any sort of comment

47

whatsoever. It didn't matter in the slightest what the hell colour they were to me if they were Wednesday.

But in a game against Cambridge United I can remember the merciless monkey chants against a player called Floyd Streete.

Every time he got the ball it would be greeted by monkey noises and I'm not talking about a few people, I'm talking thousands of people. It simply wasn't seen to be an issue then, but looking back now, it was astonishing. It seriously upset Streete though and he ended up being sent off, when his temper got the better of him.

It wasn't just racism either. Budgie-ism was just as bad!

There was a particular guy who played for Blackburn Rovers called Noel Brotherston, who would always get loads of stick. He had a resemblance to a clown called Charlie Caroli who was on children's TV a number of years before. He was 'famous' for doing tricks with budgerigars and his catch phrase was 'look at the budgies" (No it was, honestly!)

Needless to say, the crowd would always be shouting 'look at the budgies!" when Brotherston got the ball.

Is that a budgie on your shirt, Terry!

In fairness to Brotherston, though, it never got to him and he always played well against us. To us it was all part of the experience. We participated, rather than like a lot of people nowadays who simply just turn up to watch and expect an atmosphere to be generated for them.

I knew my behaviour at games was slightly borderline. Don't get me wrong, I never offended anyone deliberately, or was aggressive, but, man did I get carried away. I had a "respectable" job as a Buyer at the time and got spotted a few times, by suppliers, being 'passionate' as they diplomatically called it, but I didn't care. When that game started I was simply immersed in it and all that mattered was a Wednesday victory. I honestly didn't care how it came about. We could have been totally outplayed for 90 minutes, but if we got a very dubious penalty in injury time to win, I was ecstatic.

In 1987 I was given a wonderful opportunity to do my bit for the club, at the annual company dinner-dance. It was held at a city centre hotel on a Friday evening, which just happened to be the night before we were due to play Everton in an FA Cup 3rd round tie. Everton had a very strong side indeed at that time, so it was expected to be a very tough game.

We had been there about three hours and were pretty inebriated, when we heard that the Everton team were stopping in the very same hotel. This was simply too good to be true and so I started to hatch together a plan with a few other lads, as to how we could disrupt them. The obvious one was to simply set the fire alarm off, but we didn't want to spoil what was a pretty good night, so decided to sneak up on to the top floor, where they were all staying and run down the corridor shouting and banging on all the room doors. It would have been about 11 o'clock at night, so we figured the players would be tucked up in bed asleep, by then. There were about six of us the first time and we did a pretty successful run, tearing down the corridor, banging on the doors and making as much noise as we could.

We escaped back downstairs without incident and fell about laughing. We had another beer and waited a little longer, before deciding to give it another go. This time only three of us would do it, but we made our way to the top floor again, surprisingly without being challenged, and again banged on as many doors as possible before retreating down stairs in hysterics. About an hour later there was only me and another lad who were willing to give it another go (he was actually a Unitedite, but totally up for the fun of doing it anyway!)

This time, someone from Everton must have complained because there was a member of staff at the lift entrance. We were still intent on doing it though, so we simply took the stairs. I think we expected to get stopped, but amazingly we didn't, so for a third time, we set off down the corridor hammering on the doors. As pissed as we were though, we weren't totally stupid and only did a handful before beating a hasty retreat. As tempting as it was to knock on a few more doors, the prospect of being caught by an irate Peter Reid or Pat Van Den Hauwe, in their underpants, was a far too scary thought to risk being caught.

Satisfied that I had done my bit I was proud to share the previous night's escapades, with the lads at the match the next day and was roundly congratulated on a job well done.

We had beaten Everton 1-0 the week before in the league, so we did have a fair chance and when Colin West headed us into a 1-0 lead again, with less than 10 minutes left, I was already happily accepting the congratulations for my part in the win. Surely Everton were showing signs of tiredness from their late night, but it wasn't to be and Peter Reid scored an even later equaliser to tie the game and as they celebrated I am sure that they were looking for me in the crowd.

I can't say what it is about football that grabs you the way it does. I am sure that many people more qualified than me have tried to explain it, but I still can't say why. I guess the biggest single factor is having a team that you support. This gives you a real interest in the outcome of the game.

It becomes important that your team win.

I love football, but I have watched games, as a neutral and to be honest I can't say that it really interests me. I have no interest in say Portsmouth against Birmingham City. It doesn't matter who wins to me, they are just two more teams. As a result I don't watch it when it is on TV. Sky have done a good job of covering football. They have moved football on TV to a new level since they first started screening the game and their marketing of it is exceptional. They have helped create a massive media hype, particularly about the Premiership and sadly it seems that no other football matters, which I find sad and misguided.

The beauty of football is that clubs fortunes do fluctuate but the obscene amount of money that has been injected into the game since Sky has meant that the 'Same Old Four' (SOF) now have a total monopoly on actually winning anything. As it stands in 2009 the Championship has actually overtaken the Premiership in terms of interest. The Championship is completely unpredictable, with maybe ten or twelve clubs having the capability of going up and there are some big bloody clubs in there too. The Championship has now become what British football is really all about. It is the fourth biggest league in the world and yet amazingly gets completely and utterly neglected by the media. In comparison the Premiership is oh so predictable again. The only real question is how Man City will fare now they have also joined the SOF's ranks of obscene money.

In fact, Sky should be worried about the line up of the Premiership. Given the hype of the 'Best league in the world' there are some pretty unfashionable clubs in there for the 09-10 season. Full credit to the clubs that have got there, but the line up of Wigan, Hull, Stoke, Portsmouth, Fulham, Bolton and Burnley could also easily be a line of third division clubs.

Wigan against Fulham, is hardly any reason to stay in, is it?

At least you get to see all the goals on TV now. When we were younger, the only chance you had of seeing any of Wednesday's goals (as rare as they were in the seventies) was if they were chosen to be on the local Yorkshire TV football programme on a Sunday afternoon, which would televise one of the local games (usually L**ds, given YTV's shocking biased towards them).

In those days we didn't have video recorders or DVDs, so on the rare occasion that Wednesday were on, we would record the sound on an audio cassette. That way we could listen to the commentary and the cheers again.

I still have the cassette from a Wednesday v Rotherham game at Millmoor in 1978 which Wednesday won 2-1. We would replay the commentary of Martin Tyler over and over again, listening to the roar of the fans as the ball smashed into the top corner for the winner following Bryan Hornsby's thunderbolt volley.

"Wednesday have a corner......it's played in and headed out...it might come....down for Hornsbeeeeeeeeeeeeeeeee!!!!"

You can now see every single goal scored up and down the country, but to some extent the blanket coverage also spoils it. It takes away the specialness of it all. Football is on the TV continuously and a lot of times it is of no importance to anyone except supporters of the teams that are playing.

It is similar with Italian football, which has been aired by Channel 4, but I can't say that I ever watch it. Like I said before, to me you have to have that spark of interest in having a team to win. If Reading against Bolton doesn't inspire me, then why would Roma against Udinese ?

51

If I am honest I don't think I would watch football at all now, if it wasn't for Wednesday. I find it pretty damn dull and can put my hand on heart and honestly say that I wouldn't go to see the likes of Liverpool against Arsenal if it was played within a mile of where I live and I had free tickets. My sole interest is with Wednesday.

Once you have that magic spark, the fever gets fuelled intensely with every game that you go to, until you find that you are addicted.

Although Wednesday were pretty bloody awful in the mid seventies, there was a perverse pride still in being a Wednesdayite. To be honest we are not a massive club and never will be. It does have huge potential however and will always be a big club and in the darkness of the 3rd Division, we were without doubt the biggest. Wednesday have always had a large hardcore of support and a particularly loyal and impressive away following, so going to places like Bury and Lincoln was lots of fun as we would just about take over the ground

In one particular game at Lincoln City we were walking back, after the match, along a road that ran parallel to a further road that the Lincoln fans were walking along. There were then a series of connecting roads between the two that were obviously the width of a football pitch. Each time that we would come along a connecting road, the Lincoln fans would be mouthing off at the other end and of course as soon as the Wednesday fans charged them, they would run off, up to the next one. This carried on a few times, until some of the Wednesday lads got wise to it and ran a few roads up. There must have been about 50 lads "hid" behind the wall and boy did the Lincoln fans get a shock when they came round the corner. There were the usual fisticuffs and most escaped with a few punches and kicks, but two were "kidnapped" and brought back to where most of the Wednesdayites were. I can't say it was nice to see these two poor lads given a bit of a slapping, but no rescue attempt came from Lincoln. At the end of the day, I don't think either of them were seriously hurt, and as funny as it was to see the 50 guys hid behind the wall of the house in ambush, it still wasn't good to see the two lads get whacked.

There was a similar instance at Mansfield as well. Wednesday had got walloped 3-0 and after the match there was the usual mouthing off and then running off from the home fans "mob." You got to expect that it would happen, but the sheer number of visiting fans meant that it didn't end in a mass brawl very often. On this particular day, a similar thing had happened that two lads hadn't been clever or quick enough to get away and had been captured. One had got away with a bloody nose

52

and a few kicks, but the other lad was getting a proper hiding. To be honest it wasn't right and I can remember suddenly diving in amongst the fists and boots and trying to stop it with my brother, Mark. I would have only been about 15 and I think people were shocked that all 8 stone of little old me was pulling these guys off this Mansfield fan! We simply told them that it wasn't right to attack one kid on his own and much to our surprise, they stopped and let him go.

I'm not sure I'd be that brave now.

We nearly always went on the home end when we went to away games, particularly at local games. It was just simply the thing to do in those days. We had a lot of derby games against Rotherham and Chesterfield and from 1979 Barnsley too and we would nearly always go on their Kop end. We never looked for trouble, but we knew it would happen from someone else. It was always quite fierce at Chesterfield, but Wednesday never got to take their end, so quite often we would simply walk round to one of the two sides of the ground that were flooded with Wednesdayites and watch the game from there.

On one occasion in 1975 it got very out of hand though. It was the first game there since our relegation and was a night match played in September. We had gone on the home end but despite some serious scuffling, there weren't that many Wednesday fans on there. We had just hopped over the fence and onto the terrace along the side when a huge roar went up from the opposite end. We turned to see hundreds of Wednesday fans jumping over the wall and now charging across the pitch. The Owls on the Kop end were heavily outnumbered and up against it, so the rest of them went to the rescue.

It was pandemonium as the Chesterfield fans saw this huge wave of marauding fans coming at them across the pitch. Of course this site encouraged more Wednesday fans to run across the pitch as well, which spurred the Wednesdayites on the Kop end even more when they saw the cavalry coming.

It was amazing to see this and the Police were now really struggling to keep order. A lot of Chessy fans were bailing out of the Kop big time at this sight, but a lot also stood their ground. When the fans reached the home end it was bedlam, with brawling everywhere.

It took ages for the Police to eventually restore some form of order.

It was similar after the game as well with trouble everywhere. Cars were turned over and windows put through and the local press had a field day with the papers full of the riots in Chesterfield.

Rotherham was different though and it almost became expected that the home Tivoli end would have a mass of Wednesday fans on. I have seen Wednesday play there from all four sides of the ground and found it funniest when we were actually on the Railway end (designated for away fans). The Wednesdayites would all wave to one another from different parts of the ground to signify their presence and from the Railway end on a sunny 'shirt sleeves' day, the Tivoli looked like a mass of wiggly worms (as Graham once put it), with all the arms waving.

Wiggly Worms

One year we went on the Tivoli end and got split up as we went in. I was with a guy called John Mallard, and we went up onto the terrace through the central exit / entrance point behind the goal. I think that we just presumed that Wednesday had taken the entire end, from the noise from below, so didn't think anything of turning right and making our way up the terrace and taking a vantage point in the middle of the mob. It was only when they started singing songs about hating Wednesday that we realised that the Tivoli end had been split in two by the police and we were on the wrong side of the divide.

John was not the brightest and simply laughed and said,"Bleedin' hell, I think we are on the wrong side." I cringed when everyone around us turned round and thought, "here we go." To my relief we walked away without being hit and were allowed to simply walk off to the front

54

and onto the Wednesday side. One of our lads, "Founts" was not so lucky and got a fine kick in the nuts when he did a similar thing to us, at about the same time. A Rodger Wylde goal made it all fine later on in a 1-0 win to the Owls.

There was also an incident at Rotherham in the 1979-80 season. Rotherham had hosted Sheffield United on the 6th October and there had been some trouble on the Tivoli end, which resulted in a wall collapsing. The fixture list had thrown out an interesting week for Rotherham, as they entertained Wednesday the following Saturday, so there was a lot of work to be done to ensure that the wall was repaired and safe for the next derby. Needless to say, there was the usual large Wednesday following and there was considerable trouble again. We were on the Tivoli again, but not to be outdone by United, some Wednesday fans went armed with hammers and other tools. Not to be used on opposing fans, but to ensure that the wall came down again!

The police spokesman was quoted afterwards as saying "The supporters came here today intent on doing more damage than their rivals did last week. This was a deliberate attempt to dismantle the wall by taking sections out"

Talk about anything you can do, we can do better.

Of course our own stretch in the Third Division was dragging on now, with no signs of being released early for good behaviour. I think we all thought it would be a brief visit, but it was proving to be far too difficult indeed. We kept getting occasional glimpses that things were looking up, but never realised a serious promotion push. The travelling support particularly was superb and it made going to away matches a real lot of fun, even if the action on the pitch wasn't so good.

Half of the following at Bradford City's Valley Parade from November 1977 (and yes I am in there somewhere!) Note the amount of people stood on walls on the left. This simply wouldn't be tolerated today

55

Some twenty minutes into that game, there were still Bradford fans on the street to the left, throwing bricks into the crowd!

I can remember getting lost on the way to the ground that day and Melv stopping an elderly gentleman to ask directions to the football ground. When we followed his instructions, we found that he had sent us to where Bradford Park Avenue used to play before dropping out of the league some seven years earlier!

After the last day salvation against Southend in 1976 there were some hopes of a better time the following season and although we never really troubled the promoted three sides, it was a nice change to not be in a relegation dog fight. In fact towards the end of the season, we even had a late push, winning three games in four days over Easter (can you imagine football players now been asked to play on a Saturday, Monday and Tuesday!), but a respectable 8th place was at least an improvement.

A thumping 8-2 aggregate win over Doncaster Rovers in the League Cup, at the start of the 1977-78 season raised some optimism, but then a failure to win any of the first ten league games, saw Wednesday familiarly rooted to the foot of the table. A change was needed again and this time the change was monumental. Len Ashurst was sacked after a 2-1 defeat at Preston North End and the board approached a certain Jack Charlton to take on the challenge. World Cup winner Jack had lead a Middlesbrough side to a runaway title success in 1974 and became the first manager outside the top flight to win the Manager of the Year award. He had then steered Boro to three relatively successful seasons in the First Division, so rumours of Jack coming to Hillsborough were creating quite a stir. Jack has a way of doing things his own way and so declined the offer to watch the home game against Chesterfield from the Directors Box and instead tried to sit anonymously in the stand with the fans, to gauge the feeling for the club. He was inevitably spotted and pleaded with by everyone around him to take the helm. He sat through a terrible game which Wednesday somehow managed to win 1-0. This result was met with wild celebrations, which had a big influence on Jack and shortly after it was announced that Jack Charlton would be the next manager of Sheffield Wednesday.

It would be nice to say that Jack brought in a fluent style of football and that we soon moved up the table, but of course this wasn't the case and it took until January to eventually get out of the drop zone of the bottom four.

Results and performances were sporadic, but slowly and surely they dragged themselves out of trouble. There were many times that Wednesday would be outplayed at Hillsborough, but we would sneak a goal and then defend like mad. It was not uncommon to take the ball near to the corner flag of the oppositions half and try to keep it there and run down the clock, with ten or even fifteen minutes left!

Far from being disgruntled at this negative play, the crowd loved it and as long as the team scratched out two more vital points, we all went home happy! Jacks philosophy seemed quite simple and that was to not lose. If we could pinch a win, great, but the priority was to not lose and the team eventually learned how to do it. A run of just 3 defeats from the last 22 games saw Wednesday finish a comfortable ten points above the drop zone and hopes high for next season.

Jack had worked hard at re-organising things in the summer and strengthened the back room team with the likes of Ian St John, Maurice Setters and the wily old fox John Harris, as well as adding new players such as Brian Hornsby, Ray Blackhall and the solid Mick Pickering. He also brought in youngsters like goalkeeper Bob Bolder and Mark Smith and the side was showing distinct signs of improvement. Although the 1978-79 season didn't live up to its promise and only a mid table finish was achieved (curiously enough it ended with a run of five consecutive home games) it will always be remembered for an epic cup run that saw us get as far as the third round!

Being in the Third Division, we had to enter at the First round stage and I ventured to Scunthorpe's Old Show Ground in November to witness a 1-1 draw. It was bloody freezing, with no heating whatsoever and it is no wonder that fans had a bad habit of smashing up trains in those days. They were probably trying to find some wood to burn to keep warm.

The subsequent replay was won 1-0 and we were then drawn away to Tranmere, which was again tied at 1-1. By the time of the replay the draw for the third round had already been made and we had drawn high flying Arsenal at home. Arsenal were near the top of the First Division (as it was) with players such as Liam Brady, Frank Stapleton and David O'Leary. The draw must have spurred everyone on because Tranmere were destroyed 4-0 three days later and the scene was set.

The tie at Hillsborough almost didn't go ahead, because the country was in the middle of one of the harshest winters for some time and there had been a massive amount of snow the previous day. An army of volunteers were called on to shovel all the snow from the pitch on the morning of the game and due to their efforts, the game was able to go ahead.

Not surprisingly Arsenal took the lead and at half time they lead 1-0. The teams came out for the second half and Arsenal keeper Pat Jennings had to defend the Kop end. The problem for Jennings was that he couldn't get near the goals. The Wednesdayites had an almost inexhaustible supply of snow and poor old Pat was pelted, every time he ventured anywhere remotely near the goals! Every time he thought it safe to go near, hundreds of snowballs would come raining down again.

The ref had no choice but to delay the game, but it was to no avail and the torrent of snowballs continued. There was a lengthy delay as the snowball game continued and even Jack had to come on to the pitch to ask the fans to stop. Even this made no difference and he in turn was bombarded with snowballs. There is a clip of this on You Tube now and I must admit when I saw it recently I had tears streaming down my face I was laughing so much.

When eventually the game did get underway, it must have disrupted Arsenal because Wednesday equalised quite early on and deservedly took the game to a replay.

Strangely enough this was the last time Wednesday would play at home for nearly 2 months, with the next 8 games being played away from Hillsborough.

Sorry that I couldn't get a better picture than this, but it is the only one that I could find with Pat Jennings. Wednesday celebrate Dennis Lemans equaliser, but look at the pitch. The whole of the eighteen yard box was absolutely covered with splattered snowballs

I think we all thought that the cup run ended there, but to everyone's surprise, Wednesday took the lead with a Rodger Wylde goal at Highbury and looked as though they may win a shock victory. We went to Melvs house to listen to the game on the radio and I can still see him now, pacing up and down, biting his nails down to his knuckles as the clock ticked by. Sadly Arsenal equalised with just four minutes to go and the game was sent to a further replay.

Leicester City's Filbert Street was chosen as the neutral venue, as they had a huge inflatable, protective balloon which was pumped full of air. It covered the entire pitch, so despite the freezing weather, the game still went ahead.

Although we all expected to get thumped, there was a terrific following for the third game. So much so that Mark and Melv, who came down later on their own, couldn't get into the allotted Wednesday section, so had to go in the Arsenal end. When it became obvious this was not a safe thing to do, they escaped via the perimeter of the pitch and jumped in with the rest of the Owls.

The game itself was terrific and finished 2-2, after extra time. There was quite a lot of fighting after the game, so when the fourth game was played just two days later, again at Leicester, it was no surprise that there was even more trouble. We were in the stand behind the goal, which seemed to be full of Wednesdayites and if the third game was good, the fourth was even better. It finished 3-3, with both sides looking as though they could have won it.

For the third replay, there seemed to be a lot more Wednesday supporters than Arsenal, but the fact that the games were so good and could go either way built up a lot of interest across the country. So much so that for the fifth game there was a crowd of over 30,000 there. Again we had our chances to win the game, but finally succumbed to a 2-0 defeat. We must be the only league club in the history of the competition to play nine cup ties and still not get past the third round.

Sadly that season again failed to live up to expectations and I wondered when exactly we would get our share of glory. I honestly always believed that Wednesday would return to the top division, but it seemed a frustratingly long time away. My only "success" was seeing us avoid relegation to the third tier and fourth tier on the last game of the season.

I would religiously watch, "Football Focus," and, 'On The Ball," on a Saturday afternoon and be so envious of watching other teams success.

59

I particularly remember it showing Brighton clinching promotion following a midweek game and seeing the fans run on the pitch at the end and the celebrations that followed. I was absolutely gutted and so jealous.

I was so desperate to experience that glory and knew that one day it would come around. Seeing your team lose to the likes of Port Vale and Chesterfield would just make it all the more sweeter when it happened (well that's what I deludedly tried to tell myself, but you know what, the part timers who just come for the glory, enjoy it just as much)

Football in the late 1970s was in the doldrums for many reasons and I'm not just talking about Wednesday. The football hooligan problem was rife everywhere and particularly when England or English clubs played in Europe and whereas the press were not over interested in domestic violence, trouble abroad was a big story. Unfortunately the desire of the media to report on this trouble only made things worse and fuelled the people who were doing it into creating even more trouble. This in turn encouraged others and foreign hooligans would relish the chance to contest against the famous English hooligans. The press will obviously deny it, but they love it when there is trouble abroad. It's a great story to them. Even the BBC, with their high moral stance are as guilty as anyone of over reporting trouble. They like to be seen to distance themselves from it, yet they send their cameras and reporters and will make it their leading story over REAL news stories when it kicks off. It seems odd that a responsible establishment will report a fight at a football match over deaths, murders, corruption, world poverty etc.

I'm not saying that trouble wasn't bad, it clearly was, but the media frenzy to find it and report it got ludicrous.

I remember getting tickets to see England play in Germany for the European Championships in 1988 and being concerned over the reports of non stop trouble and fans being attacked constantly. The Sun had a blazing headline "World War 3" yet the worst picture they could find of the trouble was a skinhead pulling his tongue out.

Again, I'm sure there was fighting, but when we got there, we saw no trouble whatsoever. Everyone was mixing together, from all nationalities, drinking beer, singing and having a good time. But of course, this never gets reported. There are a number of stories of journalists actually paying trouble makers to start the violence, because nothing was happening. Surely this is more outrageous than the trouble itself, but again, it barely gets reported.

England have had to work incredibly hard at restoring the image of it's supporters and have done amazingly well, given the massive numbers that went to Germany for the World Cup in 2006. They have contained and discouraged trouble, yet sadly the press don't want to know about this. They are still there waiting for something, anything, to happen and they will jump on it.

The press coverage, together with the actual violence itself did put people off going to domestic football matches and attendances were a lot lower than they are at the moment. Having said that, it is not surprising, considering the state of some of the grounds. Conditions at most grounds, particularly in the 3rd Division, were archaic to say the least. Facilities were pretty atrocious, with very little in terms of catering. A "Wagon Wheel" or a "Bovril" was about as much choice as you were given and the toilet facilities were an absolute disgrace.

It was the norm to have to wade through urine 2 or 3 inches deep if you wanted to venture into an overcrowded smelly urinal block, so many people would simply piss against the wall outside rather than get their feet wet. The vast population of football supporters then were men (and it is pleasing, as well as a sign of progress, that there are so many female fans now), so peeing against a wall was not necessarily seen as such a bad thing in those days. In fact there were hardly any women's toilets at football grounds and there seemed little desire to attract them either. The trouble and poor facilities were enough to put anyone off. Wednesday did try in the mid 1970's to encourage ladies, offering discounts to females.

mmy Craig

Half-Season Tickets

Now on Sale.
Valid from 26th December, 1974 (v Bolton Wanderers) to the end of the season.

Centre North/South Stand
    £10; Lady £9.50; Juvenile £9.00

Back Centre North/South Stand
    £7.75; Lady £7.25; Juvenile £6.75

North Stand Wings, West Stand, South Stand Wing (Penistone Road)
    £6.50; Lady £6.00; Juvenile £5.50

West Stand—Senior Citizens
    £4.00

Ground
    £4.00; Lady £3.50; Juvenile £3.00

New Turnstile

A Juvenile turnstile will be opened for the Uncovered Seats from the 14th December. Admission 45p. This turnstile will be in the block nearest Penistone Road.

Today's Team Mascot

The team mascot for today's game is Steven

In 1974 women clearly didn't have the same comprehension of the game as men. This advertisement in a 1974 programme shows that ladies paid 50p less for a half season ticket than a man. The original advert said it was £3 for girls with big tits, but this was thought to be too sexist and so got changed

Football didn't particularly help itself around this time. Although clubs did draw a distinct line between themselves and any unruly supporters they had, there was still a shrug the shoulders attitude that there was nothing they could do. Wednesday did have regular pieces in the programme, with the very catchy "Hooliganism isn't Wednesdayism" phrase (I don't think Saatchi and Saatchi thought that one up) and regularly they would try to discourage the hardcore element that was building up quite a reputation.

The Wednesday hooligans even became well known faces at Hillsborough, with people like "Sammy" and "Anny Bovver" becoming minor celebrities.

An incident from the away game at Lincoln City which caused the club to make a statement in the programme. Note how the Police are understandably cowering from the barrage, yet the old St Johns Ambulance guy carries out his duties undaunted

Pictures that tell their own story

A POLICEMAN IS STRUCK BY A THROWN MISSILE IN FRONT OF A SHEFFIELD SECTION OF THE CROWD AT LINCOLN LAST SATURDAY. SHEFFIELD FACES IN THE CROWD REFLECT FEAR, APPREHENSION, CONCERN AND THE HOOLIGAN EXPRESSION OF JOY AT THE SIGHT OF A REPRESENTATIVE OF LAW AND ORDER BEING INJURED. THESE HOOLIGANS ARE A DISGRACE TO THEIR PARENTS, THEIR CITY AND THE CLUB THEY CLAIM TO SUPPORT

WE CAN DO WITHOUT THEIR SUPPORT: THEY ARE NOT WELCOME AT HILLSBOROUGH.

H. E. McGEE, CHAIRMAN.

The clubs official comments in the programme following the Lincoln events

Wednesday v Tranmere

Don't forget that it is OK to wave your scarf, but don't be a disgrace to your parents. I did wave my scarf and never got into any trouble but my parents still thought I was a disgrace

Most clubs had very short sighted views of the problems and caging supporters in was seen to be the common way of dealing with fans inside the grounds. The reaction from the Police was pretty similar as well to be honest. The tactics were to contain fans and prevent them from getting at each other if possible. Although these combined actions of treating supporters like animals, lead to the supporters behaving like animals, to me it was slowly the start of recognising the problem and eventually analysing and trying to solve it.

Unfortunately, the measures that had been put in place were totally fraught with danger and with the benefit of hindsight now, it is amazing to think that such dangerous acts of fencing people in were allowed to happen. It was only a matter of time before something terrible happened.

Ironically and tragically it was our own beloved Hillsborough that would be the catalyst for change following the disaster at the FA Cup semi final held there in 1989. To me all that was wrong in football, for the previous 20 years or so came to fruition and everyone should accept some part of the blame. The supporters for their behaviour, the football clubs for the state and design of the stadium and restraints in place and the Police for their approach to managing football supporters.

It could have happened anywhere and at anytime, in my opinion.

It was sadly inevitable.

I can remember being at an FA Cup game at Chester City's Sealand Road ground only two years before in 1987, where amazingly they only had one turnstile open for visiting fans. We were there 20 minutes before kick off and the crush outside was intense. As the minutes ticked by, people got more and more agitated and once the game had started this intensified. There was no way on earth I could touch the ground and the fear was that as I got closer to the entrance, I would be pushed past and have to go to the back again. The pressure on the wall would be coming dangerously high to collapsing, but thankfully, it didn't and we made it in OK. My only surprise was that a disaster didn't happen somewhere like this, instead of a large and what was considered at the time a modern and safe stadium like Hillsborough.

I have been to a hell of a lot of games over the years, where you have been crushed into small pens and been unable to have any control over what was happening to you. It was a reasonably common occurrence to be unable to touch the floor with your feet, as you were carried along by the crowd. I can't honestly say that I was particularly scared before these incidents though. It was simply accepted.

I can remember being particularly scared at a game against Nottingham Forest though in August 1985. It was less than three months after the Heysel Disaster in Belgium, where 39 people died following a crush and a wall collapsing. Wednesday had won their second game of the season 1-0 and we were all happily celebrating, before starting to make our way out.

In 1985 the away end at Forest was an open terrace and the way in and out was down quite a steep bank of steps. On that particular evening, the Police had decided to keep the exit gates closed to prevent any confrontation with the home supporters. Unfortunately they didn't tell the thousands of Wednesdayites the plan and so there was the inevitable crush of bodies. The people at the back on the terraces were still pushing forward and getting agitated at the lack of progress, whilst the crush built on those at the bottom. I was already descending the steps but quite near the top, when the panic started to set in. There was a mass of bodies, crushed and unstable on a steep embankment with that feeling of being out of control and unable to touch the floor. All around there was a real fear that something could happen. People were scared, angry and starting to panic with Heysel fresh in the memory. The feeling in the darkness behind the terraces was that it was only going to take one person to go over and there would be another catastrophe. Fortunately it didn't happen.

The message was screamed to those at the back to stop pushing and move back and slowly normality resumed. Not thanks to the stewards or Police, but because of the fans themselves.

Every fan around that time will be able to give you similar scenarios and the shock and grief following the Hillsborough Disaster, was heartfelt by us all because we all knew that it was a case of, there but for the grace of God, go I.

The changes that started to happen from 1989 was partly down to a review of strategy by the authorities and a slow but steady improvement of safety and facilities from the clubs, but I also think it was due to a change in the mentality of supporters. I think fans got sick of being herded like animals and treated like scum. There became a, maybe, begrudging acceptance of one another and the fact that we are all in this together gave us some respect for fellow fans. Yes there is still some trouble at games, but you can walk around wearing colours now, without automatically being attacked. Slowly football has learned its lesson.

It may not be perfect but it sure is a damn site better.

Sadly it took the loss of life to see it.

CHAPTER 4

Hope and Glory

Following the epic encounters against Arsenal, the rest of that season was pretty disappointing as the team still lacked that little spark of quality. The first of those sparks was to arrive towards the end of that season though. Terry Curran was signed from Southampton for £100,000 and we went down to, soon to be promoted, Watford to see his debut. He came on as a second half substitute and you could tell straight away that he had something special. That bit of flair and unpredictability that would win games (as well as drive you mad).

The main thing in that 1978-79 season was the relegation of Sheffield United to join us in the Third Division. There were five local clubs in the third division that season, with United being relegated and Barnsley being promoted from the Fourth Division, so that there was also a mini "South Yorkshire league" running (if you include Chesterfield) as well as nearby Mansfield Town.

The following season was probably my all time favourite, Jack had got the team organised and the basis of a good side was established. In the close season, Jack had brought in Andy McCulloch and Ian Mellor to add to Curran and the team suddenly looked full of goals.

I had my season ticket for the North Stand at £39.10 (The Kop was now 90 pence for a juvenile. Damn that inflation!) and the season started with 3 of the first 4 games against Hull City, having also drawn them in the League Cup.

In the Cup the first leg finished 1-1 and a solid performance saw us win 2-1 at Hull. For some reason we gave their player Trevor Phillips some stick during the game (I think it went back to a recent incident when he played for Rotherham and had gestured at the crowd). We had a few pints after the match and made our way home, stopping at a service station en route, only to find the same Trevor Phillips, tucking into his post match meal. There was some banter, as a few other Wednesday fans had also spotted him and Phillips decided it best to make an early exit. One guy spotted this and noticing his half eaten meal, picked up a sausage from his plate and went after him. Phillips walked faster as the fan kept following, before deciding to leg it with the fan chasing him shouting "OY! Trevor you've forgotten your sausage." He made it to his car just in time and with a screech of wheels and a final throw of the sausage at his car, he escaped.

We got on the Motorway to find the Wednesday team coach going past us.

I think we spent the rest of the journey home overtaking and then being overtaken by the coach, leaning out of the windows and waving to the players. They happily waved back, but after seventeen times got bored and went back to playing cards.

The first league game of the season was away at Barnsley and from what I remember was a fine sunny day, as the opening day of the season usually is. We got there at a reasonable time, for the customary pre match drink. There was as expected, a huge following from Sheffield and it seemed chaotic outside, so we went on the Barnsley end. With colours hidden, we climbed the back of their Kop and entered the terrace and it was clearly already kicking off. We couldn't see a great deal, but it was obvious from the noise that they were fighting in heaps. We made an assessment that there wouldn't be masses of Owls on here so made our way to the front and jumped over the fence and onto the terrace. Although this area was mixed support, it was apparent that Wednesday were in the majority.

What a lovely feeling opening day is.

Buoyed by a huge following, a nice sunny day and the anticipation and excitement of the new season, we were all in fine spirits. We even saw Jack walking behind the stand and along with everyone else, wished him good luck for the new season. I was amazed when he actually turned to us and said that we would do just fine as long as "us lot" behaved ourselves.

I was staggered.

I'd never even contemplated that we could ever be mistaken as football hooligans, but clearly we were and by our own manager at that.

Now it made sense why Trevor Phillips beat a hasty retreat from his sausage and chips.

Onto the game and it was a perfect start to the season, with a resounding 3-0 win and goals for new boys, Andy McCulloch and Ian Mellor and of course one from the mercurial Terry Curran.

One nil to the Wednesday boys.....TC celebrates the first goal of the season at Barnsley, with Brian Hornsby rushing to congratulate him

I think the Owls in the background were just a bit happy by this.

I think we all thought that at long last this was to be our season, but in reality the first part of the season was similar to the previous, with totally inconsistent results. I was going to virtually every game by now and we had established a good mob of regulars. We saw some great games like at Wimbledon, when Terry Curran scored one of the best goals I have ever seen in a 4-3 win at Plough Lane, as well as nightmares, such as a 3-0 drubbing at a wet and windy Carlisle, but we were having a hell of a lot of fun.

69

In November we played away at Blackpool and there was always something special about going there for a match. A lot of fans would go for the weekend and you would see Wednesday flags draped out of B&B windows. The game itself was pretty poor and we scraped a 1-1 draw.

We were hardly tearing through the league like we expected.

It got so boring during the game at one point that two of the lads, John Mallard and John Fountain, went on the Blackpool end. Their Kop in those days was split down the middle by a fence, to keep rival fans apart. Yet you could simply walk round the back and onto whichever side you wanted, so they decided to wander round. They stayed for about five minutes before coming back round.

There was no trouble during the game, but it kicked off afterwards. It seemed that all the side streets had little battles going on and we all got split up. We met back at the car, but Mark was no where to be seen. We waited five minutes before deciding to go looking for him. We were in Graham's car and he drove round the streets, with us all trying to spot Mark.

Suddenly we saw a gang of Blackpool fans charging at two Wednesday fans, just in front of us. Graham was convinced one of them was Mark that was taking a few blows, so accelerated the car straight into the middle of the fracas. I think he realised it was a crazy thing to do, as he braked hard at the last minute, so fortunately no one was killed. Instead two of them went flying over the long bonnet of his Capri and landed heavily. The others must have thought we were serious hard core hooligans after such a wild entrance and ran off quickly. The two Blackpool fans that went over the bonnet couldn't run off though as they rolled around in agony and must have feared the worst as we got out of the car. One of the Blackpool fans looked totally stunned and horrified and asked "Why the f**k did you did that" to which Graham, once realising that Mark wasn't amongst the fracas simply said "Sorry, I thought you'd got my brother" and promptly drove off again leaving the two guys bewildered on the floor. We eventually met Mark where the car had originally been parked, having simply wandered off to find an off licence.

Man, I bet those Blackpool fans hurt the next day.

Another disappointing performance along the way came at Chester City in the next away game. Again we managed to get a draw, a more entertaining 2-2 draw this time.

We had gone in the main stand at Sealand Road and had a pretty good view. Wednesday supporters were scattered all round the ground,

70

but I can particularly remember the fans gathered off to our right in a covered wooden stand. It was a freezing cold day and during the second half, some of them decided it would be a good idea to set fire to the stand. The idea was to drop lit pieces of paper through the gaps, to try and light the rubbish, which had accumulated over the years, beneath the stand. We were some way from the incident, but could clearly see what was happening. They tried several times and occasionally it looked as though the fire would take, but fortunately it never did. It seemed an incredibly stupid thing to do, yet from what I can recall, there was no official intervention from Police or stewards to try and stop them.

Of course we now know that the accumulation of rubbish under the stand was the cause of the tragic accident at Bradford City, some five years later, where 56 people died when the main stand caught fire.

The season was still going OK and Wednesday were handily placed, without managing to raise a serious assault at a promotion place, until Christmas approached and a game that would go down in Sheffield's footballing history and a game that totally changed the course of the season. I will eulogise about the game in a later chapter, but for now let's just say that the first Sheffield derby match for 10 years ended in a resounding and emphatic victory for Wednesday.

(Although my memory told me that from this point on Wednesday stormed up the league and United fell away badly, it was only when I researched it, that I found that United remained in the top three and above Wednesday, until the end of February).

Wednesday promptly lost their next game after beating United, but then won seven of the next eight games and averaged three goals per game. From this point on it seemed everyone wanted to jump on the promotion bandwagon and average crowds almost doubled.

It was still scary stuff, because you just never knew when the wheels would fall off, but it was bloody marvellous. We went to every game, except one, Oxford away, as rather foolishly Mark had arranged to get married that day (I still can't believe he didn't consult the fixture list!).

One of the games was at nearby Mansfield and so there was a huge away following. We got in reasonably early as we thought there may be problems. We were stood along the terrace, in front of the main stand. To our right the away end was packed and the little stand opposite also had a huge contingent of Owls. Three sides of the ground were bouncing in anticipation and then at about ten to three a huge roar went up on the Mansfield Kop end and Wednesdayites charged at the Mansfield fans. There was some serious fighting, before the Mansfield fans were chased

71

off the Kop and onto the pitch. This victory seemed to encourage more Wednesday fans on to their end and so all four sides of the ground were occupied by us. Of course there were Mansfield fans amongst the Wednesdayites, but the thousand or so Mansfield fans on the pitch, didn't know where to go!

More to the point the Police didn't know what to do with them either!

They stood around on the pitch, while they figured out what the hell to do. Eventually, they were put partly on the small terrace opposite and the Police made a cordon on the Kop to allow them partly back on there, in the corner.

Graham had got a new car at the time (he didn't like the dints in the Capri that the Blackpool fans had caused), a Ford Fiesta Sandpiper. It had a two tone beige and brown colour scheme and looked quite smart. He was suitably proud of it, as it was his first brand new car. He had it for a week before taking us on the short trip to Mansfield. There were two car loads of us and I ended up coming back in Gray's car, following the 1-1 draw.

We were back in Sheffield, when someone said they could smell burning. We all agreed, but thought it must be a running in type smell. We debated whether the smell was getting stronger but then, worse still, was the fact that the car was filling with smoke. Suddenly flames shot from the rear passenger door and amid lots of swearing and cursing Mallard whacked the flames out with his hand and stopped the little fire that was taking hold in the back. The stupid pillock had put his cigarette in the side ashtray and not put it out properly. It had slowly smouldered and eventually caught light, burning all the side panel of the car. Graham was not amused but Mallard simply laughed.

I don't think we went in Graham's car for a long time after that.

To be honest nobody liked to take their own car to a game. I don't know why, but the cars were treated with no respect whatsoever and it would always take ages to clear away all the mess of papers and empty beer cans at the end of the journey. As a result we would hire a van if there was enough of us, for an away match.

This was the plan for the New Year's Day clash to Gillingham. We had hired an Escort van, for seven of us to make the long trip south. Hardly well thought about, but at 18, comfort wasn't as important as being there.

Mark had a party at his house at Killamarsh for New Years Eve and it was fancy dress. The party started well, in the local pub and by midnight everyone was very drunk indeed. I can't remember a great deal about the party now, other than it was really good and that at about 3 or 4 o'clock in the morning, it was still going strong. Eventually, it naturally ran its course and slowly we crashed out for a few hours.

Getting up at 8 o'clock was tough, but nothing like as tough as the journey down. The disgusting stench in the back of that cramped little van was absolutely appalling.

It is a bloody long way to Gillingham from Sheffield when you are squashed into a confined space and sat on a bare metal floor, breathing in a constant cacophony of rancid farts, I can tell you. I'm not honestly sure how I survived that journey, but the sheer relief at opening the rear doors of that van and stumbling out into fresh air made me feel giddy!

We parked bang outside the ground, where a large number of Wednesdayites were angrily milling around and trying to knock the main doors down. We found this a little over the top, as there were plenty of other pubs around, until we found out that the game had been called off. Yes, with just over 2 hours to go to kick off, the ever so considerate football industry, had decided to call the game off, due to an icy pitch.

I mean, fine, if the pitch was a bit iffy, then it can't go ahead, but come on, two hours before kick off! No thought whatsoever to the couple of thousand people that had to drive 400 miles on New Years Bloody Day.

Oh well at least we had a lovely luxurious return journey to look forward to.

The rest of that season continued in wonderful style and life was particularly good. SKA was the in sound at the time and every away game would be accompanied by the likes of Selector, The Specials etc and the car bouncing along with us all dancing inside to " Too much pressure" at full volume.

After years of watching Wednesday struggle, at long last we seemed to be in with a chance of a little bit of glory, although it was going to be close, as to whether we got promoted or not. A terrific unbeaten run of 16 games, saw us with only three games remaining, going into an away game at Blackburn, in a second v third encounter. Wednesday and Blackburn were level on points, with Chesterfield just two points behind and a game in hand (two points for a win in those days and the top three got promoted). This was a huge game, absolutely massive, with a draw or defeat, probably putting an end to my hopes of seeing some success for the first time in my life.

The crowd was over 26,000 with a massive following from a glory starved Sheffield. Gray had been over to Blackburn earlier and got us tickets in the main Blackburn stand. Ewood Park was an appalling ground before Jack Walkers millions transformed it. A typical post war stadium, with hardly any money spent on it for decades and ridiculously insufficient leg room in the "luxury" of the one stand that had seats, but we didn't care, we were inside for the big game.

There were Wednesdayites scattered all over the ground as scuffles kept breaking out in different areas and the atmosphere was great. We were sat towards where most of the Owls were stood, but when Blackburn scored to go 1-0 up, just before half time, we knew we were sat in the Blackburn end. And of course the huge flock of budgerigars that fluttered around the celebrating players told us it was our old friend Brotherston that had scored.

Half time was terrible. We just had this hollow sinking feeling that this long awaited glory was slowly slipping away. If the game stayed like this Chesterfield would have 2 games in hand and only 2 points behind (If we could have known that we would only take 1 point from our last two games as well, we would probably have gone home there and then), but football as we all know, is a funny old game and the second half was very different.

Wednesday played superb in the second half and Kevin 'Ticker' Taylor equalised on 51 minutes and then Ian 'Spiderman' Mellor bulleted a diving header home, with just 8 minutes remaining, to send us all absolutely mental. When the second goal went in, we all jumped up and down, hugging each other and went tumbling over the rows in front falling on to people sat in front of us, as we inevitably lost our balance. I can imagine seeing your team lose a one goal lead in a big promotion decider would be pretty gutting, but can't imagine what it would be like to then have half a dozen away fans falling on top of you, wildly celebrating! There were lots of angry comments, but we didn't care by that stage.

There were Wednesdayites scattered everywhere and being seated near the away end anyway, it seemed like half of the ground was bouncing. We wouldn't sit down at all for the rest of the game, absolutely singing our heads off and screaming the lads on. Everyone around us was telling us to sit down, but we were having none of it. The noise coming from the 'away end' was phenomenal and everywhere around the ground there were pockets of Wednesdayites jumping up and down, singing along.

74

The game finished 2-1 to Wednesday and we knew that we were virtually over the finishing line. God it felt so good. Anybody that was at that game will always remember it as being a truly special night as an Owl.

Kevin 'ticker' Taylor smashes home the equaliser.........

.........and Ian Mellor's header wins promotion

We already had plans for going to the penultimate game at Exeter, but the win at Blackburn and a subsequent defeat for Chesterfield the following night, meant that a win for us would guarantee promotion.

It seemed everyone was going.

We met on the Friday night in the local pub and had a good session, before we even set off. When the pubs closed at 10.30, (Yes pubs really did close at 10.30 in those days) we got ready to leave. The banter in the pub had been good before, particularly aimed at any United fans that happened to be there. One of which was a lad called John Stainrod. He was one of the kids that was a Unitedite, but hardly went to any games.

He was still good sport to take the mickey out of though, so as we left the pub, he got bundled into one of the cars, as someone joked that we should kidnap him and take him to Exeter. Although he resisted a little, he gave in and was bundled into the back seat and we set off. I'm sure he kept expecting us to stop and let him out, but we didn't and after a while, it was too late and no one wanted to turn back and take him home. As a result he found himself on the M1 heading to Devon!

I think we stopped at the service station near Nottingham, so he could have hitched a lift back with some burly lorry driver, but he obviously decided to stay with us.

In 1980 the big rage was the arrival of the Space Invaders arcade game and I think we were all hooked on it. As a result the long drive down to Exeter took twice as long, because we had to keep stopping at every service station for another few games. We decided to go to Torquay, when we arrived in Devon, as we heard that was where everyone else was heading and we got there at about 7 or 8 in the morning. We had a wander around and grabbed something to eat and bought a cheap yellow football from a newsagent before heading to the beach for a kick about. After a while, some other Wednesdayites joined us and the game grew. I can't honestly remember what happened for the next few hours. I know we left and headed for a pub, come opening time. At about one o'clock we headed off to Exeter and laughed as we saw our yellow football still being kicked about on the beach in a 50 a side game.

After a few more beers around the ground in Exeter, we headed to the game. I can't remember why, but the day before, someone thought it would be a good idea to buy a bouquet of flowers to give to the goalkeeper, Bob Bolder. Bolder had come back into the side after about 20 games and did a magnificent job of shoring up the defence and aiding the promotion push.

The obvious choice for player of the season would obviously have been Terry Curran, but to recognise Bolder's efforts, we decided on him.

Why flowers is another question altogether.

We didn't think this through at all, though. John Fountain got a bouquet from his Dad's shop and in the car it went. How we were going to present the flowers was another thing. Were we just going to walk on the pitch and give them to him?

The next issue, was who was going to carry them. No one wanted to be seen walking to a football match carrying a big bouquet of flowers, so after some debate, Founts himself took them. There were a lot of strange looks and comments along the way and I think the rest of us were all thankful that none of us were holding them. Wednesday were given the home end, in anticipation of the large 6,000 following, so we went on there. Once inside, it was agreed that we needed to get rid of the flowers as soon as possible, so when the players came out to warm up, we went to the front and yes, it was as simple as climbing over the wall and onto the pitch. A steward came and asked what we were doing and at that stage I bottled it and stayed terrace side. Founts, Stainrod and 'Harry the Duck' went for it and presented the flowers to a rather embarrassed Bob Bolder. The moment was captured by the local press and subsequently published in The Sheffield Star's 'Owls promotion special publication.'

BLOOMIN' GOOD SHOW!

I was soooooooo jealous!
Kidnapee, Bolder, Founts and Duck
(Harry the Duck had a lovely girlfriend, called Janine. She was so
thoughtful, that on one occasion went to the local shop, to buy him a
copy of the "Green'Un" (a local sports paper that was published at five
o'clock on a Saturday with all the football scores from the day).
Unfortunately for Janine, it was three hours before any games kicked
off! Harry (John Mallard) sadly died in 2007

77

The game itself was a bit of an anti climax, with Exeter winning 1-0 and so it looked like we would need to beat Carlisle at home the following Saturday to clinch promotion. But then a very kind announcer from Exeter read the scores out from the other grounds. There was total silence as he got to Millwall 1 Chesterfield............nil, followed by wild celebrations, as promotion was secured. I know it was only promotion from the third division, but this was absolutely fantastic. Everyone was screaming and hugging each other. After a while the fans went onto the pitch to celebrate and congregated around the main stand. I went up into the stand as I knew that it would be there that the players would come out. I managed to get into the Directors box, just as they emerged. The stewards then tried to hold everybody back, but I got in just at the right time and was stood just behind Jack Charlton, captain, Mickey Pickering and the rest of the players, as fans and team celebrated the magic moment. It was truly special. It had been 14 years since there had been any kind of achievement from Sheffield (The 1966 FA Cup Final defeat) and I was there in the middle of it

I can't believe that I was cut off this picture! I am sure the photographer must have moved 10 yards to the right to keep me out of the shot!

I must say that there is something disturbing about 12 naked men getting into such a small bath. No wonder players today like their own individual baths!

The £39.10 for my season ticket for the North Stand was money well spent, with some unbelievable highs along the way. The final game was again an anti climax, with a pretty dull 0-0 draw against Carlisle, but that day we were all there to celebrate and over 32,000 welcomed the long awaited glory and saw us off to Division 2.

We had waited years for this. After seeing other clubs on the TV finally it was our turn. A packed Hillsborough swarms the pitch in celebration after the Carlisle game

The 1980-81 season started very well. We had drawn United in the League Cup, so the very first game was against them at Hillsborough. Although the attendance was only half of the same game eight months earlier, it was still a terrific atmosphere. There had been a dramatic shift in this time, however. United seriously looked a club in decline and Wednesday were on the up. This time it was expected that Wednesday would win and win they did. A very comfortable 2-0 victory was followed up by a 1-1 draw at their place and we eased into the next round. Four days later and the league season started with a marvellous fixture at home to Newcastle. It was everything you wanted it to be. A nice sunny day, a good crowd of 26,000, a few Geordies in the Wednesday end to take some stick, a strong performance and a 2-0 win. Wonderful!

We got off to a reasonable start and ventured over to Oldham for a game in early September. There was only Mark and myself for some reason and after failing to get in the away end or the home end, managed to get in one of the stands. The thing that will always be remembered for this game was the subsequent 'riot' that happened. I use the word loosely because in my eyes it was nothing like a 'riot'. As usual there were sporadic fisticuffs, from the mixture of visitors inside the home ends, but nothing out of the ordinary.

It all changed when Terry Curran was sent off by a referee who appeared to be giving everything to Oldham. It seemed an innocuous moment and most people believed it was some terrible acting by Oldham player Simon Stainrod (maybe he was seeking revenge for us kidnapping his cousin the previous season). Whatever the reason, the crowd behind the goal acted very angrily and the situation soon escalated, with fans getting onto the pitch. The Police came over to calm the situation, but as is usually the case, it simply inflames it. The players were taken off the pitch, while order was restored. I can remember loads of bricks and concrete being thrown from the Wednesday end, but no real uprising. The local announcer kept appealing for people to clear the pitch and that the game would not restart until they did, even though there was no one but the Police on the pitch.

After half an hour there was a personal appeal for calm from Big Jack, but he left the field shaking his head as the mayhem continued. Eventually it all calmed down with the players returning and the game continued.

A distraught JC after trying to restore order
(Either that or he was having flashbacks about snowballs)

We were dubbed "animals" after that and as a subsequent punishment Wednesday had the standing areas of Hillsborough closed for the next four home games and Owls fans were banned from travelling to the next four away games. All that happened was that Wednesday supporters went away and just got tickets for the home areas (increasing the chance of trouble). I can remember at Derby there being a big chant of "Clap your hands if your not here!".

As for the home games, the club got more revenue, as fans had to sit in the more expensive stands, rather than the cheaper Kop and we won nearly every game as well.

An eerily empty Kop contrasts with the packed North and South stands. This harsh measure by the FA obviously brought the Wednesday animals to their senses...............................not

The rest of the season was OK with a real fluctuation in results and although we were never threatened with struggling in the league, we weren't quite good enough to make a challenge, either.

The side was starting to change again. Jack brought new players in around this time, such as Bannister, Megson and the rather strange Yugoslavian, Ante Mirocevic. Home grown players such as Mark Smith and the soon to be legend, Mel Sterland were making a mark on the team and the feeling was that we were pushing on again. (The nickname of 'Zico' given to Sterland was created by our very own Melv.)

Local players like John Pearson, Mel Sterland and Gavin Oliver were pushing into the first team now. Here they attend a children's Christmas party. The father of the poor lad on the right must have been a huge Wednesdayite. Can you imagine the conversation the morning of the party... "Ar dunt care 'ow poorly thy ar. Thas gooin t'wednesday party and that's that!"

The second season in Division Two really should have seen us promoted. We started the season well with four straight wins, as well as playing some great football. I loved this period in my life. Wednesday were doing well and everything else was just great.

I had a great social life, a great team to watch, a bit of money to spend and the music scene was just getting better. New wave had followed punk, which was somehow more cutting and clever. I can remember being into U2 at the time. No one had heard of them and I saw them about 4 times playing in small clubs in front of a couple of hundred or so people. It was absolutely electric. It was as if we were all in a secret club that no one knew about and the concerts were just amazing. Of course something as good as that was always going to find its way in to the public domain and I can remember when the third album came out, seeing 'New Years Day' on 'Saturday Swapshop.' I was amazed, absolutely gobsmacked that they were on national TV, but of course it was the beginning of the end for U2 as they were. Suddenly everyone had heard of them and the secret was out. I can remember trying to get tickets for the tour a few months later and all the stadiums they were playing were suddenly sold out. I started to lose interest at that point and sadly the music became more and more commercial.

One of my great musical loves around that time was Tom Petty and the Heartbreakers. I saw them in Sheffield in 1978 and loved them from the word go. So did my mate Robert, so when they toured again in the early Eighties we decided to go to every concert. It was great and we even got to meet the band after the last show. Along the way we went down to London to see them at Hammersmith Odeon and set off on a mid morning train. We drank a few cans on the way down and then had a great lunchtime session. Me and Robert were best buddies and we could talk and talk for hours about everything and nothing and always got on like the proverbial house on fire. There was nothing (and I mean nothing) that we couldn't talk about. The session was great and we could have stayed in that pub all evening. We had such a good laugh that I don't think we realised how much we had drunk. When we decided to make a move and go and get something to eat we seemed quite sober. However, when we went outside into the fresh air, it was as if there were two blokes stood outside with big shovels that hit us in the face in a tango-esque way as we left.

I mean bang!

From sensible and coherent to off your bloody trolley in two seconds flat.

We were as bad as each other when we'd been drinking and did some ridiculously stupid things, but most of that evening is a loss to me. I can remember being in a sex shop in Soho at one point, shouting across at him, "Hey Robert, I've found those magazines on spanking you are looking for," at the top of my voice. All the other customers were browsing rather sheepishly and unsure of what to make of our brazen sexual perversions (we were taking the piss out of each other for the record. Robert had long since grown out of his spanking fetish by then......and was now into rubber panties).

The next thing I can remember was eating fish and chips in an office block lift. God knows why we were there, maybe it was raining, but Robert had set off the fire alarm and we stood there giggling like kids as people were frantically getting in the lift with us or piling down the stairs. They surely must have known it was us, as every call of, "This isn't a drill. Vacate the building!" just made us giggle more.

I am not sure how we got to Hammersmith, but we did and I can remember us both having headaches from hell as we listened to the support act (Dave Edmunds of "Girls talk" fame, if my fading memory serves me right). I remember being annoyed at myself for feeling so ill that I wouldn't enjoy the concert, but when TP+H arrived on stage, we had miraculously recovered and loved every second of it.

By the time it finished it was already late and we were cutting it fine to get the last train back to Sheffield. We stumbled into St Pancras station just after it left, but our concern about getting home was quickly replaced by fear. We were on the main concourse, when we became aware of a roar of angry voices and bottles smashing all around us. A mob of Arsenal fans was charging towards us armed with baseball bats and God knows what other weapons. The roar that came from the other side of us quickly told us that this wasn't aimed at us, but the West Ham fans getting off the train from a game at Notts County. It was bizarre being stood in the middle of these converging violent mobs, being charged at from both sides and we knew to get out of there sharpish. People were scattering everywhere. We jumped a barrier and dashed up a platform to escape the mayhem. I had no desire to watch what was happening, but could tell from the noise that it was kicking off big time. The frightening thing for us, was we were at that age where we would have been seen as potential targets. A northern accent trying to explain that we were neither West Ham nor Arsenal wouldn't have excused us a kicking, so we took no chances and hid. Even the officials from British Rail were hiding. It was bizarre.

Eventually it settled down and we were left with about six hours to kill until the next train to Sheffield. It would mean that I would be terribly late for work the next day and therefore get a bollocking from my miserable boss, but the day had been worth it.

Train stations are weird places to be during the middle of night, particularly in London and we saw all types of low life that night. It was

85

really uncomfortable, but we were more than ready for any pervs and weirdos that were stalking the platforms. More out of boredom than anything, we found out that a mail train would be heading to Sheffield at about 3 am, but was strictly no passengers. This seemed ideal to us as no passengers meant no ticket collectors, so we managed to get on board without being detected and settled on a pile of mail bags for the journey. We even thought that we would be back in time for work, but of course we didn't allow for the train stopping at every bloody station and the mail train actually got into Sheffield after the later passenger train. We also had to hide under the mail bags every time it stopped too and only got spotted when we got off at Derby (We got fed up of the slowness of it all, so got off there) to make our way home by normal train.

To top it off nicely, when I arrived for work over two hours late, I was told my boss was off ill that day (he was never off ill!) and by a pure fluke I got away with it completely.

Laaavvvleyyy!

In a way my drinking times with Rob echoed my football times, in that we would get into so many scrapes, yet we always managed to come out unscathed. I cringe now at some of the things we did, but I also look back knowing that I had a bloody good time growing up and did all the stupid things that young men should do while still free and single (ish).

Anyway back to the footy. Wednesday were still very well placed going into the last dozen games and as Easter approached (the period considered to be the real make or break) we were still in the top three. An away game on a hot April afternoon against Shrewsbury saw a very, very late winning goal by Gary Bannister and the whole place went berserk. I can remember the scenes still, so vividly. Late winners are always wonderful things, but that one felt really special. No one wanted to leave the ground at the end. Gay Meadow was as Gay as it was ever going to get that day and the huge travelling support was bouncing along, almost able to touch the First Division.

If we thought that was good, well it just got better. Two days later we were at home to one of our big promotion rivals, Newcastle and a 30,000 crowd saw us push them aside 2-1, with all the other results going for us as well.

Another home game against struggling Cambridge United followed, with there being a full page spread in the match programme, called 'The big race is on'. It featured the top nine clubs in the chase for promotion, together with their remaining fixtures. I can remember pouring over that page for hours after we had beat Cambridge 2-1, trying to work out the various permutations. We were now six points clear of fourth place, with only five games to play and no matter how many cynical ways I looked at the run in, I still predicted us finishing above every single one of them on that list. Leicester and QPR could be dangerous, as they had games in hand, but I still had us finishing above everyone else on that list.

As the season worked out, I was absolutely right. We did finish above everyone on that list. The unfortunate thing was that there was one team that weren't on that list that simply went on the most amazing run. Norwich hadn't got above 11th place all season and no one gave them any hope whatsoever. They weren't even considered to be contenders, yet they won ten out of eleven games, a run that catapulted them from mid table to the top three and as only Wednesday can, we slipped at the crucial time.

The run from Norwich was suddenly setting up an amazing winner takes all last match of the season, between the two teams at Hillsborough. Wednesday however, stumbled and fell badly, taking just two points from the four games before that, to leave Norwich already promoted, even before that last game.

I can remember feeling so angry, before that match. Norwich suddenly brought a huge following and I can remember there being some ugly scenes before the game.

They had just come for an unexpected party, whereas we had had our party cancelled at the last minute, after months of preparation. We were seriously bitter.

Inside Hillsborough, at the Leppings Lane end, there is a fence that runs from the turnstiles to the entrance of the terracing that separates the North Stand from the visiting supporters and I remember some real hostilities coming from the home supporters, through the fences at the Norwich fans.

I was sick to my stomach. Who were these bas***ds that were celebrating here. They hadn't probably been to a game all season and yet here they were partying instead of us.

I was absolutely gutted.

That's the problem with football. It gets under your skin, it takes hold of you, so when something like this happens, it really, really hurts.

Being Wednesdayites, we should be used to it. If ever there is a club that specialises in snatching defeat from the jaws of victory, it is us.

The game itself was quite interesting, with Wednesday winning 2-1, but there were two incidents that really stuck out in my mind. First of all, as the frustration and anger from the home end started to boil over, I can remember one guy running onto the pitch and goading the Norwich fans. From somewhere a full house brick was thrown from the Norwich fans at him (They were pretty well packed in, so how on earth someone found a house brick to throw at him is a mystery). It missed him by some way, but he did the obvious thing and picked it up. I can remember the entire ground cringing and shouting, 'NNOOOOOOO!' but it was too late. There was no turning back for him and the brick was launched into the tightly packed mass of bodies. Now there is no way you can avoid something like that, if it is heading your way, when you are all squashed in like that, so some poor sod would have taken quite a blow.

We were more concerned about the damage to the club, however. We had been made an example of after the Oldham riots, last season, so the great fear as he chucked the brick back, was what is going to happen now. There was no mistaking this. He was on the bloody pitch for the whole ground to see and on TV too.   (Strangely enough, to my knowledge, no action was actually taken for this. They probably felt that we had suffered enough by throwing promotion away)

The second thing I remember was the winning goal. Again, some people were on the pitch (They thought it was all over. But it wasn't.)

The ball was floated in to the area for Gary Bannister to plant a header into the Norwich net. The thing is, there was a Wednesdayite on the pitch just behind him, who also saw the cross coming over and absolutely launched himself with a fantastic diving header. If Banno hadn't got his head to it first, this kid would have scored the goal of the season.

I have since seen a replay of the goal on TV and it is an absolute classic. The odd thing is, that the Ref never considered not giving it and there was only a brief complaint from the Norwich players (I think one defender thought the fan was offside, although the TV replay confirmed that he was actually onside, having timed his run to perfection).

Although the win no where near compensated for the bitter failure, our season finished on a light hearted high and we had a lot of hope for more glory to come.

CHAPTER 5

Borman

By the late 1970's the balance of football power was changing. United were in decline and Wednesday had at least stabilised under Jack Charlton and were finally starting the climb back. As a result, the support across the city was around 50 / 50, which was a big improvement from my time at school when I was seriously outnumbered.

I was brought up in a district called Gleadless, which was a middle class private housing area on the south of Sheffield. Gleadless seemed to be mostly a Wednesday area, though it was bordered by rougher council areas, which were by majority United areas.

Our local pub, the New Inn, was a great little pub that had a real 'local pub' feel about it and was populated by a mixture of clientele. It had a large, number of younger people around our own age and soon became very popular as the place to be. We became friends with various people there and with a lot being Wednesdayites our number steadily grew.

It helped that Mark was best mates with the landlord's son (who was a good footballer and played with Wednesday himself, never quite making it to the first team, sadly, the selfish bas***d. Imagine the free tickets we would have got) which meant we were privileged to many after hours drinking sessions.

My best mate, Robert, wasn't much of a football supporter at that time. He 'supported' United, but I can't remember him going to many matches. Like my eldest brother, Graham, he preferred playing to watching. (In fact he always wore a Watford scarf, but I think that had more to do with his love of Elton John's music.)

We had a routine, that on a Thursday night just the two of us would go out, whereas on a Friday we would go into town with the lads from nearby Intake (sadly nearly all blades) and Saturdays were girlfriend nights.

Thursday nights would always see us meet in the New Inn and then usually go into town. However, we had devised a pub crawl (or sprint would be more appropriate, given the distance and schedule required) which we called the Ridgeway Run. This involved starting at the New Inn and taking in a total of eight pubs, having a pint in each and finishing at the Bridge Inn at Ford.

In those days the licensing laws, meant that pubs in Sheffield closed at 10.30, whereas in bordering Derbyshire, where the lovely village of Ridgeway is situated, the pubs stayed open until 11 o'clock. As a result there tended to be a mini migration to Derbyshire on Fridays and Saturdays to take in the extra half hour drinking time.

The journey to the Bridge Inn was a total of 3.7 miles and it took maybe 5 or 6 attempts, before we perfected the schedule and managed to complete the run. This left us in the middle of nowhere when the pubs closed and no way of getting home other than to walk across countryside to get back.

Inevitably this led to us getting into all sorts of mischief. Sometimes we would just lie in a field discussing the meaning of life and more importantly, girls, or sometimes we would get into various scrapes.

On the way back there was one house that was set on its own, with no neighbours for quite a distance. I don't know which one of us got the idea, but we decided it would be a good idea to set up a fireworks display in the front garden of this house on our way back one night. So we bought the fireworks in anticipation and come the next Thursday night after a skin full, quietly set them up, lit the blue touch papers and ran.

God knows what the occupants must have thought, when they were awaken around midnight by a barrage of 'wheeees' and a 'bangs' and looked out of their window to find a mini firework display going off in their front garden, but it didn't half make us laugh at the time.

Anyway, to celebrate the successful completion of the Ridgeway Run, we arranged it again in the following weeks, but this time were joined by about ten more people.

We started out at 6.30 and it was quite a boisterous night, with alcohol going down very quickly to meet the schedule, but the number of people we had with us, meant it was too difficult to keep everyone mobilised. Consequently we let the schedule go and just went as far as we could. By the time we got to The Phoenix, (God, if I was a musician that line would have inspired me to write a song) that is on the outskirts of Ridgeway village, it's fair to say everyone was pretty well pissed.

We knew them all from the New Inn, but one kid came along who was familiar to us, but not part of our little crowd and this was a lad called Martin. For some reason he came dressed in a long white coat, even though it was summer and because of this and his rather portly size, got christened with the name Borman, (due to his resemblance to the Nazi General, Martin Borman).

And so it became that Borman was born.

Later on that night, fuelled by alcohol, he swore that he was chased across a field by an angry farmer, but this soon got added to, until the story was that Borman said he was chased by an eight foot green giant.

That evening deteriorated into a drunken, chaotic, night.

We left The Phoenix, which in those days was made up of many small rooms and the entrance was a little glass porch that had two doors that opened up on themselves. As we left, someone suggested it would be a good idea to try and get a plank of wood that was conveniently lying around, to wedge between the two doors. To our total delight, the plank seemed made to measure and by wedging it against the inner door and slowly letting the outer door close, the plank slid perfectly into place, thus wedging the two doors against each other! No one was able to get in or out and we left them to it, giggling like school kids as we made for the next pub. I still don't know how they got out. I presumed that they had to smash the glass on the door, to lever the plank out of the way, but all we could think about was how funny it would be when the first people tried to leave the pub and found themselves locked inside!

The night ended one pub short of the intended destination, but that didn't matter. We stayed in The Swan, but got thrown out after the Salvation Army made a collection visit. We bought all their 'War Cry' magazines and they seemed delighted. They were happy to let us borrow

91

their hats too, but as the magazines got rolled up and turned into paper swords and sword fencing matches took place, it was inevitable that somebody's table would get knocked over and drinks spilled.

When it did, we were thrown out.

We eventually made our way back along White Lane, which is a long stretch of country road between Ridgeway and the outskirts of Sheffield. It was an unlit road, save for the passing of an odd car whose headlights temporarily lit up the darkness, so we thought it would be funny, when someone suggested that we should have a mock fight, when the next car came along.

It must have looked amazing to the driver of the car.

Driving along a dark and quiet road, when your headlights suddenly come upon a mass brawl in the middle of the road in the middle of nowhere.

When you have had a lot to drink, you tend to lose all sense of safety and realism and the fight became very real. No malice, but just punches and kicks at whoever was in range and obviously receiving the same!

One car had to swerve to miss the mass brawl as it spilled out into the middle of the road. Quite stupid really as anyone of us could have been hit and killed, but incredibly funny at the time!

After doing this a few times, someone decided we should do caterpillar bumming for the next car. Now being an innocent young man, I had no idea what caterpillar bumming was and I now wonder who on earth it was that suggested it and also how the hell they knew what it was! It was explained that we all drop our trousers and stand in line, one after another, and pretend to 'bum' the one in front, making a long gay line of 10. Again, what the hell the driver must have thought, when his headlights came on this spectacle, is something we will never know, but how we laughed about it. (Just for the record, this was my one and only involvement in caterpillar bumming, or bumming of any sort for that matter)

We slowly made our way home, and as we got closer there was now just me, Robert and Mark. The last 200 yards seemed a straight forward journey, but we decided that rather than walking down the road home, we would walk down the adjoining road and skip across the neighbour's garden and jump over the fence and into our own garden. Being totally pissed, this obviously seemed more logical, so we quietly crept up their driveway past the house, but at this point Robert decided to bang on their door, like World War Three had broken out. We then ran giggling as fast as we could up the garden and I was first to try and get over the fence and into our own garden. Being slightly inebriated, I found it difficult to get over, so as the haste of the other two took over, I was bodily pushed over and quickly followed by Mark and Robert. Unfortunately for me, as I went over, I went straight into a tree branch which ripped into my eye socket. The others thought I was messing about and so I got a couple of stones thrown at me, to give me 'something to cry about', because I was behaving like a big girl. It was only when they saw the huge red stripe of blood growing down my white jumper that they realised I wasn't messing and it was actually quite serious. We all sobered up incredibly quickly and found ourselves in casualty soon after.

I was very lucky that the branch glanced off my eyeball and didn't take it out. I thought I would get a pretty cool eye patch, like a pirate, to impress the girls, but instead I had another ridiculously giant plaster, like when I cracked my head on the crush barrier and just looked like a dork.

The main thing about that night was that Borman had been born and he would stay with us for the next few years. I always liked Borman, he was a real warm hearted guy with a great personality, but because he desperately wanted to be accepted and liked, he got taken advantage of and became the butt of all the jokes

Not long after the Ridgeway night, we were invited to a party at his parent's house. Graham was thrown out not long after arriving, for eating Borman's sister's goldfish. In reality it was a slice of peach, which he playfully wiggled about, as if the goldfish was trying to escape, but Borman's horrified Mother, only saw the wriggling 'fish' entering his mouth and was convinced he had just eaten her daughters goldfish.

On Friday nights when I was out with the Intake lads, Borman went out with Mark, Graham and Founts and their crowd, so I wasn't privy to a lot of the mickey taking that went on and the reasons why he was always on the receiving end.

He was quite gullible though and as we were all into music in a big way a rouse was made up, that our musical guru, Melv, would rave about this fab new (and totally made up) band "The Orange Boxes." Over a period of weeks we all said that we had got their new album and how great it was. Of course Borm never admitted it, but we know he must have gone into HMV or Virgin Records trying to buy it as for weeks after he would quiz Melv about them and what the album was called and that he couldn't find it.

No one particularly wanted to take their car to away matches, as we all had pretty old and unreliable cars in those days, so Borman always seemed to get pressured into taking his. He had an old, bright orange Austin Maxi, which was hardly a great pulling machine, but it got him around. Of course, no one would dream of taking more than four in their car to a match, five at an absolute push, but the 'Bormobile' would end up with six or seven crammed into it and he would be slagged off if he complained! At the end of the journey, we would share the cost of the petrol and it was inevitable that whatever figure Borm announced was due, would be met with howls of derision.

"Kin'ell Borm. How much?" and it would be argued that he had got his maths wrong and probably half of that would be more appropriate!

Poor old Borm.

The Bormobile had taken us over to Wrexham one day to see The Owls.

On the last leg of the journey home, we had been cut up by a guy and Borm had sounded his horn and the two had gestured at each other. This carried on with Borm flashing his lights and driving ridiculously close to the guy's bumper and the other guy winding his window down and sticking two fingers up. Eventually we pulled up behind this guy at the traffic lights at the bottom of East Bank Road and Borman piled out to confront him. The other driver was also a big fat guy and I'm sure Borm expected us to all jump out and help him. Instead all five of us sat there in the car and left him to it, laughing at the two fat blokes slugging it out!

You would expect two big blokes like that to paste the living daylights out of each other, yet they ended up fighting like big girly puffs, pawing at each other instead of punching.

After watching these two big blokes slap and push each other about for a bit, we were collectively wetting ourselves laughing and they eventually got back in their respective cars. The lights had changed a few times during their 'fight' and by the time that they had parted, the lights had just changed back to red, so we had to sit there for what must have seemed an eternity to Borm and the other driver.

I think the fact that we hadn't got out to help him fight the fat bloke and that we were all still pissing ourselves laughing really wound him up, as he was revving the car mercilessly. He was inches from the guy's bumper and hell bent on screeching off and overtaking him. When the lights did turn green, the tyres screamed for mercy as full throttle was applied and Borm was off like a bat out of hell and soon drew level with him. "Take that you fat f***er!" he screamed as we prepared to overtake him in a startling move that Nelson Piquet would have been proud of, but sadly six up a very steep hill in an old Maxi, was never going to out run anyone and the other guy simply drove away in to the distance, leaving the Bormobile to slowly chug up the hill, making us laugh even more.

As gullible as he was, Borman also had a great character and was full of bluster. He was very much a larger than life character He tried to put on a brave face and pretend the digs didn't hurt, but I guess they did.

He had a spell in the Army in his younger days and he liked to think this gave him an air of worldliness and when he spoke it carried some authority. As far as I know he never had a girlfriend in his younger days and the Friday night crowd would rib him about it mercilessly. It got to the stage where he ended up making someone up, which was about the worst thing he could have done. He had been dropping hints to the rest of them that he had been chatting this girl up for a while and one particular night, he left early, to allegedly meet this girl.

He said that he couldn't drink as he was driving over to her place with a lot of hinting that he would be staying over. Unfortunately for Borm, he hadn't thought this story through properly, so when the rest of the lads later saw his car parked on his drive at 11.30 suspicions were roused.

The next day we played away at Shrewsbury and the grilling started straight away.

"How did you get on last night Borm?"

"Oh yes, very good" looking pleased with himself.

"So, did you stop all night?"

"Yes, got up and left her to come to the game this morning."

"Did you drive over there?"

(Getting a bit cagey now) "Err, yes, of course."

"And you stayed there all night?"

"Yes."

"So why was your car on your drive last night?"

"It wasn't."

"Well, there was a bright orange Austin Maxi on your drive last night at 11.30."

(Boll*cks!) "Err, yes, err, that was my neighbour's car."

"But your neighbour hasn't got a bright orange Austin Maxi."

"Yes, he has. He has just bought it."

"So your neighbour has bought an identical car to you."

(Now sweating) "Yes."

"But it had the same registration number as yours."

(Oh f**k!) "Errr….No… It has one number different."

"Bloody hell, that's a bit of a coincidence. The same make of car, had it sprayed the same bright orange as yours and even an almost identical number plate. 'Kin 'ell that's incredible!"

(Please God open up a hole in the ground and swallow me.)

"Yes, its amazing, I agree."

"So why was it parked on your drive last night?"

"Oh he sometimes does that."

"Why?"

(Oh Sh*t, how did I get into this mess) "I'm not sure. He just sometimes does."

"So, let me get this straight. Your neighbour has bought an identical car, with a near identical number plate, had it sprayed bright orange and parks it on your drive?"

"Yes."

"Is he trying to put on loads of weight too?"

And so it continued all day. They ribbed him something rotten. It was merciless.

My football mates and non football mates had a very different culture and the football culture was always about taking the piss and slagging each other off. As stupid a thing as it was for him to do, Borman died a thousand deaths that day. Poor kid.

No wonder the poor guy moved to London.

Through a couple of Mark's friends in the Police, we heard about a place in London, which was supposedly quite a fun place to go, so when we next ventured to the Capital for an away game, we gave it a try.

It turned out to be like a working men's club, but had a great atmosphere and as Wednesday had won some game or other earlier, we were all in good spirits. As the night progressed, we got steadily more drunk and there was a duo singing, in the club. During their repertoire they sang "Blueberry Hill" and for some reason, it seemed to strike a chord with us.

We were all happily singing along and every time they started another song we would boo and shout for "Blueberry Hill" until every other song they sang was "Blueberry Hill".

We were obviously very loud, but not in a threatening way, just having a good time.

At the end of the night, one of the guys that had started coming with us, called Dixon, drove us across London to the M1 during which most of us fell asleep for the long journey home. Apparently, Dixon and Borman had decided to swap driving responsibility as we approached the M1 and Borman would drive the rest of the way home. The next thing I knew was waking up and it was daylight. I was slightly puzzled, as my brain slowly started to calculate exactly where I was and what happened. I think I expected to be somewhere near Sheffield, but instead we were still at the slip road at the bottom of the M1.

They had changed seats, but then Borm had closed his eyes "for a minute" and promptly fell asleep for the next five hours!

Borm and Dixon were still snoring, passenger door wide open and engine still running!

Needless to say it took some explaining when we all got home at about 10 o'clock Sunday morning where we had been all night.

My only ever fight at a football match involved Borman. We were playing Middlesbrough at home on the opening day of the 1982 /83 season. There were three Middlesbrough fans, surprisingly sat on the row behind us. Now I know this is very hypocritical, having sat in the home sections many times at away games myself, but I can't stand having away fans sat in Wednesday areas. Boro didn't bring that many fans anyway, so there was simply no need for them to be in the North stand with us.

The banter started straight away, but as soon as the first goal went in, it all changed. Wednesday had scored and my first reaction after jumping up was to turn round and give the Boro fans some stick. There is nothing worse than being in the middle of opposition supporters when they score, so I simply had to rub it in. To my great surprise, one of them (who was on crutches) leapt forward aiming a punch at me. I was more shocked than anything, the punch missed, but him only having one active leg (the other was in plaster) meant he couldn't get his balance, so we both went flying down the seats in front of us, exchanging blows. The next thing I remember was that my attempts to hit him back were going into thin air, because Borman had picked him up and flattened him. It was over in seconds and the Police and stewards were quickly on the scene and threw them out. As they were led away one of them waved his watch at us, which was a strange thing to do, until Borm realised that the impact of his fist on this Boro fan had knocked his watch off and one of the other Boro fans had promptly picked it up and took it!

At least Wednesday went on to win 3-1.

One of the rare times that the Bormobile wasn't ridiculously overcrowded was on a trip to Cambridge. There were seven of us and unusually all seven didn't try and get in his car. We actually did the sensible thing and took two cars. There were three of us in the Bormobile and having stopped at a service station on the A1, were resuming our journey when Borm noticed two young, attractive female hitch-hikers. He stopped and asked them where they were going and offered to take them as far as Cambridge and to everyone's surprise they got in. Borm was telling them all about his army days and doing his best to impress and I was quite surprised by his smooth patter, but after about half an hour suddenly announced in a very loud and confident voice. "Its simply no good, I have been trying my hardest to hold it in, but I simply can't do it any longer and I am going to have to fart!", with that he let out the most outrageous, thunderous blast I have ever heard, followed by a vile pungent green gas cloud that threatened to suffocate all of us. It was the vilest stench that I have ever known and it surely must have originated from the Devils very own bottom.

The car must have shook from the violent coughing and gagging that ensued, with one poor girl wretching and fighting to keep the contents of her stomach from gushing over the carpet. The windows were frantically wound down by those still conscious in an effort to dispel the evil, putrid smell and soon we were able to breathe again. Needless to say they didn't stay too long after that and after the colour had returned to their faces they asked if they may be dropped off at the next available place.

The guys in the car behind were obviously keen to understand what the hell had spooked these two girls, so badly that they abandoned ship so quick.

On arrival at a pub just outside Cambridge, Borm was buoyed by his amazing bottom feat and full of life. As usual he was rather loud and when noticing that a TV was showing the build up to "The Boat Race" from the Thames, he was saying rather loudly how he thought that Cambridge had a real good chance of winning this year. One local picked up on this and replied in a somewhat saddened voice that he didn't think they had a chance and Oxford were sure to win again. Borm was having none of it and his extensive knowledge of rowing meant that he "knew" that Cambridge really had a good chance and it would surely be there year after a run of eight straight defeats. We thought it a bit peculiar how they egged Borman on, but didn't think too much of it when they started exchanging bets. The race eventually got underway and I can't say that I paid too much attention to the fact that Oxford won again, by some 4 1/2 lengths and Borman duly paid up a series of fivers to the locals.

It was only later, on the way out of the pub that one of the local guys asked if we really didn't know that the boat race had been abandoned earlier and that the race shown on TV was in fact a re run of last years race.

I thought Melv was going to wet his pants he was laughing that much.

CHAPTER 6

New Gold Dream

I have already said how much I love music, but despite the Simple Minds title, this chapter isn't dedicated to music. Simple Minds did some great stuff and I loved it when Wednesday adopted the Simple Minds song 'Waterfront' a few years after it was released, as the music the team came out to.

It really gets the hair on the back of your neck standing up.

They also did a song called 'New Gold Dream 81-82-83-84', taken from the album of the same name. It may be a bit of nostalgia, but I loved those years and '81,'82,'83 and '84 were damn good years to be a Wednesdayite. Although the 1982-83 season, was not one that will go down in history as one of our greatest on the pitch, it was absolutely jam packed full of stuff for our little band of travelling Owls off it.

Our first game of the season was at home to Middlesbrough, which started well, with a 3-1 win and included my first, and only, fight at a match, as described earlier.

This was then followed by a trip to Charlton for the first away game of the season.

We got tickets for the main stand (which was the stand opposite that huge open terrace, for anyone who remembers The Valley as it used to be) and were sat amongst the Charlton fans.

We were never stupid about sitting amongst the home fans. Generally we would never go on the home 'Kop' end, but would select a safer 'main grandstand.' This still carries an obvious risk and it is awful to be sat in the middle of home fans when you lose. You tend to give yourselves away during the course of the game and become a target.

We were getting a little bit of stick at this game but nothing too much. Wednesday were playing superb, but it took until just before half time for Taylor to open the scoring for us. As the game progressed we were getting more stick, with some weird guy sat a few rows behind us, throwing peanuts at us repeatedly. It was foolish really because he was dressed in a most ridiculously garish checked jacket, which just gave us plenty of ammunition for taking the piss. The more he threw peanuts, the more comments about being able to play Chess on his jacket, he received.

It started to get more heated with Melv eventually threatening to, "Shove that packet of f***ing peanuts up his a*se," if he didn't stop it.

The really wonderful thing though, was that we were totally outplaying them on the pitch and were awarded and converted a 70th minute penalty, to our huge delight.

There is a truly wonderful (and dangerous) feeling about being sat in the middle of the home supporters and winning, so when John Pearson (A Wednesday legend now, with his totally biased radio commentaries) slid in a third ten minutes later, we were ecstatic. We were on our seats singing our heads off with the mass of Owls to our right, as the dejected Charlton supporters quietly trudged out.

We ventured into central London to celebrate the 3-0 win and the first pub that we went in Melv ordered a pint of wine. I'd never seen anyone order (or drink) a pint of wine, so we fell about laughing. The barman was equally stunned, but poured it anyway and Melv drank it,

We were all elated and intent on having a good night to celebrate being top of the league after two games. We were near Trafalgar Square and were making our way to another pub, when we were suddenly involved in a brawl, totally out of the blue. There were eight of us, from what I remember and the first couple of our group, including Borman, were a few yards ahead. They were just about to cross a zebra crossing, when a car with three young lads came round the corner and almost ran Borman over. The driver tooted and braked and Borman politely told the driver it was "a f***ing zebra crossing!". The three lads obviously thought Borman was on his own and the driver jumped out of his car to confront Borm, who naturally started to have a go back. The other two started to get out of the car as well, until they realised there was another seven of us behind. Now none of us are any good at fighting, but they didn't know that and seeing Melv coming at them, a six foot two albino with muscles bulging and a bright red face, must have changed their minds and they hastily started to retreat. It was too late now though. Melv and Borman were on the attack and a quick flurry of punches hit them as they jumped back in the car. The driver was desperately trying to start his car and get out of there, as Borman repeatedly booted his car door and then tried to re open it to drag the kid out. The driver eventually managed to get the car started and with a squeal of tyres they were gone.

The funny thing that I remember about that incident, were the number of tourists about, all happily clicking away with their cameras, catching the action!

I can just imagine them showing the photos to the family back home in the States. "This is us in Trafalgar Square, oh, and gee, that was when we saw those Soccer hooligans, didn't we Elmer."

"We sure did, honey. Look at that blonde guy, punching him in the face there. And the fat guy kicking some ass out of that quaint little car!"

I do believe the rest of the night passed without incident.

Five wins from the first six games, saw us sitting pretty at the top, so a midweek game at Carlisle was a must. It was too obvious to just drive straight to Carlisle for the game though, so we detoured to Blackpool for a few pints and the afternoon at the Pleasure Beach.

We arrived in Carlisle very early, so with nothing else to do, we went to the pub, surprise, surprise. Inevitably, by the time we got to the ground, we were all worse for wear, but settled in to the main stand, as usual, in the middle of the home fans. Now it is great, when you do this and you win, but when you lose it is bloody horrible.

Tommy Craig, a former Owls favourite in the 1970's was now at Carlisle, so he was getting some comments and a few chants from us (all good, as he was a popular player), but it ensured that all around knew we were from Sheffield. From my recollection of the game, we had a disastrous start and were soon 2-0 down. I can't remember too much, but the banter that had inevitably taken place, got too much when the second goal went in and someone launched a cup of hot Bovril at the taunting home fans, which immediately led to a fracas. As soon as that happened, the Police appeared and we were quickly escorted out of the ground.

This was to the great delight of the home fans and to our humiliation.

102

This was the first and only time this has ever happened to me and we had to give our names and addresses to the Police outside the ground.

To my surprise, it was left at that and a "Now be off with you!" in our ears. All we did was walk round to the opposite side, explained to the gateman that we had been thrown out and he surprisingly, let us back in again at no extra cost.

A sorry night ended in a 4-2 defeat.

Our form was still good though, with only two defeats in the first sixteen games. We were back to the top in November following a 2-0 home win over Derby and five points clear of fourth placed Fulham.

A visit to West London therefore at the end of November, was a big game, but the game paled into insignificance, compared to the evening that followed for us. Fulham had accumulated a good squad that season, under Malcolm MacDonald, with the likes of Ray Houghton and Gordon Davies and they won a scrappy game 1-0 with a brawl breaking out all around us when they scored. We were in the main stand as usual, with the home fans, but there was also a lot of Wednesdayites around us too, so the goal lit the touch paper for it all to kick off. When I say kick off, it was lots of handbags type stuff, as opposed to an orgy of violence, but we were right in the bloody middle of it all.

It is a strange sort of experience, because we never got involved in the fighting, so it is odd when everyone around you is lashing out, but you sort of stand still in the middle of the madness. I was just on my guard that I didn't get whacked by anybody and this strategy proved to be good. The Police had to dive in to sort it out and several people were taken out. But I noticed that, for the first time, it was all being filmed by a policeman with a very large video camera and sure enough, after reviewing the evidence, the Police came back ten minutes later and removed everyone that was involved. As totally innocent bystanders, we were left to watch the game.

Justice by technology huh! The times they are a changing.

After the game we headed for Central London again and decided to go in a pub called 'The Cockney Pride', just off Trafalgar Square. It was early but the bar was quite busy. We had been there about an hour I guess and the lunchtime session, was now fully topped up and there was some singing going off. Now I don't know whether it was just tourists joining in, but it seemed that the number of Wednesdayites in the bar had swollen, because the Wednesday songs were now booming out. By a bizarre coincidence, I had bumped into Chris, an old friend from school, who was in London at one of the Universities. Although a big Unitedite, he was a good friend and it was great catching up with him and his brother. He did give me a very serious warning though, that it was strongly advised not to be singing football songs in this particular pub and that we were heading for trouble if we continued. I passed this onto the rest of our team, but it got pushed to one side, as we were only there for a good time and not looking for trouble. Chris was serious about what he said and with us continuing singing, left shortly after, as he knew what would happen.

It all seemed innocent enough, until the doors leading up to the street, opened and about twenty or so guys came in. They were all wearing matching jumpers (which I found odd, but didn't think it was a good time to question why) and looked as though they were there for some serious trouble. It was like snow melting in an oven (only faster!) how quickly all the lads that had been singing earlier, had suddenly disappeared. I think we all sobered up very quickly and realised that we were going to get a bit of a beating here. Surprisingly it didn't kick off straight away. We expected just to get walloped, but instead they blocked the doors (so we couldn't escape) and started quizzing us (hooligans with a conscience!). They said that someone had phoned them, tipping them off that there were some Sheffield lads looking for trouble.

Now this is where history gets a little blurred. Mark's take on it, is that we all left the pub leaving him and Founts to get out of it on their own.

My recollection, is that Mark was very pissed!

I can remember whispering amongst ourselves that this was not a good situation and that we needed to get out as soon as possible. Our new friends had relaxed a bit, recognising that we weren't there for a punch up, but they were still pretty narked that we had being 'taking liberties on their manor.'

The door up to safety was now unmanned and our best plan was to quietly sneak off one by one. We passed the plan around and the first one left. We told Mark but he said that it was all OK and he had explained that we were here for a laugh and didn't want trouble. I think there was some truth in that, because they didn't kick the living daylights out of us. We managed to get out, quietly, although when we eventually met up outside, there was a row between us all, because Mark was adamant that we had left him to it. The seven of us that were there, had got out, but it seemed that word was out on the street about us because we were getting abuse everywhere we went. Mark was still seething about the situation and tensions (and alcohol levels) were high. A little later, we were stood outside a pub, that wouldn't let us in (probably for our own safety as it was full of Spurs fans) and there was a skinhead stood outside. He was an archetypal skinhead, with Doc Martens and a Cromby coat, with a Tottenham scarf round his neck, tucked into his coat. I can remember Mark going up to him and getting the skinheads scarf in his hand. The skinhead sneered at him, as if to say, 'you wouldn't try it. Not outside this pub full of Spurs fans.' Mark looked at the scarf and said, "Tottenham? Who the f*ck are they?" and in one swift movement, released the scarf and delivered an uppercut that almost knocked the skinhead out of his boots and Cromby! Of course that was it. The pub emptied in uproar and we scattered. I can remember simply running. I didn't have a clue where I was, where I was going, or where anyone else was. We all just scattered, every man for himself. I was lucky in that I got chased by some fatties who weren't very quick and I managed to lose them surprisingly easy. I could hear all sorts of commotion going off and angry voices shouting everywhere.

I was totally lost, on my own and boy was I scared.

It was like the film 'The Warriors', where a New York gang are trying to get home to Coney Island and the word is out with every gang in the city to get them.

Once in relative safety, I realised I had to try and get back to everyone else, so had to cautiously venture back to where I had just fled. I am sure it is just my memory now, but it all seemed very dark. It was a brightly lit major street in the middle of London, yet all I can remember was nervously walking down dark Edwardian alleyways, with a Jack the Ripper-esque fog swirling all around, rather than brightly lit streets!

After some time, I managed to find one of our lot, Steve. He was also on his own, but if I thought I was scared, he was absolutely terrified. He wasn't a usual member of our team and I am sure this was the last time he ever came with us again. We managed to find our way somehow to the car, but there was no one else about. Steve fortunately had the car keys, but was so scared that he decided he wasn't going anywhere and locked himself in the car.

I ventured off to try and find everyone else and soon bumped into three more and then the remaining two. I think everyone made it back with no major injuries, but we decided enough was enough and we should get out of there.

Once safely on the road, the relief set in and we started to laugh about it.

So much so, that some idiot suggested stopping for another beer, before we hit the Motorway home. Being a scaredy pants I voted, 'No', but bravado was taking over now and on the rational thought that no one in North London would know what had happened, we stopped at 'The Swiss Cottage' on Finchley Road.

It was a mistake.

As soon as we walked in, it was as if everyone knew. Maybe we were a bit paranoid. How could they possibly have known what had happened? And in the grand scheme of things, it was only one punch to a skinhead. Surely worse things happen in London on a Saturday night?

Whether they knew or not will never be known, but we had just walked back into the Lions Den.

We got served but the longer we stayed (and it wasn't long) the more apparent it was that we were in trouble. We were getting some serious abuse and even Mark agreed this time that it was best to leave. We didn't even finish our drinks, which shows just how serious it was.

Steve decided that he had experienced enough fun for one night, so stayed in the car, whilst we went in. He was probably settling in for an hours kip, before driving home, when he was disturbed with us screaming 'Steve, get the f***ing car going!'' as we charged towards him.

Melv stood in the doorway and smashed a bottle, which he pointed at the mob that was following us out. God it was like a scene from a movie, with John Wayne holding back the baddies, while we made our escape. It was not even that straight forward either. There was seven of us trying to get in a car, so it wasn't just jumping in, a screech of tyres and off we go. It takes some organising to get seven in a car! We did it, well six of us did as Melv held the mob back. It was only a matter of time before someone had a go and then we were in big trouble, but fortunately no one wanted to be on the receiving end of that broken bottle. So when we were all in, Melv beat a hasty retreat, dived in through an open window and we sped off, with a load of abuse and various objects being thrown after us and Melvs legs dangling out of the window!

This time there was no more stopping. We had had enough and mightily relieved to be on our way home in one piece.

Wednesday had now entered into a total change of form and the early promise saw us slump to nine games without a win and only one win in thirteen league games. The one win though was nothing short of remarkable and featured one of the best goals I have ever seen (well maybe not best but certainly memorable).

A holiday home game against a struggling Charlton side on the 3rd January, did not whet the appetite and a huge drop in the attendance (11,808), registered the fans disappointment at recent results. Of course we were there and what we witnessed was a stunning, if not farcical game.

It started bright enough and Andy McCulloch put us into a 5th minute lead. The rest of the half was appalling though and at half time we were 3-1 down. The team was booed off at half time and Jack must have stripped the paint off the walls of the dressing room in the interval. They came out fired up and set about getting back in the game. Within ten minutes of the restart it was pulled back to 3-2 and the crowd were now right behind the lads, in response to the obvious effort that they were putting in. Every attack was urged on and it was with great delight that the scores were brought level by another Andy Mac goal. The feel good factor lasted about 30 seconds though, as Charlton took the kick off and went straight up and scored to make it 4-3. It was like being punched in the stomach, to both fans and players alike and it showed. The stuffing had been completely knocked out of them, after all the effort they had put in to getting level only to throw it instantly away.

The depression around the ground was palpable.

The game was slowly drifting away as the ball was poorly given away again to full back Steve Gritt about 25 yards out He was under no pressure what so ever, when he turned back to his own goal and inexplicably volleyed a thundering drive, which screamed past his keeper and into the top corner!

It was so bizarre it was untrue and if I hadn't seen it with my own eyes, I would have thought the story was wildly exaggerated.

The whole ground seemed totally stunned and rather than the usual shout of "YYEEEEEAAASSSSS!" it was laughter!

From this point on it was all Wednesday and it was Charlton who had the stuffing knocked out of them. It was attack after attack and eventually it was Captain Mike Lyons that powered home the winner. It could have been a lot more, but it finished as a 5-4 victory and in contrast to half time, the team received a standing ovation.

Two days before this wild game, Wednesday visited Burnley on New Years Day, where the depressing run of defeats had continued, with a 4-1 thumping. It was also the scene of one of the funniest things I have ever seen at a football match.

We had arranged to go to the game in Melv's car and there were five of us. Graham had gone to Blackpool for the New Year with his wife and our parents so had arranged to meet us at a pub in Burnley near the ground. Graham had got a train to Burnley from Blackpool and had no way of getting home, other than public transport. This was a bone of contention, as Melv had specifically stated that he wouldn't take six in his car and he wouldn't be able to take Graham back (only the Bormobile can carry six or seven).

We met up anyway and the pub that we were in was split between home fans and visitors and of course, the nearer it got to kick off the fuller the pub got.

There was a group of Wednesdayites in the pub who were quite vocal and had come from a New Years party in fancy dress and it all seemed reasonably good natured. Eventually it started to deteriorate and the atmosphere between the two rival sets of fans was getting uglier, with insults being traded freely. The Burnley fans were seriously annoyed that their local was full of away fans and wanted us out. The pub was sort of split in two, so the Burnley lads that fancied their chances, decided to go outside and attack the Wednesday fans from the door at the other side and trap us all in the middle of the pub, in a classic pincer movement. It suddenly kicked off big style as the Burnley fans, unexpectedly, charged in from behind us all. What they probably didn't expect, was that the lads in fancy dress were pretty handy and the Burnley hooligans that came through the door were given a battering. After repelling the attack the Wednesdayites then went on the offensive and charged out of the pub to get at the fleeing fans outside. When the pub had emptied, we went out to see a totally bizarre site.

In the middle of the street Elvis was whacking someone in the face, a Nun seemed to be taking two on and some form of sci-fi robot thing was struggling (with a lack of mobility in his costume) and getting punched, by the Burnley fans, before a big yellow chicken came to his rescue.

The fancy dress guys were clearly on top and the Burnley fans started to scatter.

We were then presented with the truly bizarre spectacle of Quasi Modo, hunchback and all, chasing down the street after a fleeing Burnley skinhead.

He even ran with a limp (I don't know whether he had a funny leg or was just still in character), so I don't know how the hell he caught him, but he did. He legged him over and gave him a few whacks and boots, before letting him run off.

It was so funny seeing this bizarre battle take place and afterwards, they just picked up their bits of costume that had been knocked off in the melee, straightened their outfits and went back in to finish their pints

Although that was the end of the crazy fight, it was not the end of the trouble for us. As usual, we sat in the main stand with the usual banter, until half time, when Graham (who was in a mad phase of his life, at this time) started a fight with some gobby Burnley fans. As Graham had a habit of doing though, he starts it and then disappears. He confronts them, when we are all around, will throw a punch and then miraculously disappear, leaving us in the middle of a brawl. The Police came over and calmed things down and this time we weren't ejected, which was probably worse as we then had to endure the debacle of the second half.

It all ended in tears later though, as Melv, true to his word, wouldn't take Gray back and he was left in Burnley, after some angry words, to make his own way home. He didn't even have enough money to get home, as it happened. My brother was always very resourceful though and would have found a way of getting back without paying a fare.

One season, when money was particularly tight for him he managed to go the whole season, without paying to get in. He would use all sorts of cunning plans to achieve this. The most popular was to wait at the turnstile, until the guy in front had paid and the gateman released the turnstile lock. As the person was going through, he would then push past and be off into the ground, leaving everyone behind bemused at what had happened. The club obviously got wise to this eventually and at Hillsborough, there are now extra barriers on the turnstile making it impossible for two people to get through at once. It is quite tight now, so much so that fatter people have quite a squeeze to get in.

So if you are fat and struggle to squeeze through the turnstiles at Hillsborough now, that's my brothers fault that is!

Although the league form had slumped, the cup form was superb.

We reached the quarter final of the League Cup, which meant a repeat of the five match epic against Arsenal. Unfortunately it was a one off this time, as we lost 1-0 to a late Tony Woodcock goal. There was a lot trouble after the game, with fights breaking out everywhere. We didn't get involved of course, but two of the lads that travelled down to Highbury with us did and got arrested. The funny thing is that one of them was a Unitedite that just came down for the game.

The same progress was made in the FA Cup and an away game to Burnley in the Quarter final. As said earlier, this game was drawn 1-1 and replayed back at Hillsborough three days later, with the draw for the Semi Final taking place between the games.

I remember us gathering at Mark's house to listen to the draw on the radio. The teams that were left were two very tricky teams in Arsenal and Man United, as well as bottom of the First Divison Brighton. Consequently we were obviously all praying for Brighton and the cheers when Arsenal and Man United were drawn together, were as loud as if we had just scored a goal.

Was this it at long last ? Was this our year ? I had always dreamed of seeing Wednesday play in a Cup Final. It was the one ambition as a supporter that I really desperately wanted to see. Getting to Wembley was the holy grail for a football fan in those days.

We always watched the Cup Finals on TV. It was a magical occasion and one that I desperately wanted to experience for myself. I always thought that Wednesday would get back to the First Division, but a Cup Final appearance would be something else. Of course we still had the small matter of getting past Burnley, the day after the draw, but suddenly the golden dream of a Wembley Final was frighteningly opening up for us.

Getting to Wembley in those days was a very, very special achievement.

I cannot emphasise enough what a massive thing it was getting to the hallowed twin towers. There were only two games played there that league sides had the chance to get to. The League cup and the FA cup finals. Nowadays I believe that this magic has been totally devalued as a Wembley appearance has been made available to virtually everyone, as all sorts of minor games are now played there. Play off games, non league games and even Semi Finals are all held there now. One of the great achievements of winning a Semi was the thought of going to Wembley for the Final. Where is the glory of achieving this now when the Semi is actually played at Wembley already? It is crazy.

In 2008 John Motson was praising the fact that the semis were held at Wembley and all the fans could get to see the big game. Well, I'm sorry Johnny boy, but of the semi finalists that year only West Brom scraped above the 20,000 average that season. Barnsley, Portsmouth and Cardiff averaged below that, so all the real fans could easily have been accommodated at Villa Park as usual. In fact the Barnsley v Cardiff game could have been played at Darlington and they still would have about all got in.

What you probably should have said was that it gives a chance for all the part timers to come out of the wood work and jump on the band wagon.

When Wembley was being re-built, there was suddenly an extra special feel to a big game, by moving them to the magnificent Millennium stadium in Cardiff. It was a great incentive to appear at this fantastic venue. (Hops back on the soap box.......) While on the subject of Wembley, although the newly built stadium looks fantastic, why on earth is the pitch so far away from the fans? One big problem with the old Wembley was the ridiculous distance from pitch to terrace. Although it is a lot better than it was, why have they still left a big gap? I bet the view from the front row, behind the goal is awful....... (Dismounts soap box).

As much as it is nice that so many get to experience going to the stadium, it is definitely no longer as special as it was.

The game against Burnley couldn't have gone much better if we had written the script ourselves. It was one of the very best nights of watching Wednesday, with a 41, 731 crowd packed into a bubbling Hillsborough.

Two Gary Shelton goals and a Megson penalty had put us into a 3-0 lead and by half time the ground was absolutely rocking.

Two more from big Andy McCulloch made it 5-0 and completed a stunning night. The euphoria around the ground was amazing and I think I bought every newspaper I could the next day.

There were comparisons to the Cup run of 1966, with Wednesday being drawn away in every round, so the omens were good and I couldn't wait to experience a Semi Final, one month later.

Gary Shelton makes it two nil and my head is just about to explode!

The cup run had certainly started to get to my blunt chums, who were getting pretty pissed off listening to us always talking about the Semi Final, on Friday nights on the town. I think that the fact that we had drawn struggling Brighton also worried them, as we had a very strong chance of winning. There was a definite us and them on the final Friday before the game and for the first time ever, football was a problem between us.

In an earlier league game away to top of the table Wolves, the fans had the cup run on their minds, which lead to a very unusual heart warming experience. The game at Wolves was a midweek night game and we had travelled down to see it.

Molineaux was in a dreadful state in those days. The old Kop end was derelict and empty, as was the stand to our left, so the 16,000 crowd that night had the use of only two sides of the ground.

The standing end behind the goal was split into two sections, with a fence dividing the rival fans. In contrast to this sorry decrepit stadium, there was a new shiny state of the art stand to our right, which looked totally out of place to the rest of its surroundings.

The atmosphere under the shared roof though was superb, with both sets of supporters being so close and the noise so contained. The one wonderful thing that you do get at football matches is a fantastic, if not twisted, sense of humour that is usually aimed at the team that you are playing. This takes the form of singing, or chanting at rival teams or fans and can be quite nasty at times, but is mostly just piss taking. Songs like this are usually started by some wag in the crowd, and if funny or nasty enough, will soon be picked up by those around.

This was the case at Wolves that night, when the Wolves fans started singing, "What's it like to have a roof" (as the Kop at Hillsborough was uncovered at that time).

The way the Black Country accent is structured, meant that the unusual pronunciation of the word 'roof' (particularly as it was sung in such close proximity, as opposed to the other end of the ground), sounded to our Yorkshire ears like ruuwwff (sorry but it's bloody impossible to spell! Try your best Black Country accent and give it a go, but suffice to say, it sounded odd!)

The immediate response was then, "What the f***in ell's a ruuwwff!" Instantly the Wolves replied with, "That's a ruuwwff, that's a ruuwwff, that's a ruuwwff', simultaneously pointing up to the structure above them. Wednesday hit back with, "We'll have a ruuwwff at Wembley, We'll have a ruuwwff at Wembley, na na,na na" and so it went on. The singing between both sets of fans was fantastic and for the first time that I can remember, they could have taken the fences down and there would have been no trouble at all.

It was a very rare moment that both sets of fans shared.

Gary Shelton makes it two nil and my head is just about to explode!

It became a 2,000 a side prolonged conversation, with quick fire wit and the singing banter went on for quite a few minutes, before eventually petering out. When it finished, it was signalled by an ovation from both sets of fans, in recognition of respect for each other.

I have never experienced an exchange like that since and at the end of the game fans mixed without a hint of trouble. For the record, there were three penalties that night. Wolves scored their one. We missed our two and lost 1-0. Typical.

We had a, 'ruuwwff', at Highbury, for the Semi Final, in what turned out to be the best and the worst day in my Wednesday watching life at the time. It started out fantastic, with twenty odd thousand Owls descending on London. We got there nice and early of course and full of expectation. By twelve o'clock, we were in a pub near the ground that was already heaving. We moved from one pub to another and all were the same, bouncing with Wednesdayites enjoying the day. From what I remember it was a nice sunny day too, so the singing throng spilled out on to the streets. It was as if the whole of North London had been taken over and an absolutely wonderful feeling.

A little after two o'clock we started to head to the ground, to enjoy the atmosphere. I remember on the way to Highbury, passing a church,

113

where the happy couple had just emerged from the ceremony for the usual photographs. The couple were black and I bet they got seriously pissed off with how many times they got asked if it was 'a white wedding.' as virtually every drunken footy fan seemed to shout this original comment at them. We were all absolutely buzzing and felt like we owned the world and Melv was as high as a kite. He had his shirt off, a blue and white scarf tied round his forehead, singing "We're the Vikings from the North" over and over again.

I wish we had video cameras in those days.

The euphoria extended to the game, where a thumping atmosphere was booming out. We were on the North Bank that day, and so all we could hear was Wednesday. The Brighton fans opposite us, on the open terrace, seemed silent from our vantage point and we were all starting to believe that it was going to be our day.

We should have known better.

Wednesday had suffered a major blow, just the week before, when left back Ian Bailey, who had been in terrific form, suffered a broken leg, so we went into the game without a recognised full back.

Although there was nothing between both sides in a scrappy game, it was Brighton that went 1-0 up in the first half and the ground suddenly seemed subdued.

Early in the second half that all changed again, when Mirocevic equalised and the North Bank went ballistic!

Mirocevic equalises and we thought it was our day. Note the number of Owls up celebrating in the Brighton end

114

From here on it was all Wednesday and it seemed as though Wembley may well be in the diary after all. The second half seemed all one way traffic, so it was a sickening blow, when Brighton took the lead with just twelve minutes left. I can still see that moment in my mind with the Wednesday goal wide open, Bolder helpless on the ground and Robinson stood over the ball. I am sure there would have been a cheer from the other end, but from where we were stood, the world fell silent. After a few agonised expletives, as the ball hit the net, it went silent. I mean absolute total silence.

Wednesday carried on battering Brighton but despite several near misses, it wasn't meant to be.

Again, glory had been snatched away.

We walked back to the car in silence, but I can remember feeling so damned bitter and angry.

It should have been us, rather than this bunch of nobodies.

I have never been violent, but I seriously could have hit any Brighton fan that was near that day. I think those from the South Coast that had parked at the wrong end, were acutely aware of the hostility and threat in the air. You could see it in their faces that even a hint of a smile would bring trouble. I cannot ever describe the feeling of emptiness and bitterness that stayed with me from that game. It was so hard to take defeat from a game that was there for the taking.

The season petered out from that point. It had promised so much, but as usual, delivered little, but at least we were left with some wonderful memories.

In the summer, we were distraught to learn that Big Jack had decided to call it a day. He had been the first manager, in my time, to bring any sort of success to the club and I was so sad to see him leave. Jack will always be loved by Wednesdayites and remembered as the man who turned us around and set us back on course. He was a huge character and his successor would have a hell of a job to fill Jack's shoes.

When the new manager was appointed, it was a bit of a shock and I think everyone felt unsure about this Howard Wilkinson guy. However 1983-84 would prove to be very different.

This was suddenly a whole new era and the sadness of Jack leaving, was instantly replaced by winning, winning, winning! A record eighteen match unbeaten start saw Wednesday six points clear at the top by the end of November. I could write a whole book on this season alone, but this isn't a history of Sheffield Wednesday, so I will cut it down to highlights (with great difficulty).

Mike Lyons gets the season off to a flyer with the winning goal at Swansea. Celebrating the goal are Pearson, Lyons, Morris, Madden, Megson and Bannister, along with a few thousand blues

Under Wilkinson, Wednesday played a lot more direct, with huge passion and energy. As a result they tended to steamroll the opposition, which as a supporter is fantastic to see. Not only are we winning, we are scoring a hatful of goals to boot.

Consequently, our travelling group barely missed a game.

It had also swollen in numbers too. One of Mark's work colleagues, a guy simply called Dixon (I don't think he had a first name. It was just 'Dixon', like 'Madonna' or 'Prince') had joined us and although he had been watching Wednesday for years, became a regular at away games with us. The only problem was the matter of travel. Dixon was always willing to take his car to away games, but after a few trips, we realised that going in the Dixon Volvo, meant paying not only for the petrol but his car loan as well and would cost well over double or triple in petrol money, as opposed to the Bormobile.

As we were all such a bunch of tight arses, it therefore became a real battle to avoid having to go with Dixon to away games.

For a game at Portsmouth in October, me and Mark decided to get to our meeting place a good fifteen minutes ahead of the agreed time, to ensure a place in the Bormobile.

It was therefore with great horror, that myself and Mark walked to our local pub car park, to find the Bormobile already parked up and full with the doors locked. The rest of the bas****s had got there half an hour early and dived in with glee. I can still see there grinning faces in the window, as Dixon's Volvo pulled in and no amount of pleading was going to make any difference.

They had locked themselves in and weren't going to get out for anything.

The trip was worth it that day though, with the Owls winning 1-0. It was a very windy day, so a 35 yard screamer from Gary Megson made it very pleasurable. We were sat in the South Stand that day, towards the end where most of the Owls fans were getting soaked and after the final whistle, as we applauded the team off, can remember being attacked by some disgruntled Pompey fans wielding umbrellas. Fortunately none of us got hit and we exited the ground. As we made our way back to the petrol guzzling machine, we had to get past a line of local hoolies, who were asking people the time, to try and identify Wednesdayites.

They weren't very bright though, because as I got to their cordon, they asked a kid wearing a Pompey shirt and so I slipped through unchallenged.

The huge petrol bill for the Pompey trip meant that I sadly couldn't afford another trip in Dixon's taxi for the following Saturday's trip to Brighton. It meant that I missed the 3-1 revenge for the Semi Final defeat six months earlier and was one of only three games I missed that season.

Another highlight was the home game against third placed Newcastle in November. A crowd of 41,134 produced a thundering atmosphere to justify a wonderful game. Newcastle had the likes of Kevin Keegan, Peter Beardsley, Chris Waddle (x x x x bless him), and Terry McDermott in their side, but we still brushed them aside in a pulsating 4-2 win.

I love this! Varadi jumps on the fence to celebrate putting us 2-1 up, only for one of the players to pull his shorts down as he is stood there arms aloft! (I'm not sure if the ballboy to the left is rubbing Varadi's leg or just clapping politely)

A few weeks later we were at second placed Manchester City, in another 40,000+ crowd. Maine Road in those days had the Kippax divided into two, with both fans under the same roof, so again the atmosphere was electric.

This was Wednesday's biggest test of the season and going a goal down in ten minutes didn't help, but two Imre Varadi goals gave us a 2-1 win as well as a three point lead with two games in hand.

We got bombarded by coins when the second goal went in (very brave I'm sure) but that just seemed to crank up the volume from our side. That was a thoroughly enjoyable afternoon and we left truly believing.

A 5-2 and a 6-1 home thumping over Cardiff and Swansea, respectively, kept us bubbling in the league, before a Quarter Final League Cup tie with Liverpool followed. A crowd that slightly bettered the 49,000 attendance for the Boxing Day game against United in 1979 saw a thrilling 2-2 draw, in a game which Wednesday always seemed capable of winning.

Victories just seemed to come rolling in, yet it was still tight at the top as we entered April. A home win against Portsmouth saw Wednesday, Chelsea and Newcastle, level on points, with Man City just behind.

This game against Portsmouth was also the day of one of my rare sojourns into football violence. It was the day I took on about 12 hard core Portsmouth hooligans, single handed....and won!

I was driving back after the match along Penistone Road towards the City centre, when a removal type van about 30 yards in front suddenly screeched to a halt and the sliding door at the rear opened up. The van was full of Portsmouth fans and they stopped to attack three Wednesday fans who were walking along. I was incensed by this and in a total rush of blood to my head and in an echo of the Blackpool trip many years before, drove my car straight into them! God knows what I was thinking. I had a white TR7 in those days, it was my pride and joy, so what on earth possessed me to run over a dozen blokes I don't know. Fortunately most dived out of the way and the ones I did hit, seemed to roll over the wedge shaped bonnet. Fortunately for me the traffic kept moving, as Lord knows what I would have done if the traffic had ground to a halt at that point (probably locked the doors and told them to go away, in a firm voice).

Luckily I escaped comfortably and I hope the three lads did too.

About a mile or so later I pulled up at some traffic lights and the car next to me, which was also full of Wednesdayites, pulled up alongside. The driver wound down his window and in a really broad Yorkshire accents said, "F*****g hell, thar wur braave runnin em oo-er, back theer. That or thas f*****g stupid! Well done mate!"

I took it as a compliment and felt like a hero!

The following week we were up at Newcastle, for an absolutely massive game. A midweek 3-1 win for us over Derby had opened up a three point gap, but everyone knew that this was the crunch game.

A win would almost certainly cement our place back in the top flight, so a huge following ventured north as expected.

We were in Borman's car that day, which had not been in the best of health due to the constant hammering it kept taking, but it got us safely up the A1.

I remember as we got to the North East passing a few coaches carrying Newcastle fans to the game. As is customary between rival fans, we got the usual two fingered greeting and abuse as we passed and I thought it would be funny to reply with a cheery 'thumbs up' greeting instead of replying with the same. From that point on, every time we passed Newcastle fans, we would all give them big cheesy grins and a matey thumbs up. It was so funny seeing their response, as they didn't quite know what to do. Instead of the usual two fingered reply they were getting thumbs up. The initial response was still to be abusive, but then they questioned it and slowly raised their thumbs back, almost against their will and it total confusion.

The game was not the best and we all seemed content to come away with a 0-0 draw, when Gary Shelton, with back to goal, hit an overhead kick of wonderful quality to win the game 1-0. We went absolutely berserk, screaming and shouting and hugging each other!

The remaining ten minutes were fantastic and when the entire Wednesday end joined in with my, "Put your thumbs up for the lads" song, aimed at the angry baying Newcastle fans on the terrace to our side, I almost peed myself.

Shelts hits a stunning overhead kick to win the game.
Look at the crowd jammed in there too. This is so typical of a lot of
pictures I have from this era. Deemed unsafe now, but what an
atmosphere it created

The total joy at the end of the game was quickly dampened however, as we left the ground. It was one of those classic moments when we needed to go left to our car, while EVERY one of the dancing, singing happy Owls turned right.

We asked a policeman for advice, who was part of the cordon holding back the hostile Geordies, who were seeking physical revenge on us for the result. He said that we had to take our chances, so that is what we did.

We casually split away from the happy revellers and as much as we tried to look as glum as possible and blend in with the Geordies, I am amazed that no one sussed us out.

It was a strange experience, listening to the voices around us threatening all sorts of violence against anyone from Sheffield and being stood in the middle of them.

The atmosphere was still very hostile and you knew that if any one of them realised we were Wednesday fans, we would get absolutely hammered, so it was with some relief that we made it back to the Bormobile.

We relaxed a little, but still had the slow crawl through the City before we could get to the A1 and safety.

Almost as soon as we set off the Bormobile started to struggle.

We anxiously discussed what to do, as we were still in the middle of the angry crowds walking away from the ground.

Several Geordies tapped on the window to tell us that we had a flat tyre, but we had no intentions of stopping in the middle of that lot and changing a tyre. With our best "Why aye man, thanks fo' telling us like, bonny lad" we pressed on. Borm was seriously worried about driving continuously on a flat, but we were more worried about our safety and made him keep going until it was safe.

We eventually hit the A1 and were doubly happy.

Just to finish our day off we gave lots of thumbs ups to the departing Geordie coaches. This time they knew exactly how to respond and there weren't any thumbs held up in reply. One guy totally lost it on a coach and was going absolutely mental at us. Borm let the coach overtake us again and again, so we could goad him a bit more. He ripped his shirt off and threw himself at the back window of the coach. He was like a total raving lunatic, foaming at the mouth and screaming God knows what at us. We absolutely wet ourselves laughing at him, which of course just made him worse. In the end, we gave a final cheery thumbs up and headed ecstatically back south.

Indeed, it did prove to cement promotion back to the top flight and a late Mel Sterland penalty at home to Crystal Palace a couple of weeks later confirmed promotion. Along with half the crowd that day, we took Champagne with us and thoroughly enjoyed spraying bubbly everywhere and relishing every second of it, when the final whistle went (You could tell the part timers that were there that day, because they were complaining about getting wet).

Three days later we won at Huddersfield and headed into the last three games of the season already promoted and five points clear of second place Chelsea.

We also had the easier run in.

The title of Champions was ours as well.

What a perfect season! (Insert sound of record scratching)

But, of course this is Wednesday we are talking about. Come on you should know by now.

A surprise defeat at mid table Shrewsbury, cut the lead to two points followed by a disappointing home draw with Man City, whilst Chelsea won their games. This meant that going into the final game, we had totally thrown it away and were now second on goal difference.

Bloody typical.

So off we went to Cardiff for the last game of the season. We did it in style of course, by a Friday night session in Sheffield before setting off at midnight. Of course there was the obligatory scuffle with totally pissed off Blades in a late night wine bar, but it was nothing more than handbags.

We were going up. Nothing could stop our enjoyment.

We had hired a mini bus for the trip and Dixon had kindly volunteered to drive. The trip down was totally forgettable, as I think we all slept right the way through it.

The first thing I remember on waking was someone shouting, "Bloody, chuffin' hell!"

This cry seemed to wake everyone up to see what was happening. We had stopped at some traffic lights, on the outskirts of Cardiff and stood almost next to the mini bus was a pair of copulating horses. The stallion had just finished his performance and was just dismounting. The first thing we saw on waking that morning, on already fragile stomachs was a huge horses kn*b that was covered in.....well you can guess, and it sort of hung there with a big wad of semen dripping, wobbling, yet still hanging on to the horses kn*b.

It was certainly not what you wanted to see first thing in a morning and combined with the usual smells you would expect with sharing the back of a van with eight men, after a night on the town. I seriously didn't feel well.

I don't think anyone had a giant hotdog with mayonnaise that day.

As for the game itself, we played very well and went on to win 2-0. About half way through the first period, I can remember a cheer starting on the opposite side of the ground, amongst Wednesdayites and it was clear, even from where we were, that the buzz was to say that Chelsea were losing (and so the title would be ours). It was amazing to see this 'rumour' physically move around the ground and soon the 8,000 travelling fans were jumping and shouting in celebration. Why people start these rumours is beyond me, as it does nobody any good. The official score over the tannoy system, at half time confirming that Chelsea were actually winning.

It was exactly the same at Full Time, when a rumour shot round the fans that were by now gathered on the pitch, that Chelsea had conceded a late equaliser, giving us the title, but again it wasn't true. The celebrations continued anyway and I can remember a real pigs head, complete with Sheffield United scarf, being passed among the happy crowd. It wasn't the end of the world that we let the title of Champions slip through our fingers on goal difference, but it was disappointing. It should have stood out as a clear message to everyone there, that even in times of success, Wednesday have a way of pulling the rug from under your feet.

If we all understood this, it would make life more bearable.

I always believed that we would get back to the top tier of football and at long last in 1984 it happened. It is frightening to think that something that still seems so fresh in the memory is now a worrying 24 years ago, as I write this.

Where the hell have those years gone?

So many games that I lived through, agonised through or rejoiced for yet I can't even remember anymore. So just as we had done four years earlier, we welcomed promotion to a new division on a nice sunny day, in front of a good sized crowd against a 'big' club. This time it was Nottingham Forest, the team that had finished runners up the previous season and recently won the European Cup two seasons running in 1979 and 1980 and like Newcastle before, it couldn't have gone much better. We won 3-1 with an absolutely stunning goal by Imre Varadi. From a Forest corner, the ball was headed clear to Varadi, who was just clear of our own penalty area. He ran with the ball, and just kept on running, until just outside the Forest 18 yard box, thundered a shot that screamed into the top corner. Stunning.

When Sheffield United got promoted to the Premiership for the 2006-07 season, their fans went on and on about it like it was something unique. They lasted a season, losing almost every week, before being relegated. When we were there, we didn't just stay up, we lit the place up. We did the double over Man United in our first and our second season. We won at Anfield, we beat Arsenal, teams like Spurs and Everton were brushed aside, as irrelevant. We got some stick in the press for the style of football, but this was out and out attacking football and we were ripping these sides apart.

Varadi has just thumped a late headed winner in front of us all at Old Trafford. I think I remember this being a rather nice feeling

Cup runs became commonplace and quarter finals were the norm, although the holy grail of a Cup Final, always seemed elusive.

Looking back I am surprised that this golden spell on the field provided so few memories off it. Don't get me wrong, it was an absolutely fantastic time and after visiting so many grounds in the bottom leagues, it was nice to add the famous ones to my list too, particularly as we were winning, but the funny situations and scrapes got less and less.

My theory on this is that football went through a hell of a transition around this time. For a long, long time football supporters had been treated absolutely diabolically, by clubs and the Police alike, although you can argue that this was deserved by the way a lot of fans behaved, particularly in the 1970's.

Segregation was not the norm in those days. Yes there were popular ends (usually behind the goal), where home fans would congregate and as a result became a target for visiting trouble makers, but areas designated as strictly only for visiting fans were not common place until the 1980's. You only have to see TV clips of games from the 1970's and look at the crowd when a goal is scored. The fans are all mixed in together, you can tell by the pockets of those celebrating against the ones stood still, who have just conceded.

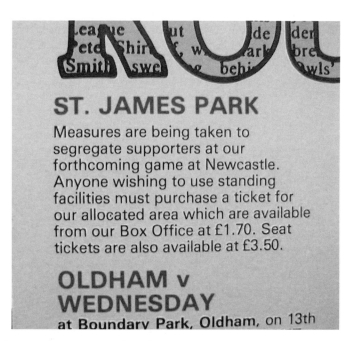

ST. JAMES PARK

Measures are being taken to segregate supporters at our forthcoming game at Newcastle. Anyone wishing to use standing facilities must purchase a ticket for our allocated area which are available from our Box Office at £1.70. Seat tickets are also available at £3.50.

OLDHAM v WEDNESDAY

at Boundary Park, Oldham, on 13th

Taken from a 1982 Wednesday programme, where the introduction of segregation was slowly being enforced

Eventually the problem got so bad that action had to be taken. Segregation of supporters became more rigorous and following several pitch invasions, fences were put up, to cage fans in. Policing of fans became more professional, with measures taken to keep fans apart, outside the ground as well as in. These measures were not instantly successful nor were they welcome. Being a football fan means that you have precious few rights and being treated like animals often meant that fans behaved like animals. Police heavy handed tactics often incited trouble rather than quelled it and as recent as 2002, I witnessed appalling scenes, all through terrible policing.

The game was a League Cup Semi Final at Blackburn and as a struggling second tier team, that had lost the first leg at home 2-1, we didn't expect to get anything out of the game at all, so expectations weren't high. However a semi final is a semi final, so there was a large following that ventured over the Pennines, in the slim hope of something happening. As it happened we were right and lost 4-2 on the night.

(Ironically the two scores of 2-1 and 4-2 were the same scores that we beat Blackburn by at the same stage of the competition nine years earlier).

I was sat about four rows from the front of the lower tier that night. I was on my own as my brothers had tickets for the top tier and late in the match, with the game already lost, the atmosphere was pretty quiet. For some unknown reason, whoever was in charge of policing that night, thought it would be a good idea to send in the riot squad, despite the fact that there wasn't even the slightest hint of trouble. They marched out unannounced, all fully kitted out as if ready to face the anarchists from Trafalgar Square and stood in line, right in front of the Wednesday supporters behind the goal. Being quite low down, neither myself, nor anyone around me could see anything of the game at all. However that was not really the point. Such an unnecessary and provocative action, merely inflamed the lunatics that were in the crowd and from nowhere, there was suddenly an ugly and tense atmosphere. It didn't take long before the Police started pulling people out of the crowd and it was all down hill from here. This was a signal for the hotheads to come charging down the terrace and all hell let lose. I was quite lucky, in so much as I was out of reach of the flailing truncheons that were being wielded indiscriminately into the crowd, but there were a lot of people in front of me, who were not so lucky.

Being in the middle of it, it was difficult to get out of the way, as the gangways were full of the trouble makers, who had been goaded into chasing down the aisles to get into the thick of the action. As a result there was no obvious means of getting out of there. As a fit male adult, with no one else to look out for, I managed to fight my way back over the rows of seats to a safe distance. However, it was sickening to see this needless violence erupt from nothing and the thing that stayed with me most of all afterwards, was seeing the terrified faces of women and kids that were caught up in it. The battle raged on for quite a few minutes and fortunately for me, I got out of there unscathed, unlike some. The really galling thing though was that the person that created this violence, I doubt, would even be questioned as to why they caused this totally unnecessary situation.

Back in the 1970's I guess this sort of incident was to be more expected, but by 2002 Policing had improved no end, which made the Blackburn incident even more alarming.

Caging fans in was also something that was applied at the vast majority of grounds and there were some absolutely shocking examples.

127

Away games to places like Luton and Notts. County were to be dreaded simply because you couldn't see hardly any of the game. These clubs installed double fencing, that created a passage way between the two lots of fencing, so as a result of the thick metal fences, you couldn't see any action that was taking place on the other side. I guess this wasn't so bad for clubs of their size who didn't have many fans, but when your small corner of the ground is sold out, there is no where to go to get a better view. Consequently, you don't get to see what is happening on the pitch.

Bristol Rovers moved to Twerton Park, Bath in the early 1990's and I can remember visiting there for a league game once.

I was 'lucky' enough to have got a ticket for the game, as we quickly sold out of our small allocation. We mixed quite happily with 'Gas' fans in the pubs beforehand, with no hint of trouble and all seemed well. That is until we got in the ground. Twerton Park was a bloody horrible ground anyway, totally inadequate for the second tier of football, but the thick fencing there was a joke. It was about ten feet high, so we could see nothing of the penalty area of the nearest goal.

And so it was that in the 28th minute Trevor Francis latched onto a bad back pass and.......... Well to be honest, I don't know.

It was impossible to see anything so, we just watched the reaction of the players that we could see and waited to see if the other fans that could see cheered. They did. I would like to say that I saw Tricky Trevs first goal for us, but sadly I can't.

It was the appalling way fans were crowded into totally unsuitable areas that started us going into the Main Stand at away games. At least from there, you could get a reasonable view of the game, even if you were mixed in with the home fans. It just seems bizarre paying to be squashed into an unsafe cage, where you can't even see the most important part of the game.

What sort of industry would allow this situation to happen to its customers?

Eventually I think fans themselves got totally sick of it and so rather than turning on each other, for supporting different clubs, they started to acknowledge that we were all being treated the same and so stopped treating each other as the enemy per se.

As a result a certain amount of tolerance of each other occurred and we are now left with a lot more civilised way of watching football.

I think to those brought up in the era that I was, for a long time it was difficult to take seeing fans of opposing clubs walking along Penistone

Road, openly wearing there team colours, without any form of intimidation, but thank God that this did happen. Watching football now is very different and I cannot say that I have seen any trouble between rival fans at Hillsborough for a very long time.

Having said that, there was still an air of uncertainty about going to away games, particularly going to clubs who had a bit of a reputation.

A trip to Millwall in December 1988 was a prime example of this.

A few years earlier, one of our lads had gone down for a night game in the cup. He had managed to get himself lost after the game and got chased a few times around a very rough looking council estate. He managed to escape and decided to get the tube out of there and then get a train home. He obviously wasn't too familiar with 'The Jam' at the time, otherwise he would have known that you, "Don't ever go down in the tube station at midnight."

He dismissed Paul Weller's advice and soon got sussed out and took a severe beating, including being hit with a motorbike chain.

With this in our minds, two car loads of us ventured to London for the game and given Millwall's reputation our tactics were to set off nice and early. The idea was to park the cars right outside the away end, so at the end of the game, when the trouble was most likely to happen, we would be in the car and safely away without coming anywhere near any Millwall fans.

When we got to Cold Blow Lane, it couldn't have been any better, as we parked the car within spitting distance of the turnstile.

The only problem with our plan was that it was only twelve o'clock and the ground wouldn't even open up for at least another hour and a half!

We sat and discussed what was the best thing to do, before deciding that it was plenty too early for any trouble and as long as we kept a low profile, we should walk down the road and find the nearest pub. As soon as it started to fill up we would quietly slip out and head to the ground. Brilliant!

The problem about going somewhere like Millwall, was that you expected to see trouble. It was in your mind that this was a dangerous place, so to say that we were all apprehensive is an understatement.

Within a few hundred yards we found a pub and cautiously went in.

We were all mightily relieved that there were only three people in the pub, so joked a little as we stood at the bar and ordered our drinks. The pub had Millwall stuff on the walls, so it was pretty safe to say that we were in the Lions Den, literally.

Even the hastily drunk first pint didn't ease the nerves, but we still knew that we were, for the moment, safe. Certainly the two old geezers in the corner reading "The Sporting Life" didn't worry us, but very soon the one bloke on his own, sat at a bar stool did.

He had obviously sussed that we were from Sheffield and as soon as we all sat down at a table, he started singing and I mean real top of the voice singing.

We all fell silent, amazed at this one guy on his own, singing at us!

I really don't think any of us knew what to do. It was surreal.

He wasn't just singing nice Millwall footy type songs either. He went through the full gambit of, "We are Millwall, no one likes us," to, "You're going to get your f****ng heads kicked in!"

It was crazy, I mean there were eight of us and one of him (even three of our eight were Policeman for heavens sake!), we could have pulled him off his stool and pulled his head off, if we were that way out, yet we sat there like scared mice, listening to this lunatic singing at us. After a few minutes of this we returned to talking amongst ourselves, thinking if we ignored him, he might disappear, but he didn't. By now I had quickly drained two pints and was bursting for a pee and although a little apprehensive, decided I could wait no longer.

I sort of hoped someone else would go too, but no I was on my own.

I quickly reasoned that our psycho friend wouldn't attack us on his own and very warily off I went.

I had only been stood there having a pee for a few seconds, when the door burst open and I heard a gruff cockney voice say,"You fackin' norvern barrstud." I swear my heart stopped beating as I turned to see Psycho boy with an iron bar in his hand about to splatter my brains against the wall.

If I wasn't already pissing, I would have wet myself.

But instead of the lunatic it was my bloody stupid brother walking in taking the piss out of me in a stupid cockney accent!

I am sure I called him some pretty unpleasant names!

Not long after we sat back down, our Cockney lunatic got up and walked out casting a nasty look over at us as he left. I think it took us five seconds to unanimously agree that he was off to get his mates and we should get out of there damned sharpish. Our pints were finished within one minute and we were soon banging on the turnstile doors to be let in!

As an aside to this adventure, I think the game was one of the all time lows of watching Wednesday. Although we were still in the top division, the side was being slowly dismantled and Peter Eustace was now the manager. A very poor Wednesday side went out with the sole intention of playing for a draw and used every negative, offside and time wasting tactics they could. It was a totally awful display and when Millwall eventually scored the only goal of the game deep in injury time, it was as low as I had felt at a game for a long time (but at least we were in our car and away in seconds after the game!)

CHAPTER 7

pigs

There is nothing like a derby match in football.

Let's get one thing straight here. I absolutely hate Sheffield United. I despise their very existence. It is a hatred that is totally irrational but I can't change it. I loathe them and would happily have done anything that I thought would make them extinct. It is a very strange feeling really, as the Unitedites that I know are great and now that I live in West Yorkshire, there simply aren't any Unitedites up here, so it isn't as if I take a lot of stick from them. Yet that strong feeling of hatred is still there. I hate their players. I hate their fans. I hate their crappy red and white colours. I hate their ground. I hate their badge. I absolutely f*****g hate everything about them.

I do wonder sometimes which is the greater. My love of Wednesday or my hate of United. I hate it if Wednesday lose, but it certainly lightens the load massively if United have lost too.

Over the years I don't think the out and out loathing of the pigs has lessened, but in a perverse sort of way I am actually pleased that we do have them to hate. Every team has its rivals but I feel sorry for clubs who only have the one club in their town or city, as they will never truly appreciate what a real derby is all about. Yes I am sure that they still have their enemies, their rivals, but it isn't the same.

Clubs like L**ds have no one. The sad L**ds fans I know, say their rivals are Man United. Man United? Come on! For a start they aren't even in the same bloody county and I am sure Man United fans will have a list of half a dozen clubs on their 'derby' list long before L**ds even get a second thought.

No, there is nothing that compares with a real, same city derby.

So how does Sheffield compare?

What makes a Sheffield derby so special?

Well, I am not sure what it is to be honest. If you compare it worldwide to the likes of River Plate and Boca Juniors or to some of the lunatic games in crazy old Turkey, then it doesn't compare in the slightest.

In the UK there is only one derby that stands out and that is Rangers and Celtic. I would dearly love go to a Glasgow derby, as this is the derby in this country to see.

A Sheffield derby however is as nasty a derby as there is after Glasgow.

I know that all derby games have a special edge and I am sure that the rivalry is very genuine, but Wednesday / United really is absolute hatred of each other. The chapter title "pigs" (no capitals used intentionally) refers to the name that both sets of supporters call each other. Wednesday call United 'pigs' as they play in a streaky bacon, red and white stripes kit. United call us pigs because.........well I don't know. I don't think they know either. It is just a derisory name we invented and they probably couldn't think of anything better. Whatever the reasons, that is now what we call each other. They also have other more polite names, based on the nickname of 'the blades', such as 'blunts' or 'bladies', as well as pig derivitives, such as porkers, squeelers, etc. etc.

So why in Sheffield are you blue or red? There is no real explanantion for this either. As a general rule Wednesday always drew their support from the more affluent areas, whereas United took theirs from the more working class council areas. This is not the golden rule however and you will obviously find mixed support for all areas, but certainly the south side of the city, where we lived, was as a general rule, divided into areas that were prominently Wednesday or United.

There has always been a massive argument in Sheffield as to who is the biggest club and my honest and biased opinion is that there isn't one. (oooooh that's shocked a few people!)

I think the footballing public in Sheffield are pretty fickle to be honest. Both clubs have a hard core of fans, that will go to see their team regardless and from this I would deduce that Wednesday have the largest hardcore support. As bad as Wednesday get, they can still rely on a good number of fans to still turn out week after week. United can do the same, but on a smaller scale and undoubtedly both have a huge pool of fans that will come and watch them when they are doing well.

(I may be wrong on this but I think the reservoir of glory hunter fans are two different groups of people. i.e. this group of people will only go to see one of the sides when they are succesful and not either of them).

It is strange that a city that can consistently pull in a cumulative support of 40,000 to 50,000 every week gets such little press (especially when the quality of football has been so poor over the years). Of course this opens up the debate about merging the two clubs in Sheffield. I don't think that anyone really wants this, yet it does make perfect sense. A major city like Sheffield, the home of the game, that is a football city through and through would definitely become a major force with the one club, I am totally convinced. The difficult thing would be the short term aspect of this as the rivalry is simply too deep and bitter. It would take a generation of "Sheffield City" before acceptance and I just cannot see this happening. (Of course there would be debates about what to call a merged club and what colours to play in. However, I will resist putting in the bit about how we could make up the kit by taking the white stripes from Uniteds shirt and the blue stripes from Wednesdays shirt and the "Sheffield" part of Uniteds name and the "Wednesday" part from ours to make the clubs name..............Doh!)

The hatred is so deeply rooted in both sets of fans that there has always been a lot of fans trying to get one up on each other. There are great stories about Wednesday fans breaking in to the sty the night before a derby game and painting the goalposts with blue and white.

There was also a poster campaign carried out by Holsten Pils a few years back which gave us great pleasure. The ad showed a picture of a pig and the caption "It's what's inside that counts." The pig then had lines drawn on it to show pork chops, sausages, etc. Now either by incredible stupidity on behalf of the piggy board or genius by a Wednesdayite, that ad was actually put up right by Bramall Lane! The sheer pleasure from this was immense to us. Of course United were totally embarrassed by this, but the damage was done.

Bramall Lane..... Its what's inside that counts! I love the way United fans tried to rip down the poster, but there is no hiding it!

The same poster re-emerged later on about half a mile away from the Wednesday ground and this too was used for our pleasure. Someone had the vision to take a couple of tins of paint and a ladder up one night and painted the pig some red and white stripes!

The story goes that a united fan was so incensed by this that he went up with a tin of blue paint to paint over the red, but got disturbed by the police, fell off the ladder and broke his ankle!

Another lovely story that I like is one of the shoe burning ritual. A Wednesday fan has set fire to his shoes following every trip he has ever made to United's ground. It has become a family tradition now, that they all burn their shoes to "disinfect" themselves after setting foot in their ground!

Of course this works both ways and they must have lots of similar stories themselves. I just don't know of any and can't say that I am interested anyway.

It just goes to prove the intensity of the rivalry and I absolutely love it!

Shoe burning time!

As I grew up it was Wednesday that were the stronger club. They had been in the First Division since 1959 and their appearance in the 1966 FA Cup final underlined their 'big club' status. In fairness to United, however, they overtook us in the early 1970's with a good side

136

made up of the likes of Currie, Woodward, Salmons (God do you know how hard it is for me to type this), while Wednesday started their slippery slide to the Third Division.

It was against this backdrop that I was cast as a Wednesday supporter.

I went to the derby games of the 1970-71 season, but was way too young to understand the importance of it. I can also remember being taken to Bramall Lane for matches when they were in the First Division and always ended up shouting for the other team. In fact, we used to go a few times and stand with the away fans to cheer on the other team. I think a lot of Wednesday fans did in the early Seventies (It was probably the only way of having a chance of seeing 'your' team win!)

One of my first recollections of trouble between fans came strangely enough in a game against Doncaster Rovers. We had played Donny at Hillsborough in a League Cup game in 1977 and was making my way back into the City centre following a 5-2 win. In those days both clubs were allowed to play at home on the same day and United had also had a home cup game.

Unfortunately I was on the bus that day and it was one of the very first buses back into the main terminus from the match. United's ground is close to the City centre, so their fans were already there. As we got off the bus and started to walk cautiously towards our next bus stop home, they came pouring out of the main terminus. There were probably about 200 or so of them and about thirty of us. I was with a mate from school, called Robert Smith, that day and as everyone around us ran, I don't know what it was inside me that said 'No' and I refused to run. Now don't get me wrong I wasn't hard and about to take them on, I just didn't want to run away. Even at that early age of 16 I felt a deep hatred for the enemy and I guess I didn't want to think they could beat me. Instead I grabbed 'Snags' as he was nicknamed and pulled him into a conveniently placed phone box. Fortunately none of the marauding piggy mob had spotted us, as they milled around outside, happy they had chased Wednesday off. It was still pretty scary stuff though, as we tucked our scarves quickly into our pockets. They seemed to hang around for ages and we were both sweating knowing that at any time we could be pulled out of the phone box and given a serious hammering. Fortunately we weren't spotted and as soon as they left, we headed to our bus stop and got out of there.

Given Wednesday's demise in the 1970's we didn't have a proper derby game for a few years, so the only time we encountered each other was at friendly games. We actually played each other a few times and this was seen as a golden opportunity for Wednesday to make up for events on the pitch by extracting some pride off it.

I can remember one testimonial game played at their place particularly. It was a night game and we had a simple single bus ride to get to their ground, just minutes, from where we lived. We had heard rumours all week that Wednesday were going to attack their Kop end, so decided that we would go on the Shoreham end also. Not that we were going to get involved, but it was the place to be, should it happen. As soon as we had paid to get into the ground we heard the roar. "Wednesday! Wednesday!" was booming out and we ran with glee up the steps to the terracing to add our numbers to the cause, pulling our scarves out of our pockets in pride. It was an awesome feeling joining the mob in the middle of their Kop end and belting out the repertoire of Wednesday songs with so much pride. This was great and made up for all the stick that I used to get at school from my piggy chums. Better still was seeing the Unitedites around us, unable to do anything than stand there in humiliation. Oh how we enjoyed it!

There was another testimonial game there, the following season and I obviously expected a repetition. For some reason I went with two friends who were both Unitedites that night and when we were stood on the United Kop, I waited for the conquering heroes to appear. That night was different though and when the charge came, this time they were beaten back. United had obviously learnt their lesson and weren't about to let it happen again.

As much as I was disappointed, we stayed on the Kop however, and stood towards the front. It was expected that United's much better side would win easy, so when Wednesday scored to go 1-0 up I was ecstatic. As far as I can remember, there were no other Wednesdayites near me, but I jumped up and down and shouted anyway. This obviously drew some attention to me and although no one particularly did anything, I can remember that some bigger lads clearly came down from the back to suss me out. On finding that I was only 14 nothing was done, except blowing smoke in my face constantly. I do remember getting a few whacks across the head later, though when United equalised. From here on I expected it would be all downhill, but no, Wednesday scored again and won 2-1. I must have been a right arrogant (or stupid) little tw*t in those days, because I was simply asking for trouble, behaving the way I did. I was shouting my head off and joining in with the Wednesday fans songs on the other side of the ground. Why I didn't get a beating that night I will never know, but I didn't.

The following season the teams played at Hillsborough in the County Cup Final and there was no way United were going to even get a sniff at getting on the Kop. Wednesday had posted groups of hard lads at every entrance to the terracing, so every fan was checked out before being allowed on. Any Unitedite that tried was whacked and thrown out again. As a result there was no attempt on the Wednesday end. In fact as long as I can remember United have never had a go at taking Wednesday's Kop, whereas Wednesday would always have a go at their place, even up to the 1980's, before all seater stadia meant it couldn't be done anymore.

Around the 1970's our next door neighbour tried desperately to convert me to United and would take me to their games regularly. As much as I enjoyed the whole experience, I could never see it any other way, than wanting the other team to win (Sorry, Les.)

The good news was that United, like Wednesday before them, also had a death wish and after a brief spell of having a bloody good side, eventually chased us down the leagues (we even teased them with going tantalisingly close to being relegated to Division Four) but eventually they caught us in Division Three in 1979 and the scene was set for one of the biggest derbies in Sheffield history. The date for the first game was set for Boxing Day, so we still had some time to wait, when the fixtures were announced, but already this game was bigged up as being absolutely massive.

United set off like an express train that season and were soon top of the league. Wednesday weren't doing too bad themselves, but were inconsistent, so by the time the big game came round we were in 6th place and 4 points behind them (two points for a win in those days). I think Wednesday fans were dreading it to be honest and rightly so. Our home form was poor, with only four wins from eleven games and the banter was getting more hostile, the closer it came. I can remember in our local pub on Christmas Day, Mark getting pretty irate with one of my friends Chris (the same guy from the Cockney Pride night) and it seemed like it would come to blows at one stage.

The day eventually came around and we had planned to meet up at a specific location near to the ground. The match was an all ticket affair and brought forward to an eleven o'clock kick off to try and combat the realistic fears of there being a huge amount of trouble. As a result we took a load of cans with us to drink before the game but it was nothing to do with the early time that meant none of us could face a drop. I felt sick to my stomach at the prospect of the game, my nerves were that bad.

We therefore made our way to the ground a lot earlier than planned and it was absolutely heaving when we got there. We had season tickets that season, but for some reason we went on the Kop. Only Melv took up his usual place in the North Stand. We stood where we used to stand too, in the middle about three quarters of the way back. The game itself was unbelievable from our point of view as we hammered them 4-0. I can still see Ian Mellor's shot whistling past the piggy keeper and into the top corner to open the scoring.

Terry Curran absolutely ran United ragged that day, scoring the second and setting up the third. It was an awesome day. Even my chum Robert, who was a part time Unitedite in those days, got carried away and cheered when the third went in (He of course flatly denies this now) and it would be hard for anyone in the middle of that jubilant, ecstatic mass of people not to get carried away with the passion of it all. It was absolute heaven.

In total contrast this was a United supporters view that was recently posted on one of their websites.

"Oh yes. It took a few therapy sessions to get that one out the system. Turning up full of hope and expectation, then just standing there in horror as it unfolded. Kenworthy having a nightmare, Speight injured, we were just there for the taking, and didn't they do it. The overriding memory I have is standing on the Leppings Lane End, about the edge of the Penalty area on the right, and hearing 'Boxing Day, massacre, etc. etc.' and looking up into the main stand, and the North Stand and the whole sty were singing it, the loudest chanting I'd ever heard before or since. I left after the last goal, and there was an 82 bus just pulling in as I got to Middlewood Road. I jumped on and sat down, and the conductor came up to take my money, and he said, 'how are we doing?' I just remember saying, 'don't ask, mate, don't ask.' Work was hell on the Monday, and it lasted for at least a couple of weeks before the Pig fans got bored of singing 'massacre' as any Blade walked past. I don't ever want to go through an experience like that again."

After the game we met Melv and piled on top of each other celebrating it all again.

Amazingly enough, there was no trouble that day. I guess we were all too happy and they just wanted to disappear.

We headed back to our local and sang our heads off until the pubs closed (Yes kids, in those days the pubs closed about three o'clock and didn't re-open until the evening. The governments didn't trust ordinary people to not drink themselves stupid during the day, so passed a law to close the pubs. It was all for own good though)

I even got the pleasure of having a pint poured over my head as I was on my knees singing, by Robert, but you know what, nothing could take the gloss off that day.

Ian Mellor is congratulated by Mark Smith and Terry Curran following the first goal.

It's official! Boxing Day Massacre became legendary to Wednesday fans

By the time the return game came round at Easter, the season had been totally transformed for both clubs, with Wednesday riding high at the top, while United were now sliding out of the promotion race.

We had tickets for the South Stand at Bramall Lane and this time we were really looking forward to the game. We met in our usual pub and then decided to go nearer the ground for a few drinks. Someone suggested we head to London Road, which is close to the ground and populated by a lot of pubs.

Mistake.

Big mistake.

Now we really should have known this, living in the City, but London Road, is a United stronghold, so when about ten of us started walking up the road, in blue and white, we were a magnet for trouble. They must have obviously thought that we were well up for it and that was why we were there and boy did they whip up a welcome. Of course we weren't, we simply naively came for a drink, but now found ourselves the centre of attention.

By the time we realised we had made a big mistake, it was too late and we already had a mob of about two or three dozen following us, kicking at our heels and goading us. There was simply no way we could turn round and go back. The pubs seemed to all empty and we were very quickly massively outnumbered, as we went further into their territory. I can remember them looking incredulous at us, amazed that we were there, as they ran out to taunt us. If I am completely honest, I was absolutely terrified. You could feel the hatred coming at us and it was simply a matter of time before we got seriously pasted.

None of us said a word, even mighty Melv, as the abuse rained down on us. Things were being thrown at us, we were spat on and we got the odd slap and kick but still nobody started the attack. I actually think they were enjoying our agony, like a cat plays with a mouse, as they knew there was no escape. We also knew we couldn't get out of there. We were dead meat.

We walked on further, because we didn't know what else we could do. A little huddle of Wednesday surrounded in a sea of hate. The worst part was the waiting. We knew we would get hammered. It was inevitable, but the delay in the attack, as they ridiculed us, just made it worse. I don't know how we could have been so stupid to put ourselves in this situation, but I think we thought we were untouchable. We had done it so many times all over the country, so why would it be different in our home city?

It was this delay that ultimately saved us though, for all the time it went on we continued walking. We were incredibly lucky because one of the lad's Dad was very good friends with one of the landlords that had a pub on London Road and by a wonderful stroke of luck he was outside his pub talking to his door minders as we approached. He recognised Kev and immediately saw our predicament, so just as the attack was about to start, we dived in there and the bouncers on the door, stopped anyone following. They did have a hell of a go though and the pub sustained some damage as they tried to get at us, but we survived in tact and mightily relieved is an understatement. The landlord was absolutely livid with us, but he had let us in and we had miraculously escaped. The baying mob were also furious as they had unwittingly let us escape and continued to batter the pub for a while.

It took some time before any sort of real relief set in and the realisation that yet again we had come out of it unscathed. Someone up there must seriously have been looking after us, because I can't believe how many times we voluntarily put ourselves into dangerous situations, yet always managed to come out unharmed.

The South stand seemed full of both sets of fans and the atmosphere was electric and full of tension. There was loads of abuse thrown at each other and quite a few punches too with scuffles everywhere as the game unfolded and as scary as it is, this is part of what makes derbies unique.

The game was cracking and finished at 1-1.

Terry Curran celebrates scoring the equaliser in the 1-1 draw. In the earlier game at Hillsborough TC slid on his knees in front of the Unitedites after scoring the second goal. This time his feat is to a more appreciative audience. Curran later signed for United in a bizarre move that was never, ever going to work, following his heroics for Wednesday

Wednesday were promoted that season, but played United again very soon, as we were drawn together in the League Cup. Wednesday won the first leg 2-0 and drew 1-1 at Bramall Lane, but surprisingly there wasn't the usual passion about the games, although we all went home very happy.

The course of the two clubs went happily opposing ways, with Wednesday going from strength to strength whilst United plumbed new depths.

The following season United went into their last game against Walsall....

It was something that United have come to specialize in over the years. Turning a tricky situation into a deadly one by not only cocking it up themselves, but by other fixtures also contriving against them to send them down. Spookily enough this day was the first of three in a thirteen year cycle that saw them relegated in 1994 and again in 2007. (I can't wait for 2020!)

The Walsall game though became legendary to Wednesdayites as "Thank Givens Day."

Neither Sheffield clubs had ever been as far down the leagues as the Fourth Division and this looked unthinkable after five games of the 1980-81 season with United winning four and sitting at the top of the table. However, as we fast forward through the season with just one match to play, United had slowly slid down the table. They did seem just about clear of relegation though, placed eighth from the bottom, having Swindon, Oxford and Chester between them and Walsall in the final relegation place. United even had a significantly better goal difference too, so relegation seemed highly unlikely.

Results conspired against them that day though with Swindon, Oxford and Chester picking up the point that they needed, making the Walsall match, effectively, a loser goes down game.

You can imagine my excitement then on the Saturday afternoon, when the local radio interrupted the music to tell us about a late penalty drama at the Lane (no match commentaries in those days, kids!). To my relief it was to Walsall and they duly scored it. The way the results were at that stage, this meant that United had amazingly slid into the bottom four for the first time with just five minutes left of the whole of the season!

I was ecstatic.

I couldn't believe that this could happen.

It was agony waiting for those last few minutes to tick away, so when the music was once again interrupted to tell us of even more late, late drama and another penalty at the Lane, my heart was in my mouth. To my horror United had been given a last minute penalty and scoring it would keep them up.

Jammy ba***rds!

It was Don Givens who stepped up to take it and although I have sadly never seen it, I am told that it was as bad a penalty as is possible and the keeper saved comfortably.

I was at my girlfriend's house at the time and I can remember dancing round the room laughing my head off like a lunatic! My

145

girlfriend's mother always thought I was a bit odd, so seeing me behave like this merely confirmed her suspicions.

The funny thing that day was that a lot of Unitedites had foolishly believed a rumour that went round the ground at full time, that Swindon had lost and they had been reprieved. I saw two blunts later, who I half knew, that were on their way home from the match and had enormous pleasure telling them. Although they denied it was true, I could tell from the expression on their faces that they knew I had been listening to the radio and what I was telling them was the truth.

Oh Joy! Such sweet, sweet Joy!

How the local sports paper presented the disaster. For once I didn't care about how Wednesday went on!

When you have such bitter rivals, you do take a sadistic pleasure in watching them struggle. As I said before, at times it is a close run thing between whether I loved Wednesday more or hated United more. Although, I think Wednesday always shaved it, it is always so blissful to see them struggle.

During that same 1980-81 season, we were due to play Preston away one Saturday and had all assembled to venture over the Pennines. We had only got as far as Barnsley, when it came on the radio that the game had been postponed due to an icy pitch (You see Gillingham, it can be done!). We stopped to consult the second car load as to what to do and pulled into a nearby pub to decide. After a few beers, some decided to go home, while some of us decided we would go to Bramall Lane. Their early promotion push had faltered and they were now seriously struggling, so it could be fun to stand with the Gillingham fans and cheer them on.

I can't remember too much about what happened before the game, other than it deteriorated badly. The pub we were in was in a rural area and for some reason I can remember someone throwing a load of hay round the Gents toilets. I don't know who and I am not sure why, but when the landlord found out he was furious and threw us out. I can't even remember why we ended up falling out amongst ourselves either, but I remember Graham head butting me for some reason! (It was during his mad spell).

It all fell apart at that stage and so just four of us went to the Lane.

When we got there, we had a change of plan and decided to stand on the John Street terrace, instead of the away end. The game was pretty drab to be honest (which was a good thing) and the mood of the fans was not good. The then manager, Martin Peters was under pressure so as undercover agents, we seized on every bad pass and poor shot, to help influence those around us. When challenged about our negativity, we sited that we had been down to Newport the previous week to see the 4-0 drubbing and this seemed to give us credibility to those around and slowly a few more joined in the boos. Just as things were starting to look good for us, United got a penalty.

Disaster.

All our good work was about to be undone, but instead the penalty was missed and we masked our delight by vociferously shouting abuse, to which quite a lot were now happy to join in.

The day got better too as Gillingham were also awarded a penalty later on and unlike United, they converted it.

I remember me and Mark walking out in supposed disgust, saying that was it we had had enough. Instead we went into the toilet and jumped up and down. Fortunately no one was about as I am sure we would have been sussed out and in a lot of trouble (nerve wracking stuff these undercover operations!).

We couldn't resist going back on the terraces to stir things up a bit more and when we left in injury time, it was wonderful to hear "Peter's out! Peter's out!" booming round the ground.

We smiled to each other.

Our work here is done.

I don't know whether we were just young and foolish in those days, as I wouldn't dream of doing something like that now, but in those days we just saw it as a bit of fun.

We did a similar thing, when United played Bristol City in a play off game in 1988 as well.

In those days plays off were held between the teams who finished third, fourth and fifth, but also included the team who finished third from bottom in the division above. On this occasion United were in the bottom three and City had finished fifth in Division Three. As is the case now, there was a two leg Semi Final and then a play off final with the winner being "promoted', while the other three teams would be 'relegated.'

The games were played over two legs, with Bristol City winning the game at Ashton Gate 1-0.

Just me and Mark went to the return leg and I arranged to meet him in a pub off Shoreham Street. It was so strange going in there as an undercover Wednesdayite and it was about as nervous as I have ever been at a football match. The thing is, if you are spotted, if you give something away, you know you are in a hell of a lot of trouble and no one is going to get you out of it. I was very pleased to see Mark already in the pub when I got there and he also felt very vulnerable. In some ways it was crazy, as we were from Sheffield, so it was going to be difficult to be caught out, but deep inside you knew you were deep in enemy territory and that it was wrong and dangerous.

Having said that, once inside the ground we didn't even try to disguise our feelings. We sat in the South stand, towards the Kop, which was a relatively safe place to be, but on such an emotional night, still carried quite a risk. We were definitely not alone though because when former Wednesday player Carl Shutt scored for Bristol there were quite a few people around us that also cheered and I don't think any were from Bristol. The game finished 1-1 and United were relegated and we went home happy. Looking back I am still surprised that we did it and got away with it. I can't imagine for a second that you could be so brazen now, so in the more violent days of the past, it seems even more surprising that we escaped unscathed!

Young and foolish indeed.

It is funny now looking back at how many times that I actually visited the sty. I must have been pretty sad really, because if they were getting beat, I would often tear down there to watch them suffering. I would never ever pay to get in and it became part of the fun to get in without paying. Usually turning up for the last twenty minutes or so was easy, as you could simply walk in the ground anyway, but it was always fun to see the pigs streaming away from the ground as I was rushing in. I usually had a few comments of, "I wouldn't bother mate," but what they didn't realise was that was simply adding to my glee. Fortunately for me, I never regretted once making the drive to see the last ten or fifteen minutes, as they never once came back. Instead I took great pleasure in witnessing their displeasure and listening to the boos and jeers and fortunately in the 1980's it happened a lot.

The next time we faced each other in a competitive game was November 1989, in the prestigious Zenith Data Cup!

That season will always be remembered by United supporters with glee, as we were relegated and they were promoted on the same day and so swapped places.

AAAAAAAAAAAAAAAAAAAAAAAAAAAAAAAARRGGGH!

The game itself was a corker though with Wednesday winning 3-2 and John Sheridan scoring a stunning winner in front of a 30,000 crowd.

The next league derby didn't come around again for 11 years and that was a bit of a disaster to be honest. Wednesday had a very good team and ultimately qualified for Europe, whereas United struggled and finished well down the table. Consequently, you would have thought we would win both games comfortably.

Wrong!

The first game was at Bramall Lane. The away end sold out quickly, so we, like thousands of other Wednesday fans were scattered throughout the ground. We were in the South stand again that day and once more close to the Shoreham end. There were absolutely loads of Wednesday fans in there that day, so we did nothing to hide our allegiance and when the first chant of "Wednesday!" went up, it was amazing how many of us there were.

149

The number of Owls there meant that we got some abuse from their Kop, but I think they had enough to deal with, as about 500 Wednesdayites had got on to their end and massed in the top corner near the South stand. The brawling was pretty fierce, but the Wednesday mob were not going to be shifted. We had a great view of the ongoing battle and it only settled down when the Police got sufficient numbers involved to keep the two factions apart.

I don't know what it is about the derby games, but Wednesday always had a big presence in the United sections at the Lane, yet I can never, ever remember them having a mob, of any sort in the Wednesday areas of Hillsborough. I am not saying that there aren't Unitedites scattered around the ground, because there clearly must be, but I have never heard any sort of singing, other than from the Leppings Lane end.

Maybe it is because, the away end at Hillsborough is considerably larger than the away section at Bramall Lane and so they don't have the need to be in other areas of the ground.

The return game at Hillsborough was eagerly awaited, particularly by Wednesday, having been surprisingly beaten in the first game. The atmosphere in the Travellers pub beforehand was superb. Normally it is quite full, but very rarely is there any singing before a game. This night everyone seemed fired up and the pub was rocking. We eventually made our way out towards the ground and noticed a mob of well known Wednesday hooligans were a few yards behind us.

There was an incredible atmosphere hanging in the air that night and you could sense such massive anxiety and aggression.

Any male adult, foolish enough to be walking in the opposite direction to the Leppings Lane, in red and white, was getting hit. Nothing incredibly violent, but a kick or a slap was aimed at everyone and certainly lots of verbal abuse. It was like being back in the 1970's.

As we walked down Penistone Road you could see that something was going off ahead and as we got closer, there were about ten of Uniteds hard core hooligans coming the opposite way and they had the same intention of most Wednesday fans going the opposite way. Everyone knew not to particularly have a go at these though, as they were serious hoolies. They were clearly enjoying the fact that they were walking behind Wednesday's Kop and no one was daring to have a go at them. What they didn't know though, was that about twenty yards behind us, there were about twenty of Wednesday's nutters. It was obvious it was going to kick off big time and the gobby piggies were going to get a hiding, so we stopped to watch the fun. Sure enough the two sets clashed a few seconds later and I think everyone enjoyed watching the blunt thugs get a good kicking. It was actually nice to see their gloating faces change to horror and panic and see them scattering everywhere. I gather it was the same all round the ground that night, with trouble flaring up everywhere and both sides on the receiving end.

Playing United is so different. I wouldn't dream of getting involved in trouble ordinarily, but against them it is completely different. As an ordinary non violent fan, it is an odd feeling when you have an inner turmoil inside you that wants to start a fight, just because someone is in red and white.

I can just about say that I managed to not get involved, but boy I have come close a few times.

The games that season though were a disaster, with Wednesday losing both. I think the odd thing too, was that we really expected to win both. The feeling after was absolutely gutting and for as high as you are after winning, the stomach wrenching pain you feel in defeat is just as strong. It is even worse when you consider that two wins that season would also have won us the Title.

The following season, though, would be as sweet as revenge could ever get.

Both league games finished 1-1, but the drama that year was reserved for the Cup.

United had already drawn their game at Blackburn in the Quarter Finals of the FA Cup, as we travelled to Derby County (who were in the league below us at the time) for our Quarter final tie on a Monday night.

I think the game was played on a Monday because it was live on TV and because of this we already knew the draw for the Semi Finals and it was massive.

If both Sheffield clubs won their ties, they would play each other in the semi final.

I don't know what it was that season, but you just knew that United were on for a good cup run, so the trip down to Derby had the added pressure of knowing we had to win, as we were the only ones who could stop them. After our exploits of winning the League Cup in 1991, we really had one over them and the thought of them getting to a final, or worse, even winning something, was too frightening to contemplate (How Man City fans cope with Man United winning stuff every season I will never know).

We knew that if we lost to Derby, then United would be playing a second tier team in the Semi's and therefore, as far as we were concerned, may as well face a bye to the FA Cup Final.

It is weird how we looked at it, that Derby was a tricky game for us, yet it would be an easy one for them!

It was another cracking game that ended up 3-3.

I won't bore you with the details, but with time ticking away, we trailed 3-2 and looked to be on our way out.

All I could think of was United getting to the FA Cup Final.

The delight and relief was shared by us all when Paul Warhurst hammered a late, late equalize for us, to earn a replay.

The replays the following week saw United draw 2-2, but win on penalties, so the pressure was heaped back on us the following night.

Fortunately Wednesday pushed Derby aside, winning 1-0 and the first ever all Sheffield Semi Final was on.

It was a strange feeling really, as you were excited about probably the biggest derby game of all time but the fear of losing totally outweighed the excitement.

The game was originally scheduled to be played at L**ds, but after a campaign from Sheffield was switched to Wembley. This switch only seemed to raise the profile of the game even higher.

The Sheffield 'Star' newspaper carried an article, by United reporter Tony Pritchett, the Friday before the game stating that regardless of what had gone on before, this was the game to end all games and that the winning team would carry the bragging rights for ever.

My nerves were just about shredded by now.

When we got to London on the Saturday morning, the atmosphere before the game was very strange, with none of the expected hostilities. I don't know what it was, but both sets of supporters just seemed to ignore each other and though mixed in together before the game, there was no violence that I saw, or none of that aggressive atmosphere in the air that you always experienced before a Sheffield derby match.

I think both lots of fans were simply dreading the possible outcome.

Once inside the stadium, that all changed completely. It was absolutely awesome. The crowd of 75,365 was split pretty much down the middle, with a very colourful Wembley half blue and white and half red and white.

There had been an ongoing rivalry in the City for over a week about things like, who would have the biggest flag and who would have the most balloons. Reports in the local media that a United supporter had ordered 5,000 red and white balloons being bettered the next day by a Wednesdayite that had ordered 10,000 blue and white balloons and it went on and on.

The old stadium was rocking as the atmosphere built towards kick off and when the teams emerged from the famous old tunnel, I could barely see them from beneath the enormous mass of balloons that were released. (I remember listening to the radio commentary the next day of the other Semi Final, between Arsenal and Tottenham, which was also played at Wembley. The commentator kept saying that the atmosphere for this game was simply not a patch on the Sheffield encounter the previous day and that the colour and passion was nowhere near as good as 24 hours earlier).

The teams come out to a sea of balloons

The atmosphere was electric and the game couldn't have started any better for us with Chris Waddle hitting a stunning, near 30 yard free kick home in the first minute of the game.

153

I cannot possibly imagine trying to describe words to express my feelings at that time.

It was just absolutely manic.

The whole of the Wednesday end went absolutely mental. It was a mass of people screaming and shouting and punching the air. People were falling over seats as they lost their balance. Hugging complete strangers in delirium.

We were going nuts piled in a big heap on top of Melv, screaming our heads off!

It took me a minute or two to get my breath back after the goal, to be able to join in the singing that was booming out.

Goddle is Wad (out of picture) slams home the opener

The first half was one way traffic with us hitting the woodwork twice and the piggy keeper making several fine saves and we really should have been more than 1-0 up, so it was with horror that just before half time the blunts scrambled in a scruffy equalizer. It was totally against the run of play and resurfaced all the fears of losing.

The fact that Wednesday lost both games the previous season, despite having a far better side, really un-nerved us I think and the fear was that it would happen again, in this the most important derby of all time.

This unease that it just wasn't our day, continued in the second half, as Wednesday totally controlled the game, but couldn't find the finishing touch.

The game went into extra time and my nerves were severely frayed.

I don't think I had any fingers left, let alone finger nails.

Extra time was going the same way as the previous ninety minutes with Wednesday doing everything but score.

The feeling that we were going to be undone by a rare United attack was getting stronger, until the 107th minute when Mark Bright finally headed home, from a John Harkes corner.

Inside I was going barmy, but I remember just standing there arms aloft, in silence, as the world went mental all around me. I think mentally I was shattered and didn't have it in me to leap around like a lunatic. The relief and joy was overwhelming.

Absolutely indescribable.

The remainder of the game stayed one sided and unusually we never looked like conceding a goal (although the fear was there). The scenes at the final whistle were extraordinary. People were crying, laughing, screaming and hugging each other.

Just complete and utter ecstasy.

The whole end was absolutely crazy, which contrasted massively with the quiet and quickly emptying tunnel end of the ground. Wembley is not an easy place to get out of quickly so how must it have felt having to witness your bitterest rivals celebrate like that. The noise was booming out and they couldn't even escape.

We were in no rush to get out of the ground. I wanted to stay and party there all night.

I can remember as we did make our way down the exit steps, everyone leaning out of the "windows" and hurling abuse and insults at the departing blades below us. There was such a mixture of glee and hatred pouring down from the victors and you just knew it would kick off big time when we got outside.

Instead it was exactly the opposite.

I really don't know why, but the outpouring of joy and ecstasy was replaced with calm. It was as if someone was injecting us all with sensible tablets as we left, because the difference was staggering. Both sets of fans mingled outside with no tension, no aggression, no malice.

Extraordinary.

The journey back up the M1 was not quite the same though. With 75,000 people all heading back up North at the same time, it was a very slow drive home, but I don't think any of us cared. We were hanging out of the windows of the car all the way back, laughing and screaming. It must have been torturous for the pigs though.

Unlike the Liverpool Everton Cup Final a few years before, there was no mixing of fans on the way to London. Coaches and cars were either blue or red, so when we passed a Wednesday coach it was bouncing and singing, whereas United coaches were deathly quiet. I remember passing many United coaches as we all hung out of the windows sharing our joy, but mostly they just sat there staring blankly back.

What a horrific journey that must have been for them.

One of the oddest environments I have ever watched a derby was in 2002. Our son was six months old at the time and so we had booked to hire a nice cottage in Cornwall with some friends in September.

Of course, when the fixtures were announced later, the game that I would consequently miss would be the one that I was praying that it wouldn't be.

United at home.

Part of me was telling myself that it would probably be a blessing, as recently they had the edge in derbies and without Wednesday mustering a single win in the league that season still, the omens were not good.

I thought therefore that it was probably a good thing that I wasn't there.

I even tried to be a good parent too and promised myself to not even think about the game until it was over, but when it got to three o'clock, or whatever time it kicked off, I was drawn like a magnet to a pub to see the game on TV. I couldn't fight the anxiety and turmoil that was building up inside me, so I left the rest of them in the town and sprinted to the nearest pub that was showing the game, as fast as I could.

It was so weird watching such a huge game in a crowded pub, with absolutely no one interested in what was going on. I managed to find a quiet-ish corner to watch the game and I promised myself to stay calm whatever happened.

Some chance!

The thing is that you get so engrossed in the game, so consumed by it that your passions get the better of you. Despite telling myself that I was in a very crowded pub with apparently no one interested in the game and therefore not one of these strangers would comprehend my actions, this was a derby game.

All sense of reason goes out of the window.

Because of the noise of the general chatter in the pub, my ooohs and ahhhhs went mostly unnoticed, but when Wednesday scored to go 1-0 up late in the second half, I went absolutely mental!

The whole pub stopped dead in its tracks and went deathly quiet to look at this middle aged bloke screaming and jumping up and down like a lunatic on his own.

God my wife would have been so embarrassed had she been there. It was bizarre, because I was very much aware that the entire pub had stopped and they were all staring at me, yet there was no way I could stop. The total and utter joy of taking the lead against those b******s was overwhelming.

The second goal was not so bad, as although again I brought the pub to a standstill when I jumped up screaming, at least this time everyone knew what it was about.

At the full time whistle I went back out to find everyone and again it was strange that the world was going on as normal, with no one around me wanting to sing and shout at the top of their voices. It was so difficult to not come out singing football songs as loud as I could, but somehow I contained it and I returned to my family holiday with a deep warm glow burning inside me that lasted all week.

A few years later and the good old fixture list threw up a similar situation, in that I had booked to go on holiday in Spain and when the fixtures eventually came out, it was bloody inevitable that the game I would miss would be United again.

It was.

FFS! Does the fixture list man check my holiday dates before releasing the fixtures?

Of course I re-assured myself again that it would probably be a blessing as we would most likely lose. Being in a different country does remove some of the pressure from you, as you aren't subjected to the local media build up as the game nears. I even told myself that I wouldn't watch the game on TV but of course on the day of the game, the feeling started deep inside me and built and built. My wife is wonderful, but simply doesn't understand what it is all about and how it consumes me. I kept my inner turmoil to myself, until it grew so much that I excused myself and left.

Driving to a bar was just like driving to the game for real. My stomach was in absolute knots.

Remembering what happened in Cornwall 6 years earlier, I was delighted when I walked into a sports bar to find only 5 people there. They were all English too, which meant I could explain my behaviour if necessary.

I was concerned that the build up to the game wasn't on the big screen but was assured that they were trying to get the game on. As kick off time neared and there was still no sign of the match appearing, I was getting more and more agitated. Fortunately one guy there was good

157

enough to understand my anxiety and rang a friend to try and find where the game would be showing. He explained that my best chance was a bar in some unheard of town about 10 miles away. I thanked him and armed with some vague directions, I hastily departed. I was sweating profusely now, but it had nothing to do with the temperature. I was panicking because the game had started.

To compound the situation my mobile phone beeped a text message to me. I worked out that the game was maybe 2 minutes old, so was horrified to see the message was from my good friend, but piggy fan, Robert. Sadly as a 40 something, my eyes aren't what they used to be and I really struggled to read the message without my glasses, as I drove. I glanced down, fearing the worst. I couldn't quite make it out, but it seemed to say, "Are you disguised?"

What the f**k!

I looked again……….. "Are you disguised?"

What does that mean? Why would he send a message like that two minutes into the game? My brain was swimming trying to work it out, as I tried to find this bloody town. Did it mean we were losing…..or winning?

Eventually I found this tiny, sleepy town and to my relief a bar with football on. I was delighted when it was the derby game that was on. At least I could see the game, which earlier looked doubtful.

I was even more pleased when I saw it was still 0-0 and worked out that the message actually read "Are you excited" and was sent 5 minutes before kick off. I laughed to myself with overall relief more than anything and ordered a beer. The bar was packed with locals and no one seemed remotely interested in the game. In the back of my mind I knew I had a Cornwall situation brewing, but as I quickly got engulfed in the game I still tried to tell myself that whatever happened on the pitch, I would stay in control. Even I didn't believe myself! No bloody chance!

To my delight when Wednesday had a near miss, three guys in front of me gave a collective 'Ooooohh.' I wasn't alone.

No one else in the packed bar seemed interested, until United had a near miss and two blokes somewhere over to my left gave an'Oooooohh' as well.

Suddenly the atmosphere changed. The temperature rose significantly a few minutes later, when a high challenge by a piggy player resulted in a straight red. Instantly I found myself up cheering with the other Owls, whilst the two blunts complained bitterly. The bar sort of stopped to see what was going on, but despite it being full, it seemed as if there were only the six of us in there.

Now we had given our allegiances away, we all suddenly became more vocal. Yet no one spoke to each other. It was weird really. We were all from the same city, hundreds of miles away from home, with a deep love for the cities football clubs, yet we couldn't even acknowledge each other. Our bitter rivalry and resentment was too deep. The atmosphere was so charged it was untrue.

A few minutes later and Wednesday's Steve Watson lobbed in a beauty from 20 yards. As soon as he struck it I knew it was going in. I found myself out of my seat. It was like slow motion as we all watched the ball sail over the defenders heads before finally seeing the beautiful site of the net bulging confirmation of the goal. I went mad, screaming and punching the air in delight. Of course the bar stopped to take it in, but this wasn't like Cornwall, for it still felt like there were just the six of us there. From that point on it got seriously heated and there were quite a few words exchanged during the remainder of the half. With great relief the half time whistle sounded. The TV briefly showed the Wednesday fans bouncing and I so wanted to join in.

I couldn't believe that I had walked into this bar in a tiny remote town (miles from any tourist area) in Spain and yet there were still Owls and Blades there. Glowing from the half time victory I chuckled to myself picturing similar situations all over the world. To outsiders it means nothing, but to fans from Sheffield, there is nothing, absolutely nothing, that is as important as this.

The second half was just as heated and I really thought that it would escalate into a brawl. All sorts of abuse was being hurled at each other. I knew it would be hard to explain to my wife what had happened, yet I couldn't back down. One of the piggies was quite a big guy too, yet it didn't make any difference. The rivalry is so great and the hatred so deep, you can't help yourself.

I could even see the headlines in the local Spanish papers, that six English football fans had been arrested following a mini riot in the middle of nowhere!

Thankfully it didn't quite get that far and even more important Wednesday won 1-0. At the full time whistle I delightedly punched the air and noticed the two blunts quietly walk out.

I drove 'home' singing Wednesday songs as loud as I possibly could, honking the car horn in jubilation, to the bewilderment of locals.

Although I wished I could have been there, it still felt as good as ever to beat our hated rivals again and I was absolutely ecstatic.

I will give a mention to one very good moment between the clubs that happened recently. During the 2005-06 season, two Wednesday supporters were tragically killed in a car accident, on the way back from a Wednesday away game. The club had arranged a minutes silence out of respect, before the next home game, which just happened to be against our old rivals.

It was totally expected that this silence would not be respected by the United supporters and there would be an explosion of anger from the Wednesday supporters in response, but when the referee signalled the start of the minute, you could have heard a pin drop for those sixty seconds.

It was a truly moving moment and when the minute finished the United fans were given a standing ovation for respecting the silence.

Very special and rare indeed.

Of course there have been other derby games and they will go on and on. We have won some, we have lost some. I don't know whether it is me that is simply getting older now, but the games don't quite seem the same anymore. They are still intense and unlike other games, there is still a high chance that it will end in trouble, but that edge seems to have gone. Maybe it is the all seater stadiums now, but I am glad that I experienced the derbies at what I think was their best.

CHAPTER 8

Tasting Success

I think before we go any further into what surely must be the most joyful chapter (and indeed recognise how lucky I am to be able to include such a chapter, because most real footy fans would struggle to put much in here), we need to just try and define what success is (which will give me a great chance to get back on my soap box).

Football has changed such a huge amount that success has now become quite difficult to define. It has always been different depending on who you are and what your circumstances are, and will remain so.

In the past, smaller clubs could always dream about getting into the league, climbing through the divisions and winning the Cup. Wimbledon, being the perfect example of how a tiny club rose from the Southern League, to beating Liverpool in the FA Cup Final. (How sad also, that such a fairytale rise then ended in their demise).

What is the chance of that happening now? True, it is probably easier now for "amateur" clubs to get in to the league, but winning something major? No chance. Even the likes of alleged major clubs such as Aston Villa, Newcastle, Everton, etc. have almost no chance of ever winning anything anymore. Success to them now is probably qualifying for the UEFA Cup and having a decent run. Even the pompous, "Champions League" is pretty much out of their reach, with the "Same Old Four" securing the top four places year after year. Just me having a rant again! Well, since the arrogant Premiership was created, the League and FA Cup has been played for 34 times (to 2009). On 31 occasions the SOF have won it and on 3 occasions someone from the rest has had the luck and audacity to win it. (Yes, but isn't it exciting! Almost like Rangers and Celtic in Scotland, but with four! Wow!)

The only chance anyone has of ever breaking this monopoly is to have obscene money thrown at them. Someone from Everton was recently quoted as saying that they don't need a multi millionaire to make them successful, they need a billionaire! Football has sadly come off the rails and you know what, your average fan is getting really pissed off with it all.

To put it into even more context, Benitez, the Liverpool manager, was quoted having a dig at Chelsea, before their Champions League semi final in 2007, saying that winning the League Cup, was hardly successful, for the millions they had spent. Chelsea that season finished runners up in the League, were semi finalists in the Champions League, won the League Cup and subsequently won the FA Cup. In Benitez eyes, this wasn't very successful. Try telling that to Rochdale, you stuck up git (Dismounts soap box).

Sadly promotion to the Premier League now means something like £60 million per season, so to teams in the Championship, promotion is as successful as you ever want to be. Unfortunately, such wealth means that staying there becomes imperative, so success to teams like Sunderland, Wigan, Fulham, etc is avoiding relegation. The money has become everything, so much so that Sheffield United's exceptionally funny collapse and relegation from the Premiership in 2007, resulted in a long drawn out battle of legal claims and disputes, doing everything they can to avoid being relegated. I know I am biased, but their terribly undignified behaviour over the Tevez saga, has lowered football even further. They blamed everybody but themselves for their relegation and tried to get off on a technicality. They should have accepted relegation with dignity and admit that they got relegated simply because they weren't good enough and didn't win enough points. But, of course it is about money. What they did by pursuing this through the courts was, I think, an absolute disgrace and has now opened up a massive potential problem for football. Clubs can claim against others for almost any misdemeanour. Where will it end? Hypothetically, what if a striker gets elbowed in the face that seriously, that he is hospitalised and misses the rest of the season. His team then get into a relegation battle because they

162

didn't score enough goals. Should that team sue the club of the player that elbowed him?

Surely serious foul play on the pitch is much worse than paperwork? Apparently not.

I would guess a booking for the offending elbower should suffice.

So is this what the modern game is about now. An elite group of four squabbling for the silverware while the rest try and avoid relegation?

Not impressive is it?

I still think it would be best for everyone if the "big four" buggered off to form a European League and left the rest of us to it.

The way things are going at the moment, it is as if the Premier League want to go the same way as American football, with everyone supporting a "big team" and the rest becoming 'inconsequentials.'

I can see a situation where we will end up in a loop of the same teams vying for promotion and almost a premier league of some probable twenty three/twenty four teams, with three or four of those having to spend a year in the Championship, before their millions from the Premier League, supplemented by the parachute payments, buys them their place in the money league again. If we are not careful, it will become, as impossible as it seems, for the likes of Bolton or Middlesbrough to win the Premiership, and soon it will be the same for the likes of good clubs, with terrific support, such as Norwich or Nottingham Forest, to get to the Premier League.

Something must be done before this ever happens.

It is time for football to take a long hard look at itself.

Anyway...................

So now that we know that success is all relative, I will thoroughly enjoy sharing with you how we enjoyed our little slug of success.

Following the promotion season of 1979-80, the next piece of glory was not too long away, when we finished runners up in 1983-84 and got promoted back in to the First Division. From here on it seemed to be Quarter Finals of both cups almost every season, but elusively never quite making that extra step forward. Wilkinson had put a good side together and were a lot more skillful and entertaining than they were ever given credit for. Players like Brian Marwood and Lee Chapman made a big difference to what was already a good side.

As much as Chapman was a great player for Wednesday, it all turned very sour after his four seasons with the Owls. Wednesday rescued his career, which was seriously going backwards at the time, and made him

163

into a solid all round first class striker. Yet we were repaid by a very dodgy transfer that saw the club lose out massively financially.

He was seeing actress, Leslie Ash, at the time and I saw her a few times at Hillsborough, which was nice. Then, all of a sudden he announced that he wanted a transfer because he needed to be nearer London for Leslie. Now I can't remember the full facts here, but he ended up signing for some second rate French club called Niort, which is about double the distance to London from Sheffield. After a lot of wrangling the fee was decided by a UEFA tribunal and Wednesday were only allocated £290,000, which was absolute daylight robbery. Niort then amazingly declared that they didn't have anything like that type of money and the next thing was that he signed for Nottingham Forest for a fraction of his true market value. Only Lee, Nottingham Forest and Niort will know what really happened, but to the outside world it looked like an appalling stitch up.

In 1984 -85 we finished a good season in 8th place, just missing out on a European place in the last game at Tottenham.

Earlier in the season though, the biggest heartbreak was in the League Cup. We had drawn away at Chelsea in the Quarter Finals, so two days later we were all packed into Hillsborough for the replay.

The draw for the Semis had already been made and we had been paired with later to be relegated Sunderland. To us this seemed a free ticket to the final, if we could just overcome the old foe Chelsea.

You can imagine the scenes therefore when Wednesday went two goals up in 22 minutes. Chelsea weren't in it and when on the stroke of half time Marwood curled in a beauty to make it 3-0 the ground was going crazy. I can remember at half time, the concourse under the North Stand singing its head off and all the songs were about the Holy Grail that is Wembley. How could we fail now?

Well it is all history, but a guy called Cannoville came on as sub and within ten seconds of the re-start had pulled a goal back. What followed was the probably the worst, most agonising 45 minutes of football I have ever seen. It was as if the whole ground knew what was going to happen. As long as we held that two goal cushion there was a chance of hanging on (hanging on at bloody 3-1!) but, it was all Chelsea and I mean total domination.

We couldn't get out of our own half. When the second one went in, it may have well been all over as a third was now inevitable. It came just nine minutes later and worse was to follow. With just four minutes left that man Cannoville, who had ripped Wednesday to pieces, tapped home a simple goal to make it an amazing 4-3 to Chelsea. From 3-0 to 3-4 in about 40 minutes!

We were totally stunned.

The game wasn't quite over though as with literally seconds remaining, Sterland knocked in an injury time penalty to make it 4-4. Yes we cheered but I think deep down everyone knew it was gone. At 3-0 up Wembley was in touching distance, but was again agonisingly taken away.

I don't know what it is about Wednesday, but we have lost a three goal lead at least five times that I know of. This game against Chelsea, away at Hull and at home to Arsenal, Man United and Norwich. Whereas I have never ever seen us come back from that margin ourselves. They say that these things average themselves out over the years.

Well, I am still bloody waiting!

The replay the following week at Chelsea inevitably ended in disaster. It was 1-1 in the 90th minute, when they scored an injury time winner, just to twist the knife that little bit more and once again our Wembley dreams dissolved like mist.

The following season, Wembley became agonizingly close again, when we reached the Semi Final of the FA Cup, only to lose to Everton 2-1.

Everton had a very good side around that time, but hopes were still high, with Everton losing several key players, like Gary Lineker and Neville Southall, but despite the game going to extra time, we fell short once again.

A Quarter Final defeat at home to Coventry occurred twelve months later and a Quarter Final defeat at Arsenal the season after that.

It seemed as if we were fated never to see the twin towers, but 1988 was to be different and I got to see Wednesday play on the hallowed turf in a competition that I think is now sadly forgotten.

To celebrate the Football Associations 100 years, a special tournament was held in April.

It was held between the sixteen teams that had the best league record over a given period of time and Wednesday qualified!

How could we not go!

Myself, Mark, Steve and Rob the blade went down to London and had a great time.

It was a really strange event, because although there were 60,000 fans there, the ground would be almost constantly empty. The ground was split up into different sections, so fans could be segregated, but all that happened was these sections would be packed full, when their team were due to play, but the rest of the ground was empty, as no one really wanted to watch other teams play.

Our first game against Crystal Palace was one of the last of the First Round, so we headed for the pub when we first arrived. It was terrific as the pub was full of loads of different fans, who were all mingling together wonderfully. As each game finished, new fans would come in and others depart to watch their team.

There was loads of good banter between all the fans, until the doors burst open and a coach load of rather rough looking Wolves fans came in. For a few seconds there was a bit of silence as we wondered what their intentions were, but they were a great set of lads and really added to the atmosphere. They were singing a song about living in "Wonderful Wolver-hamp-erton", which was a real piss take about themselves. They had the whole pub in uproar and singing along. It was absolutely fantastic.

It was getting time for us to go, when a similar incident occurred, but this time it was L**ds fans coming in and as usual they had different ideas to the rest of us and just wanted to cause trouble.

Typical L**ds really. No wonder everyone hates them.

We drew 0-0 with Palace, in a game that was 20 minutes for each half, but we won on penalties, so then headed back to the pub before our next game. The lads we had been talking to earlier, said that there had been a bit of trouble with L**ds, but it was good to hear that all the other fans ganged together against them and kicked them out.

Fortunately L**ds lost in the first round, so didn't stay around.

We went back for the Quarter Final against Wigan, which we also drew, 1-1 this time and again went through on penalties.

It had been a good day and we were through to the Semis as well, which meant a return to Wembley the next day.

We met up with our old friend Chris at night, who was still in London and after a few beers, went to a Greek restaurant that he knew.

It was a great place in a large cellar somewhere and there was all the usual plate smashing and Greek type dancing, which we were all up for.

When dinner and the traditional dancing finished, they put on a disco. There was a table near us with about ten black people on. The guys in the group, definitely looked as though you wouldn't mess with them. As a result I can remember us all being amazed when, without a word, Chris suddenly got up and asked this attractive girl at their table if she wanted to dance.

I thought her boyfriend would try and kill him.

There was a long silence as he stared at Chris and looked him up and down. He then stared at us before he laughed out loud and said OK.

They got up and danced to the song and the restaurant watched as just the two of them danced away. At the end of the song he thanked her and escorted her back to her table and rejoined us. We were stunned, but from then on, everyone got up and filled the dance floor. It was great.

It was as if that moment broke the ice for everyone there and the atmosphere was fantastic.

We were all totally drunk and having a great time. We seemed to have brought a lot of fun to the night and everyone was having a good time.

We had particularly attracted the attention of two rather wealthy ladies, who seemed totally over dressed for the night and it was obvious that they were very well off (I think it was the tiara's that gave it way). They took a real shine to us rather common Northern lads and we were happy to let them join us and took it in turns to dance with them.

All sounding good so far, until I tell you they were well into their late Seventies. The scary bit was to come though, when one of them asked if I wanted to come back to her palace, err, I mean, place, and then tried to snog me! (I think it was when her teeth nearly fell out that I thought this wasn't a good idea!) I made some rather lame excuse, trying as hard as I could not to hurt her feelings, before she understood and moved on to the next target.

We made our way home in a very drunken state, walking through the streets of London, singing, "I'd rather be a cock than a drunkney," (Don't ask, because I don't know why).

We got followed by a small gang of lads for a while. Chris had gone in a different direction and I think Steve and Rob had realized what was happening, because I can only remember there being me and Al at that point. Fortunately for us they disappeared without anything more being said, once we decided that it might be best to shut up.

Rob and Steve stopped in a hotel that night, while me and Mark crashed out in the car (cheapskates).

The next morning we headed to Harrow. Again I don't know why, but we did. We found a very nice pub, but it was only twenty to eleven, so had twenty minutes to kill before opening. Rob was driving and thought it best if we drove around for a bit, so that is exactly what he did. It was a large car park, so he put the driving wheel on full lock and left the car to go round and round in circles for twenty bloody minutes.

Talk about car sick!

We had a great lunch time session, before heading off to Wembley again. This time we played Man United in a game that was 30 minutes each half and won 2-1.

So, even if it wasn't quite what I had in mind, at least my dreams of a Wembley final had come true.

We slipped out to the pub, while the other semi final took place (not that we needed any more beer) and came back an hour later to see Wednesday lose to Nottingham Forest on penalties in the Final.

Wednesday entered a poor period around this time, which ultimately saw Wilkinson sacked. Peter Eustace had a brief spell in charge, before the best manager in Wednesday's history took charge.

Big Ron brought a real smile back to everyone's face associated with Wednesday, but even he had to learn that we are a strange team, before he could eventually work his magic on us.

His first season saw the team changing, with great players like John Sheridan, Carlton Palmer, Roland Nilsson, Dalian Atkinson (what a talent. What ever happened to him?) and Trevor Francis brought in and slowly we adopted to his 'beautiful football' philosophy. But, even he must have thought we were safe when we were 9 points clear with just five games to go. Yet that still wasn't enough and we were amazingly relegated on goal difference on the last game.

The thing that was so difficult to grasp that season, though, was that we played some fantastic football and really didn't deserve to go down.

If relegation was tough, it was made even worse as on the same day United were promoted and the clubs traded divisions.

As hard as it was to endure, it was ultimately totally worth the price, because the next season was unbelievable.

Ron had moulded together a terrific side for the 1990-91 season and it was fun right from the start. I have never known a time when everyone believed that we really shouldn't have been relegated and that this season our place would be restored. It seemed to come from the fans, the players, the management and right through the club.

The opening game was at Ipswich and about 9,000 Owls descended on Suffolk on a gorgeous sunny day. I don't think Ipswich expected that many visitors, considering that we had just been relegated and there were Wednesday fans everywhere.

I watched the highlights on video recently and was amazed to see how many Wednesday fans there were, just stood behind the goals, watching the game. The away terrace was dangerously full and all the seats were taken, so they just stood on the pitch behind the nets! We scored both goals at that end, so when we did there were loads of fans just ran on the pitch to celebrate with the players!

Wednesday won 2-0, although 5 or 6 would have better reflected the game. That season was superb, with some delightful football taking place and a richly deserved promotion back to the top flight.

Danny Wilson opens the scoring against Plymouth in a 3-0 win. That's me celebrating, in the striped shirt directly above gangway 'C'. Graham is on the right in a black t shirt and white trousers (very 1980's!)

There were two great little fan quirks that came out of that season and both, from my memory happened at West Brom. The game was played in November with Wednesday still well placed in the league, although their form was a bit inconsistent, particularly at home. At half time I can remember two cuddly toys being thrown around the crowd, which for some odd reason the crowd latched onto and was met with a cheer every time a teddy bear was thrown. This went on for some time, more out of boredom I think, as we weren't playing well at all and losing 1-0. I don't think many people thought too much about it, but at the next game there were more cuddly toys and the idea had suddenly caught hold.

By the time we played Hull at Boothferry Park in January the cuddly toy craze had really escalated and the Police were totally perplexed as how to deal with it.

Big roughty-toughty lads carrying teddy bears was not something they were ready for. It obviously didn't look quite right and suspicions must have been raised as to what was happening, yet what could they do. Several teddies were searched in case they were concealing weapons, but they obviously found nothing.

It was only inside the ground that they probably realized that this was the latest craze.

It was impossible not to get carried away with it. There were literally thousands of cuddly toys flying around and it was common to be hit on the head by a pink fluffy elephant, if you weren't concentrating.

The other 'craze' that caught hold that day was bouncing. West Brom fans are probably best known for their 'Boing Boing', but Wednesday were doing it before them and I am sure that this was where the Baggies got it from. I am not saying we have sole rights on it and I am sure other fans have done it too. Fair play to West Brom, they took it on and carried it to a new level, but at that game in November, there was no Boinging (spell check will have fun with that) from any Baggies. There was no song that went with the bouncing. It was probably done again from boredom and cold, but bouncing up and down on the spot took off that day. (In actual fact it wasn't jumping. It was more a running on the spot, hopping from one foot to the other, in a "Zulu stylee.")

It actually looks great from a distance. We played at Mansfield in an FA Cup game that season and we were stood on the terrace, near to the Mansfield Kop end. As a result we had a great view of all the bouncing around the ground. It must be dead weird as a home fan, with no inclination of what is happening when half of the ground suddenly starts bouncing for no obvious reason!

The bouncing has been revived in the past few years, but this time with a song.

Hardly great lyrics but.......

"If you don't f***ing bounce,

If you don't f***ing bounce, then you're a blade."

This caught on and must look great from the rivals end. As at most clubs, the great atmosphere from Wednesday fans is usually reserved for away matches. Wednesday's home support, like most clubs does not create the best atmosphere, yet away from home is absolutely superb.

I can remember whupping Barnsley 3-0 at Oakwell in 2006 and 8,000 of us bouncing.

Barnsley's biggest rivals are Wednesday (which is obviously not reciprocated) and so the visit of Wednesday is usually their biggest game of the season. To get stuffed 3-0 at home and have to listen to 8,000 fans taking the piss must have been horrible. (I know it is because we have been on the receiving end as well.)

I won't go into all the details of that season, but of course I do need to touch on the Cup.

I was fortunate to go to every round of both cups that season but it was the League Cup that will go down in history.

It didn't start too convincingly, either.

We eased past Brentford over two legs, but then stuttered at home to Swindon 0-0, winning the replay 1-0. The same happened in the Fourth Round when we could only draw at home to First Division Derby 1-1 and so weren't favourites to progress.

The thing I used to love about Cup games was playing sides that you hadn't played for a long time, or were unlikely to play, but that Cup run saw us play someone that we had already played against in the Cup over the last few years and there was a lot of revenge about the run too.

We had lost to Swindon at the same stage in 1985 and Derby had dumped us out of the third round of the same competition just 13 months earlier in a particularly hurtful way.

We had scored in the 86th minute, so at that stage you expect to go on and win the game, but of course with it being Wednesday, we managed to concede two very late goals and lose 2-1. I can remember being absolutely gutted that evening, so hopes weren't too high for the next visit to the Baseball Ground. The old Baseball Ground was a great little ground that generated a terrific atmosphere (unlike the new soul-less Pride Park), but a visit there always caused problems. The away end had God knows how many posts to hold the roof above and so if you were unlucky you had a great big bloody post in front of you blocking the goals. I can remember Mark sulking the previous year, because he was late taking up his seat and had the post in front of his view of the goals. He claimed that this wasn't his seat and tried to make everyone sit in the seats according to their ticket, but no one was having it, so Mark ended up with a Wimbledon (tennis) like sore neck!

In 1990 there would be no repetition and there was a rush to assess and get the best seats from the row of ten that we had bought. Some other unfortunate missed half the game this time!

The game will probably be remembered most of all for John Harkes stunning 30 yard goal against Peter Shilton, but more than anything for me it was about revenge for the previous year.

A Paul Williams goal early in the second half put us 2-0 up, but when Derby pulled one back, we were all very fearful of history repeating itself, but it was Wednesday who dominated still and the usual massive following was overjoyed at full time.

Keeping on with the theme of revenge, we were drawn away to Coventry in the Quarter Finals. We had lost at home to Coventry in the FA Cup Quarter Finals in 1986, in a game that we expected to win.

Coventry, like Derby, were also in the Division above us, so we knew it would be a tricky game again. Wednesday had sold out their 6,000 allocation and had the usual vociferous following urging them on.

The game was nerve wracking, because of the pressure that Wembley was getting alarmingly close again.

We went 1-0 up early on in the game and although we played superb, we kept missing a string of chances and the last fifteen minutes seemed to last forever. It was as if the "W" word couldn't be uttered, for tempting fate because although the noise from the Wednesday end was phenomenal, there were no 'Wembley' songs. That is until the final whistle went and then that was all that was sung. Everyone seemed to stay behind for a good ten minutes after the final whistle to celebrate. It was absolutely superb.

Sadly time erodes your memory, but I remember that being one of the great nights of watching Wednesday. It had everything emotionally. Hope, anxiety, joy, fear, tension and ultimately, ecstasy.

Watching Wednesday was exhausting at times and you could come away from a game mentally drained, but over joyed.

The draw for the Semi Final had already been made and we knew we would face either Tottenham or Chelsea. At the time Spurs had a very good side, finishing third in the First Division the previous season, so the preference was that Chelsea would go through. It was as if we knew that we would lose to Spurs, but Chelsea gave us a chance. They had drawn their game the previous week 0-0 at Stamford Bridge, so it was expected that Spurs would win the replay at White Hart Lane.

As we left the ground still singing and dancing the announcer told us that Chelsea had surprisingly won the replay 3-0 and we all believed even more!

Now given the way we crumbled in 1985 against Chelsea, when we are talking about revenge, this was now at an altogether higher level. The pain from losing that three goal lead still haunted us all, so revenge in this game would be as sweet as it could get.

We had to wait another month for the Semi and were drawn away for the first leg.

It was an early Sunday morning kick off for some reason that day, which meant a ridiculously early start. We had sold our allocation of over 7,000 but the early start made the game a little surreal. Almost like watching it on TV. Stamford Bridge at that time was a terrible place. It was a big open ground, with the terraces sited miles away from the pitch. It was quite a windy day too, so any chanting was swept back over our heads.

There was a lot of noise generated, but it all seemed to be blown away. It was obviously a nervy game with chances for both sides but remained 0-0 at half time. Like our previous two opponents in the competition, Chelsea were in the league above us, so a draw in the first leg would be a good result for us.

The second half went our way though and goals by Nigel Pearson and David Hirst gave us a 2-0 victory. You can therefore appreciate what a bloody great time we had. Wembley had never been closer. You could almost taste it.

There had always been quite a history of violence between Wednesday and Chelsea and Stamford Bridge was an intimidating place to go. I like many others had endured some unpleasant visits there before and so boy, did we enjoy giving some back after the game. The streets were alive with jubilant Wednesday fans, as we made our way back and any Chelsea fans stupid enough to be caught in the middle of us, were totally intimidated back, to put it mildly and politely!

It was a fantastic feeling being part of this army of ecstatic supporters that had taken over the streets of one of the most feared sets of fans in the country. Chelsea fans did have a go in fairness, but were given a bit of a beating from what I saw, but most of all we were there to celebrate and we did it in style.

To make matters even better, the second leg of the other Semi Final was taking place later that day, between L**ds and Man United, with Man U holding a slender 2-1 lead from Old Trafford.

We all knew that IF (and it was still a big if) we should get through to the Final, then a game against L**ds would be particularly unpleasant, with non stop fighting all weekend long, whereas Man U wouldn't be a problem.

Again it was as if everything fell into place that year, because Man United won at L**ds 1-0 to go through to the Final much to our delight.

Now you would think that being 2-0 up from the away Semi Final, we would all be so happy and excited about the prospect of actually getting to the Final itself.

The truth was so different. It was only three days before the return leg, but those three days lasted forever.

I couldn't sleep, I couldn't eat and I permanently felt sick.

The fear of throwing this lead away was over powering.

I was terrified.

We had been so close so many times before and blown it, but this was worse. We were 2-0 up for Gods sake, with the home leg still to come!

It couldn't have been set up any more perfect for the ultimate kick in the teeth. Defeat was inevitable.

The closer the game got the worse I became and when match day eventually came round the anxiety inside the ground was tangible.

As it happens we had nothing to worry about at all. Particularly from the 34th minute when Nigel Pearson put us 1-0 up.

The ground went absolutely crazy in a massive outpouring of joy and relief. No one was counting any chickens, but this was the first sign that we might, just might, not cock it up!

This was the biggest night in Wednesday's history for years and it was like being in heaven. I don't think I have ever known a night like it and when Danny Wilson thundered a volley home just eight minutes later, the ground exploded.

Unfortunately so did a Chelsea fans nose.

There were a group of Chelsea fans about five rows in front of us and I don't know why, but when that second goal went in me and Mark ran down the steps at them. I think it was a combination of the joy and the pent up nerves and the history of trouble between the clubs, but we headed straight to them. We had no intention of doing anything other than rubbing it in, when a fist appeared from nowhere and slammed into one of the Chelsea fans faces.

It was Graham.

Again I don't know why he did it, but next thing it all kicked off big style. Gray did his usual "start a fight and run' tactic and we were left in the middle of it!

At the time that we should have been celebrating that long awaited, never to be forgotten moment, we were involved in a brawl!

Both me and Mark scarpered, as the last thing that I wanted, was to be in a fight, or even worse, thrown out of the ground and miss the moment I had waited a life time for. There was a lot of finger pointing as things settled down, but fortunately the Police moved the Chelsea fans out and we could relax. The thing is though, I didn't want to relax. That second goal really did kill the tie and put us in the final and I didn't want to be looking over my shoulder and worrying, I wanted to scream and shout with the rest of the ground, which at this time was going absolutely ballistic!

Fortunately it all died down and we could enjoy the remainder of the first half.

As crazy as it sounds, there still wasn't the massive celebrations at half time that you would expect. Don't get me wrong, everyone was going nuts, but still trying to keep their feet on the ground. We had been here six years earlier and thrown away a three goal lead, so we knew Chelsea could score four in 45 minutes.

We still weren't quite there and were acutely aware of it.

I think a lot of fans knew that the opening ten to fifteen minutes would be crucial (hang on we are 4-0 up on aggregate and three quarters of the way though the tie!) and as the minutes thankfully ticked by, the situation looked more and more comfortable. Chelsea did pull a goal back on 64 minutes, but by then I even think that we knew that it was too little, too late.

With ten minutes to go the mood changed and there was a wave of excitement spread round the ground, as if at long last everyone realized that now, even Wednesday couldn't throw this away. For the first time ever the song that we had all waited to sing was booming out of the stands, but this time it was true.

"We're the famous Sheffield Wednesday and we're going to Wembley

WEM – BER- LEE! WEM – BER – LEE!"

It went on and on and on and on and when with just two minutes left, Paul Williams lofted the ball in to the net to make it 3-1 the night was complete.

175

I don't need to tell you how good it felt. It was like a two day orgasm on happy pills! Nothing could make you as happy as we all were that night. It was absolutely f*****g awesome!

At long last, after so many disappointments, we were there, we had done it and it felt like the best damned feeling in the world. We partied all night and the glow inside, when I woke the next morning was to last for weeks.

The final was still two months away and I could have waited two years to be honest. It was the most wonderful feeling and the only fear now was getting run over, although I think I would have needed to have been killed outright to have stopped me going.

The club managed to make a cock up over our tickets though.

Despite us all being season ticket holders and applying bang on time, we still hadn't received our tickets for the final and most had now been snapped up when they went on general sale. The thought of not getting a ticket for the Final didn't bear thinking about. We were getting frantic so ended up all going down to the ground in the end and meeting Secretary Graham Mackrell, who eventually managed to get us the tickets we so desperately wanted.

They weren't the best seats, sadly, but at least we were going.

We set off early on the Saturday morning, intent on making a brilliant weekend of the event. We had even made a fanzine for the occasion (remember fanzines?) with all of us submitting our own articles and only Graham as 'publisher' saw them until they were dished out.

We stayed in a hotel on Lancaster Gate and had a big Wednesday flag hung outside. Also in the hotel were a number of Man United fans, including former player Paddy Crerrand. The banter was great with no hostilities whatsoever and Paddy was great, buying us drinks and having a good laugh with us all. In fact every pub we went in around London had a great atmosphere. Some times they were mostly full of Wednesday fans and others mostly United, but it was always great, with loads of singing and every one in good spirits with no trouble.

Thank God it wasn't L**ds.

I remember waking up at about six o'clock the next morning, without the slightest hint of a hang over and just feeling dead giddy.

We got down to the ground really early. Although we had a few beers, today wasn't a day for drinking alcohol, it was drinking the atmosphere.

There were no nerves. None whatsoever (Except the odd perverse thought of still having a car crash or a heart attack on the way). There were no reasons to be nervous.

We were there to enjoy the day.

A life time of waiting and wondering if it would ever come, had finally arrived. Wembley Way was awash with blue and white. I think to Man United, it was just another final. They were used to it they had been to so many, whereas to us it was something very special.

When the team coaches arrived, I think that situation helped Wednesday on the day too. Man United turned up to a slightly hostile reception, nothing nasty, just that they were the opposition, and Wednesday turned up to a heroes welcome. On Wembley Way there must have been ten Owls to every one United fan and this must have subconsciously affected the players. To United it was just another Final, to us it was amazing.

We even got on the official club video, which was filmed from the team bus. There we are as plain as day, at the top of Wembley Way, welcoming the lads.

We went into the ground particularly early. I don't think any of us could wait (and it would also reduce the chance of still being run over at the last minute!).

In the concourse under the stands the atmosphere was electric. The place was bouncing and I could have stayed there all day. It was only when Graham told us that he had been into the stand and that if we thought it was good down here, we should get up on the terrace.

It was even better than I dreamed of.

The Wednesday end was already pretty much full and the noise was something else.

I had been to Wembley before to see England games, but the atmosphere here was incomparable. The old Wembley may have been past its sell by date, but the atmosphere that it could generate was amazing. It was so much better than I could ever have imagined. I think everybody had such a glow about them that day. It was unforgettable.

Of course the cuddly toys were out in their thousands (something I was really surprised that the TV cameras didn't pick up on). The terrace was just awash with every sort of soft toy going, which was amazing to see. This was why I had followed this stupid club for all those years at crap places like Oxford and Luton.

It was my reward, along with thousands of others.

177

I could have savoured that feeling for ever, but very quickly the game itself came round and if we thought it couldn't get any better, well it bloody well did.

On 38 minutes John Sheridan blasted a shot into the net to put us 1-0 up. This was a real bonus, as I didn't expect to see us score, yet here we were celebrating a Wednesday goal in a real cup final!

Bloody amazing!

Our view was not the best and I honestly thought that their keeper had palmed out the shot and someone else had put the rebound in. I was amazed to see what really happened when I saw the replay on TV.

The game wasn't the best, but we were there to enjoy the day rather than the game and actually being in front, rather than being humiliated 5-0 just made it even better. The atmosphere was incredible and I felt so alive and happy.

It was only in the second half that I stopped enjoying it. With about 15 minutes left, Graham turned round and said,"You know what, we could win this."

As ridiculous as it may seem the thought of actually winning it never entered my head, until that point. Yet he was right, we were still winning and time was ticking away. The next fifteen minutes took a lifetime as we oh so slowly, slowly, tiptoed towards the final minutes. The agony intensified as it got to 80 minutes played, then it was 85......86..........87.............bloody bleeding hell...88!

About two hours later it was 89 minutes! and then, the unthinkable happened.

It was full bloody time!

I can't think of any way of describing that feeling, other than pages and pages of superlatives like chuffin', bleedin', pissin', giggly wee your pants fan-f****n;-tastic! So I won't.

Use your wildest imagination (especially if you are a piggy fan, as this is as close as you will ever get to understanding) to try and feel what a massive cocktail of get happy drugs, alcohol, 100 orgasms and a parachute jump, all mixed together with a gold spoon and times it by a thousand and you still won't be close to that full time feeling.

We had won! We had bloody well won! No one expected it. It was a great big, fat dream with custard on top and it had happened.

I don't think it sunk in for a few days. It was surreal and the next thing we knew Nigel Pearson was leading the team up those famous old steps. The same steps that I had watched so many teams walk up over the years and now it was our turn!

Un- f****ng- believable!
The rest of the day was a blur. I can't remember anything except us all being uncontrollably happy.

The sheer disbelief of winning a trophy! Me, Mark and Founts at the full time whistle

The moment that you live for as a football fan. Your team picking up a major trophy in a Wembley final. Probably the greatest football moment in my life

WE WON THE CUP

Glory, glory day for the Owls and Big Ron's Barmy Army

BIG RON'S army had every reason to go barmy ...

By Mike O'Sullivan

Carlsberg don't print newspapers............

The season was fittingly finished off with promotion back to the top flight, to end an unforgettable season.

So we were one down one to go. My ambitions as a fan were to see Wednesday in a Cup Final and see them play in Europe. We had gone one better and actually won a cup, so now it was time for Europe.

We had already had near misses with qualifying for Europe.

Firstly, missing out in the final game of the season at Spurs in 1985.

Then we actually qualified the following season, finishing 5th, but because of the rioting Liverpool fans at Heysel the previous May, all

180

English clubs were banned from European competitions (one of the reasons why I hate Liverpool).

Our League Cup win in 1991 was also badly timed as English clubs had only just had the ban lifted and so the League Cup winners didn't qualify that season either.

However, Man United went on to beat Barcelona and win the Cup Winners Cup a few weeks after our League Cup Final clash, which opened another European place to English clubs for the 1991-92 season.

In those days the European Cup was strictly for the Champions and the other places went to the UEFA Cup.

In 1992 we would finish 3rd (see Chapter 11 "Executive Boxes" for the full story) and finally clinch that coveted European spot and life as an Owl couldn't have got much better.

It makes you wonder what would have happened then, had the Champions League had the current format with the top four qualifying and we would have been awash with money. This book would probably have been written by a sad and bitter Arsenal fan, complaining about life in the Third Division and how wrong it is that clubs with millions like Sheffield Wednesday, don't want to share it. (Phew, that's a relief then.)

It also makes you wonder how we would have performed had we hung on to a certain Eric Cantona. Cantona came to Wednesday in January 1992 but due to bad weather the management team never got to see him play outside and so asked him to stay another week. Cantona being Cantona duly said "Non" and we let one of the most talented footballers in the world slip through our fingers.

I write about the Cantona situation and laugh now, but can you just imagine for one minute if we had signed him. A few months later we also signed Chris Waddle (I can't say that I was overly excited when we signed CW at the time, but what an amazing player he was. Surely one of the most incredibly gifted players ever to grace the blue and white. His performance in a 5-0 win against West Ham in 1993 will be remembered forever).

But think of the players we had then. Chris Waddle, Des Walker, David Hirst, Paul Warhurst, Roland Nilsson, Carlton Palmer, John Sheridan, John Harkes, Nigel Pearson, Mark Bright, Chris Woods, Andy Sinton, Trevor Francis etc. etc. and then Eric Cantona on top! Bloody hell we would have won everything!

How did we let all that go?

Eric in the famous bleu et blanc. I was lucky enough to see him play his only public game for Mercredi. An indoor six a side game against an American 'Baltimore Blast' team.

So we embarked into the new 1992-93 season full of hope. Some silverware at long last and a European trip to look forward to.

I did however have a slight problem. I had a holiday in Vancouver booked for the second leg of the UEFA Cup. I prayed that we would be away for the first leg, as I wouldn't mind missing the home game too much, but missing the first European trip was unthinkable. When the draw was made, we were inevitably drawn at home for the first leg, thus missing the return leg.

There was only one thing I could do. Cancel Canada!

It cost me a fortune to put the trip back a few weeks, but at least I would get to see the first European game and we were lucky because we drew a plum tie against Spora Luxembourg!

The fact that we hadn't drawn a major club was irrelevant to be honest and as it turned out Luxembourg was a great venue for us.

We only just scraped through the home leg 8-1, so there was still all to play for, when we set off.

Eight of us headed south that day and we all rendezvoused in Dover for some alcoholic refreshment. We bumped into some Hibs fans who were returning from a trip to Germany, which made us feel like we really had arrived on the European scene. Hob-nobbing with other European experienced fans!

We made our way to the ferry and I remember there being a conveyor belt that ran alongside the walkway which kindly took the weight of your bags. It was just too damn tempting and we all piled on. Kneeling up, forming a close line (Here we go, more caterpillar bumming-Ed), we all started 'paddling' as if in a large canoe and singing the theme tune to 'Hawaii-five-O'

By the time the ferry had docked in Calais, it is fair to say that we were all pretty pissed, so weren't in the best state to handle our first mini crisis. We had hired a van, which we were due to pick up in France and drive over to Luxembourg. However when we arrived they had no van or no booking and all the car hire places were closing up. The thought of missing out on actually getting to the game was frightening, so there were some pretty frayed tempers to say the least.

When it started to get very heated the local Gendarmes were called and we had visions of spending the night in a French Police cell. Foreign police are not the most tolerant when it comes to English football fans, but fortunately a quick flash of Mark's American Express card ...... ooops, I mean Police card, did the trick and we were told a van would be found.

I remember us having a Bruce Springsteen medley sing song (with "Thunder Road" being belted out at full volume, to the delight of our French cousins) before lo and behold, "Un petite camion" turned up (well done Borman, even if you did spit)

With Melv at the wheel off we set. Destination Brussels!

We seemed to have been driving for hours (probably because we had to stop every twenty minutes for someone to have a pee), but here we were living the European dream. Driving through France in the back of a transit van. Although when in the back of a transit van with seven smelly blokes it may as well have been through Oldham.

After a few hours we seemed to enter a built up area and presumed this must be Brussels. We were anxious to find our hotel as quick as we could to get out on the town, so rather than drive around aimlessly, we thought we would stop and ask someone. We pulled up outside a bar, where an elderly gentlemen, who seemed a little worse for wear was asked in our best French. "Ou est le Rue de…" (Whatever it was called). The old guy looked at us totally bewildered but after some hesitation pointed in the direction that we were heading, so off we went.

It was about ten minutes later, when the built up area had become countryside again, that we saw a sign saying that Brussels was still 80 kilometres away! The poor old guy must have wondered how the hell we expected him to give precise details of how to find a road about 90 kilometres away to a load of drunken non French speaking football fans.

He took the easy option and just pointed!

When we did get to Brussels we were lucky enough to find the hotel very easily and were soon out on the town.

I can't remember much about the night. Nothing wacky happened. We didn't get into any scrapes. It was just a really good night.

I do remember waking up the next morning in the hell hole that was our hotel room. When I say hotel, it was more like a YMCA, but it was the revolting stench rather than the room that was most alarming.

Suitably showered and fed we drove on to Luxembourg and headed to the main square for a lunchtime session. When we got there it was great. The place had been taken over by Wednesday fans and it was just like a big party. Steadily the effects of all day drinking took hold on a few, but there was no trouble. I think a lot of us were conscious of the trouble there in 1977 and 1983 when England fans had rioted in the city, so fans were going out of their way to show how good we could be. The bars around the ground were heaving with Wednesday supporters all intent on having a good time and songs were continuously being belted out. It was all good natured though and any locals in the bar were bought drinks and they were soon joining in with the singing.

The song that became our particular anthem for that trip was Cliff Richards "Summer Holiday" and it was great when we started this going to hear the entire bar singing along at the top of their voices.

Eventually we made our way to the ground. We had tickets for the main stand, rather than with the rest of the Wednesday fans, so were heading in the opposite direction to most Owls, when my brother spied Clive Betts, heading towards us. Betts was in charge of Sheffield City Council, at the time the City hosted the "World Student Games" in 1991. This was a very costly event for the City, with precious little publicity or reward. It left the City in a financial mess and resulted in higher council tax for the residents of Sheffield for quite a number of years.

As he walked towards us Mark greeted him with "Clive Betts!" He smiled knowingly enjoying his minor celebrity status, only to be hit with "How dare you show your face here, the state the bloody City is in and you are wasting money coming here, you should be ashamed of yourself, you absolute w***er" and walked off leaving Betts stood there, open mouthed.

The atmosphere inside the ground was still like a party. One of the great mental pictures I have of that night, was Mark stood at the front of the stand, looking back at the fans with the most ridiculous, drunken grin, playing air guitar, while we sang another rendition of "Summer Holiday." How I wish I had a photo of that.

The game was won 2-1 on the night and we all stood and applauded when Spora scored, which went down very well with our Luxembourg hosts.

As the game drew to an end I said to Mark that I fancied one of the Spora shirts. He asked me to take off my Wednesday shirt, which I did and he promptly put it on and simply walked down the stand and on to the side of the pitch. He waited around the dug out for the final whistle and then calmly walked on the pitch and swapped shirts with a Spora player. I don't know whether he thought Mark was a player or what (most of the Spora players had been marking Chris Waddle for the last two minutes to try and swap shirts with him), but Mark emerged later with a (very sweaty and smelly) Spora shirt.

I have still got that shirt to this day.

We went out for a few more beers in Luxembourg after the game (me in a sweaty and muddy Spora shirt) and I remember that by the side of our hotel was a place used by local prostitutes. (We stopped in some classy places, huh).

There was a piece of waste land nearby and a queue of cars parked outside with single male drivers, patiently waiting their turn. When one had finished and driven off, the next would drive in and she would get in the car.

Not kerb crawling, kerb queuing! Very orderly, these continentals you know.

We couldn't resist sneaking quietly up, when the car started rocking and simultaneously banging on the windows and shouting either "Zis is ze Police" or just "Waheyyy!" The punter looked horrified for a split second and as we walked away laughing the hooker shouted something pretty uncomplimentary to us in Flemish.

The European adventure only lasted one more round sadly. We were drawn against Kaiserslautern from Germany next and as tempting as it was, I decided not to postpone another trip to Canada. We lost the first leg 3-1 in a harsh lesson of what European football is really all about. Wednesday took the lead, with a vital away goal, but were cheated out of a result, with some serious diving by the Germans. A penalty and a sending off were the rewards the Germans got from conning the referee and there was a real sense of injustice about the whole thing. Of course this sort of thing is widespread throughout the English game as well now, sadly, but at the time everyone was infuriated.

The upside of this however was probably the best atmosphere that I have ever known at Hillsborough for the return game. The local media had done a commendable job of building the fans up and the hostile reception that greeted Kaiserslautern that night was superb (We bumped into a Kaiserslautern fan in London later that year. He came up and said that he was at the game at Hillsborough and it was the best atmosphere he had ever known. As a result he came over to see us play when he could – I bet he has long since stopped coming before our relegation back to the Third Division though!).

We needed to win by two goals and when Danny Wilson put us 1-0 up, it seemed as though it might be possible and the noise was deafening. Despite an equaliser, we again went in front, but unfortunately they equalised again and it finished 2-2 on the night.

Despite our early exit, it was a fantastic experience and it really made us yearn for more. European nights like that are superb. It is such a pity that no one else gets a look in any more.

It is sad how the European competitions have changed over the years. The Cup Winners Cup has been cancelled altogether and the UEFA cup is very poorly supported and seen as a distraction, to those in it now. It is as if only the Champions League is of any importance.

The 'glory' kept coming that season for Wednesday though.

We had two cup runs, getting to the final of the FA Cup and the League Cup, but sadly so did Arsenal. We ended up playing Arsenal four times in just over four weeks at the end of that season and won one of the games. Unfortunately that win was a league game sandwiched between the two cup finals and the one game that we probably didn't mind losing. Bloody typical!

Wednesday also had a series of big flags around that time too. Theses huge flags would be unfurled and passed among the massed crowds, which was always great fun. Eventually they had to stop doing it though as people had a habit of jumping on the flag and surfing down it! I think someone at the club decided it was best to stop it before someone got injured.

A few years after this someone had the great idea of getting the flag out again for some reasonably big game. Sadly the flag had been in storage for a few years and when it was unfurled you could hardly see it for the great clouds of dust that billowed out. It also looked rather tired and so was never seen again.

The flag in its heyday at Wembley

187

The league cup run that season was very good with some great performances, such as the 7-1 win over Leicester, but I think that it is only when you get to the Quarter Finals of the League Cup that people start to give it much attention. Our Quarter final was at Ipswich that year, which we drew 1-1.

I remember that we drove out of Ipswich after the game, before stopping to find a pub. We had pulled off the main road trying to find some form of village pub and seemed to be driving for ages through rural Suffolk, without success. In fact it was quite surprising how many sleepy villages there were that were publess.

I thought it was the law that every village or town in Britain HAD to have a pub.

We were seriously lost and even having difficulty finding villages, let alone pubs, when we spied something that looked hopeful further ahead. Sure enough it was a little pub, but when we walked in the whole place went deathly quiet, like we were aliens or something. It was that bad that I was frantically looking around for a pentacle on the wall and Brian Glover sat in the corner!

It was a real odd pub and I was waiting for the land lord to say "We don't loike strangers rownd 'ere."

I'm not sure what they made of us, but I know that when we left, none of us dare stray from the path in the swirling fog, that appeared from nowhere!

We beat Ipswich in the replay and played Blackburn in the Semi Final.

The first leg was at Ewood Park, which was at the start of its transformation. They had taken the roof off the Darwen End, where we were, but the steel structure still remained, which gave a slightly strange feel to the night. We went a goal down quite early on, but then followed one of the best footballing spells I have ever known from Wednesday. To say we ripped them apart is an understatement. We went from one down to 4-1 up in about half an hour and another Wembley appearance was looking good. The atmosphere that night was absolutely superb and all our goals were scored at the end where the Wednesday fans were. Although Blackburn did pull a goal back a 4-2 away win was pretty bloody good and we had very few of the nerves and doubts that were experienced against Chelsea two years before.

The second leg was played on a Sunday and didn't go quite to plan to start with.

188

We went a goal down, making it 4-3 on aggregate and it could have been worse, with the majestic Roland Nilsson turning and hitting a back pass to keeper Chris Woods without looking. He was under no real pressure when he knocked it back, only to everyone's horror, to see Chris Woods at the other side of his goal and unable to get near it. The ball agonisingly rolled goalwards and hit the inside of the post, before being gathered by a relieved Woods.

I presume the team got a right rollicking at half time, because we came out transformed and goals by Bright and Hirst sent us back to a second Cup Final in three years. Fantastic!

We subsequently lost the final 2-1, but I don't think many people were too upset. We had a great weekend away again and I think now, it was the FA Cup that everyone was eyeing up. Without being arrogant, I think it was a matter of, we have won the League Cup, it is the FA Cup we want now.

The FA Cup Final was a month later and we went down for the weekend as usual. We even managed to find the same Greek restaurant that we used for the Centenary tournament in 1988. There were about ten of us and as we entered we were stopped and told that we couldn't go in as it was couples only. Quick as a flash Gray said, "that's OK, we are all Gay" and we all walked in holding hands before the guy could figure out a response!

Although the evening wasn't quite as good as the last time, it was still a good night and in a bizarre quirk of fate Melv ended up snogging a pensioner.

The game the next day was very special. This was the FA Cup Final. Something that I had watched on TV, pretty much every year for over twenty years and at long last here we were being part of history.

The traditional "Abide with me" bringing a tear to our eyes and an unbelievable lump to the throat that made it hard to sing.

In true Wednesday style we had a major injury crisis before the game losing both our centre halves, Captain Nigel Pearson and Peter Shirtliffe to injury. This not only weakened the heart of our defence, but also our attack, as the prolific Paul Warhurst was switched to centre back and I remain convinced that with a 'normal' side we would have beaten an average Arsenal side (They finished below us in 10th place that season).

We went a goal down before David Hirst equalised. From that point on, we should have gone on to win, as we were the better side, but it wasn't to be and it finished 1-1, after extra time, with a fourth trip to Wembley in six weeks.

I was no different to anyone else in those weeks, in that financially it was very difficult, but this was the bloody FA Cup Final and I was damned if I was going to miss this.

I 'wagged' the afternoon off work, which was a bit obvious as everyone knew what a big Owls fan I was, but I seriously didn't care.

The trip down on the Thursday afternoon was a nightmare, with a major crash on the M1. Fortunately we heard about it on the radio and diverted down the M40. We arrived in time, but despite the kick off being put back, thousands didn't make it until well into the first half.

Again we were robbed of our centre backs, but this time we also had to do without the experienced Viv Anderson as well, so were missing our three normal centre backs for arguably our biggest game for decades.

Typical bloody Wednesday.

As in the first game we found ourselves a goal down at half time and having to fight to get back in the game. The equaliser duly arrived by the fantastic Chris Waddle on 69 minutes and we were all over them. A few minutes later came what I believe was the turning point of the game, when Mark Bright hit a relatively simple chance against the post. A goal at this point would have killed Arsenal, who were already on the ropes.

Instead it finished 1-1 again and extra time.

The game could have gone either way but with time ticking away it looked as though for the first time in FA Cup history, it would be decided on penalties.

We were even talking about it as the game petered out. Penalties are a total lottery and I really wasn't sure if I could face the torture of watching a penalty shoot out in a Cup Final. The stress would have been absolutely over powering.

We were already in injury time when Arsenal won a fortuitous corner and the rest is history. As that winning goal crossed the line, part of me died deep inside. I don't think I have ever been so gutted in my life.

The last f***ing seconds of injury time, of extra time, of a replay of a Cup Final.

It simply doesn't get worse than that.

All the superstitions and rituals we went through were for nothing. There simply weren't any 'soccer Gods', because they couldn't do anything so cruel.

This was absolutely heart breaking.

At the final whistle we left the stadium. We walked back to the car with thousands of others in total silence.

Nobody said a word.

Nobody.

There were no words to say. How could any words sum that up.

The drive home was agony and in total silence.

I stopped believing after that day.

The following season was still good and we finished seventh, with another Semi Final appearance. By now they were becoming common place, although we did lose convincingly to Man United in the second leg, when the tie was evenly balanced. One funny thing I remember from the first leg at Old Trafford was when we were walking to the ground. There was quite a nasty atmosphere in the air that day both before and after the game and there was some nasty banter being exchanged between fans. One Man United fan said to us in a belittling way, that this game was our cup final. "Yeah," replied Mark, "we only went to Wembley four times last season!" The look of horror on the guys face was an absolute picture as he realised what he had said.

Sadly that was the last real highlight for a long time as Wednesday started another scary slide down the leagues.

I think collectively we had the stuffing knocked out of us after the FA cup final defeat and it took some considerable time to get it back. We still went to away games but that passion that burned so fiercely inside had been diminished and the trips were becoming less frequent.

We had a good trip to Celtic for a pre season friendly to see a 1-1 draw and still went in the main stand with their supporters. We were a little bit concerned, especially when we saw the IRA publications, openly on sale outside the ground, but the Celtic fans were great. We had decided to keep a low profile, but we got picked out straight away. We needn't have worried though, as we were made very welcome and even when we cheered Warhurst's equaliser there was nothing said.

Despite the premature dismantling of a very good side, we still held our own in the Premiership, but success was becoming harder to find.

Francis was replaced by Pleat and things were looking bleak.

In the 1997-98 season, with us cut adrift at the bottom, the board sacked Pleat and brought back Big Ron. It was a master stroke and the fans loved it. We instantly started winning games and Ron started to re shape the side, as he did in 1989 and slowly managed to drag us out of the mire and reach a safe position.

What happened next was the biggest single incident that started our sorry fall that we still haven't recovered from ten years later.

The board sacked Ron (or rather, didn't renew his contract, to use their words.)

It was total madness and in my opinion done out of spite, because he left us in 1991.

Admittedly I was gutted when Atkinson left us the first time. He had assembled a superb squad of players, got us promoted, won a cup and we were playing beautiful attacking football.

I am convinced that had Ron stayed we would have gone on to massive success and established ourselves as a major force for years and years.

That is why everyone was so angry. We could see what had been taken away from us. Yes, we had two or three good seasons still, but we knew it wouldn't last.

Ron, old lad, why did you do that to us?

His re-instatement six years later meant that he was totally forgiven by the fans and we were on our way back again. The stupidity of the board cost this club dear and we never recovered from that blow.

Danny Wilson was made manager for the following season and as much as Danny was loved by the fans for his time as a player, he didn't quite cut it at Hillsborough as manager.

We had the fantastic and extremely volatile Italians playing for us, Di Canio and Carbone and looking back at the old videos of their time at Wednesday they were absolutely stunning players, with some incredible goals scored.

Di Canio, as everyone knows was an amazing talent, but very fiery and the crowd loved him. The guy could do nothing wrong and I think it needed a special type of manager to control and get the best out of him (and Carbone for that matter).

Sadly I don't think Danny did that and when his infamous sending off happened against Arsenal for pushing the referee over (and I know it has been said a thousand times, but that referee was a disgrace and his ridiculous theatrical dive should have been punished by the FA), the club handled it terribly. This incident made Paolo an even bigger hero with the fans. When his ban was due to end, tickets sales for his return game were almost double the average, as everyone wanted to see him.

He would have received a hero's welcome.

Instead the board made a total pigs ear of it and off loaded him to West Ham for a ridiculously low fee.

West Ham must have pissed themselves laughing at us.

Very predictably we slid out of the top flight the following season without a whimper.

There followed a succession of struggles and chopping and changing of managers, that inevitably took the club nowhere except back to the Third Division.

Premier League, Silverware, Europe and Cup Finals to the Third Division in a few short years.

How on earth did we manage that situation so badly?

No one has still explained that to me.

Ironically it was at this point that I started to rediscover the passion again.

I guess it was like being a big fish in a small pond rather than an also ran in the Premier League.

That first season back in the third tier came full of expectations that we would walk it and that belief seemed spot on as we started the season well.

As I have said before, to me it is about winning at any level and as long as I came away from the ground with a win I was happy. If I am honest I really enjoyed our time back in the Third Division. It became exciting again and I genuinely went into every game thinking we could win, which was a massive change to the last seven or eight years.

The really disappointing thing was that we should have been putting teams away a lot easier than we were doing and the promotion run changed into a relegation battle, finishing that first season back down, only three points from relegation.

Little clubs came to Hillsborough as their big day out and invariably soaked up the pressure, caught us on the break and left with three points.

The following season followed a similar pattern in that we started the season really well, but soon started slipping up and fell back to mid table.

The manager was Chris Turner at the time and I always liked Chris. He was an ex player as well as a fan of the club and I think he needs some recognition for actually stopping the slide.

When he was sacked, he was replaced by Paul Sturrock, who became a crowd favourite very quickly.

He stopped us being mugged by teams and brought some happiness back to the club.

With nine games to go we were in third place and looking unbeatable, but then did a Wednesday wobble (mostly due to a horrific injury list) and only just managed to scrape into the play offs at the end.

Now the play offs were totally uncharted waters to us, so we really didn't know what to expect.

We were drawn with Brentford and won the home game 1-0 before a partisan crowd. Sadly we couldn't get tickets for the second leg so watched it on TV in North Nottinghamshire.

There were eight of us there and we were the only Wednesday fans in the pub.

When Wednesday went a goal up, we went crazy. I think the rest of the pub thought we were mad. This was only a Third Division play off semi final after all. The thing is that we have all grown older, yet we still behave like 18 year olds and so seeing 40 and 50 year olds screaming and hugging each other, knocking drinks and tables flying, must seem a bit odd for such a low profile game. But football still has that effect on you.

The added incentive to winning would be a trip to the Millennium stadium in Cardiff. With Wembley nearing completion, we knew there wouldn't be many more chances to get to Cardiff and I had heard so much about what a great venue it was.

A second goal in the second half meant more screaming and drinks sent flying, as that pretty much secured our place in the final. We ended up winning 2-1 on the night and we were bound for Wales! Despite being middle aged blokes, the passion still burns as fierce as ever and just remembering that win against Brentford gives me goosebumps.

It might sound crazy to a lot of people but that weekend in Cardiff was as good as any of the Wembley trips in the 1990's.

Yes, it was only a Third Division play off game against Hartlepool, but the thrill was as good as ever.

We had a good night in Cardiff on the Saturday and it was nice to see fans mingling together. Lincoln and Southend had played their play off game earlier in the day and there was some good banter exchanged between all fans. The night was a wonderful mixture of Hen nights and Wednesday fans singing their heads off. I guess Cardiff got used to the influx of footy fans, but they were very tolerant, as behaviour like that wouldn't be accepted in most places.

The amazing thing about the weekend though was on the Sunday.

We drove out to Newport on the Sunday morning and got the train back in to Cardiff, as we were told that this would be the best way to get away after the game, as Cardiff tends to get gridlocked with traffic.

We were surprised when we got to Newport station, to find a massive queue of Wednesday supporters trying to get the train also, but that was nothing compared to when we arrived in Cardiff itself.

It was absolutely awesome.

As soon as we left the station we were greeted with a mass of fans and a wall of noise. There were over 40,000 Wednesday fans down for the game and the sight and sound made the hairs on the back of your neck stand up. (that following still stands as the largest attendance from one single club at the Millenium stadium).

We instantly got engulfed by it all and everyone was on a high.

The roads simply got taken over by the fans and a massive street party ensued. Full credit must go to Cardiff for exceptional organisation. They closed the roads down and let everyone have a good time. The attitude of the Police was outstanding and as a result there was no hint of trouble whatsoever.

It was still three hours before kick off, yet the place seemed packed and still more and more people were arriving.

All the pubs were open, so the atmosphere was absolutely fantastic.

There were a load of plastic footballs flying around and the atmosphere was like a carnival. It was so good you didn't want to go to the ground.

We got chatting to a couple of Policemen who had been on duty for the FA Cup Final between Arsenal and Manchester United the week before and they said what a massive difference it was. "The fans of the 'big' clubs were obnoxious, arrogant and hostile, whereas you lot are great. You all just want to have a good time." I thought that was what we all went for.

England cricket captain Michael Vaughn has a drink with Me and Mark in the streets of Cardiff, before the game. He told me that he urged the team to beat Bangladesh in the First Test at Lords by Saturday, so he could get to see the lads at Cardiff

We eventually moved onto the stadium and what a stadium.

The Millennium stadium is spectacular and the atmosphere was every bit as good inside as it had been outside.

The game was cracking too.

We went 1-0 up on the stroke of half time, only to go 2-1 down in the second half and looking to be on the way out. It was horrible to see the minutes ticking away and realising that we were enduring yet another kick in the nuts and the prospect of yet another season in the Third Division.

But with just eight minutes left we were given the lifeline of a penalty.

Steve Maclean was our regular penalty taker, but he had been out injured for over two months and surprised everyone that day by being announced as making the subs bench for the game.

He had only been on the pitch for five minutes and now lined up to take the penalty.

There is such a lot going through your head at that point.

The ecstasy of getting the penalty. A lifeline when it seemed we were lost.

Who will take it?

Maclean! Yes, he has never missed a penalty for us.

Bol**cks, he is due to miss one then! Oh please not now. Don't let this be the moment he misses.

He has scored 11 out of 11 penalties, but he hasn't kicked a ball for twelve weeks! The pressure on him is immense.

The tension is unbearable.

Will he score and save the season or will he miss and condemn us?

I look to Mark but he has his back to the pitch. He can't look.

Maclean puts the ball down.

Hartlepool fans are whistling trying to put him off.

He walks back.

Wednesday fans are in agony waiting.

Steps up.

Hits the ball.

For just that split second all 60,000 hold their breath. It is total silence.

The ball hits the net and 40,000 go mental.

Mark knows what has happened without having to see as we all go absolutely crazy. The joy and relief is indescribable.

From this point on there is only one side in it.

It finishes 2-2 and so to extra time, but it is still one way traffic and when Whelan cracks in a beauty to put us 3-2 up it is like heaven.

We still anxiously count the remaining 26 minutes down, but the lads are playing so well it only looks like us scoring again.

In the very last seconds Drew Talbot, scores one of the most memorable goals that I have seen. He wins the ball on the halfway line and sprints forward. He only has the keeper to beat and takes it round him. Just as it was for the penalty, for a split second the entire stadium falls into total silence as he strikes the ball goalwards, only to be shattered by screaming voices as the ball is clearly goal bound. What a great moment for that young lad and what a moment for us all, as promotion is won, with that single kick.

As I have said before success is all relative, so don't tell me that beating Hartlepool United in a Third Division play off is irrelevant, because at that moment (and still in my memory) it was the most wonderful feeling in the world.

CHAPTER 9

England

From being young I have always followed England.

This may seem an obvious thing to say, but in the 1970's following England was nowhere near on the scale that it is now.

In the last ten years it has become the trendy thing to do. People who have no interest in football, will be seen wearing England tops and watching the 'big' games. There has of course always been a big interest in the national side, but back then, it was more of a cult following than a mass following. The tarnished image caused by "rioting' fans abroad, meant that most 'ordinary' people didn't like the association with England.

We followed every game with passion on TV and made several trips to Wembley to see 'home' games.

Like with Wednesday, my interest started to take hold in my early teens, which was unfortunate, considering that England failed to qualify for the World Cup in both 1974 and 1978. At that time, everyone got behind Scotland instead, being the next best thing, as they did qualify.

This has also changed, I think, as I'm not sure people would 'support' Scotland to the same extent now. I think most English resent the fact that the Scots will always want anyone to win but England and so slowly they have lost the English support (not that I think they will lose any sleep over it.)

Back to England and the first real tournament I can remember watching them play in was the European Championships, held in Italy in 1980. The European Championships being held every four years but then on a much smaller scale to the current format. The first match against Belgium was drawn 1-1, but will be remembered more for the riot in Turin than anything else, yet bizarrely I felt some sort of misguided pride in the way the England fans fought so hard. The attendance at the game was only 15,000 and the other group game against Spain, was 14,000. As I said the interest in England was still not that great. Compare that to the recent World Cup in Germany where an estimated 230,000 went to Germany, just "to be there", even though they had little chance of getting a ticket (There were even an estimated 12,000 went to Prague, in the Czech Republic.)

Mostly my experiences of watching England were left to the TV. We loved the old Home Internationals and particularly the England v Scotland games. It became one of the highlights of the season to get together, get pissed and watch the game. We even set a "clothes horse" up one year to act as a crash barrier, so we could stand up to get, "the atmosphere!"

I was particularly jealous in 1975 when my brother Mark got tickets for the England - Scotland game at Wembley. Again, in the 1970's things were very different and the Wembley game had been a pilgrimage for the Scots for some time. London got invaded every two years and out of the 98,000 attendance, probably 70,000+ were Scots.

Mark was 17 at the time and he and his mate Kevin were stood up behind one of the goals. They had managed to find a small pocket of England fans up in the back corner amongst a sea of tartan and so stood with them. England scored twice after only seven minutes and so they were instantly under threat. It got very ugly and a barrage of cans and bottles were hurled at them (Yes bottles were allowed in grounds in those days) England went on to absolutely murder them 5-1 and it was fortunate for Mark that some older Scottish guys decided to protect them from a severe beating that day.

The first World Cup that England qualified for in twelve years was in 1982 in Spain, so there was huge excitement and anticipation, as the tournament grew closer. I had booked holidays from work to make sure I saw all the games and the opener against France was perfect. We had started drinking early on for the afternoon game, which about ten of us watched at Mark's house. England scored after only 27 seconds and the room went ballistic!

We went on to win 3-1, with a terrific display and everything in the world was good.

We went down to our local, The New Inn, to celebrate some more and had great fun watching Algeria beat West Germany 2-1 (*West* Germany? I hear our younger viewers cry. Yes, boys and girls. A long time ago there was a big war, which we won, and because Germany had been so naughty, we decided to split it into two to teach it a lesson. The West Germany part was annoyed and so beat us at football every time we played them to show that they were angry at being cut in half. That is all except one game, which we won in 1966. It is the law in England that this will be the only game that is ever remembered and must always be talked about, particularly if Germans are near. Because despite them getting to seven World Cup finals - winning three - and six European Championship finals – winning three again, Germans still think that 1966 was the most important tournament).

Anyway, after the West Germany game, apparently I got barred from the pub, for swearing at the TV at the final whistle, but if I am honest I was too drunk to remember. The drinking continued all night until it was decided that we would go to someone's house that we knew, that was apparently having a party. It was at the other end of the City, so we jumped in a couple of cars and off we went. Absolute madness, after drinking for about 9 hours, that someone would drive, but off we went anyway. This guy lived in a quite upmarket apartment and he hadn't lived there long, so when ten completely drunk and very loud 'mates' turned up, he thought twice about the invite and decided not to let us in. I can't say I was too bothered, but I remember a couple of the lads being pretty annoyed and trying to force their way in anyway. I'm not sure whether it was his neighbours that didn't like the noise or someone from inside his apartment that took offence to one of our lot pissing through the letterbox, but the police were called. (That was a pretty risky thing to do. There is no way I would have put my considerable size equipment in such a vulnerable place!).We were already on our way out when the police arrived and we quickly dispersed. I still think it was an over reaction, but they had brought Police dogs with them, so when they let them out, we panicked.

Me and Robert ran to a park on the opposite side of the road.

I can't remember who suggested it, but we decided in our drunken state to jump into a nearby river. I think the idea was that the dogs wouldn't pick up the scent and we would lie Red Indian style, under the water, breathing through a broken reed! Looking back I can't believe how stupid we were, but that's what we did.

I'm sure the dogs would have seen us anyway and ripped us to bits had they come after us, but luckily for us they didn't. We emerged about ten minutes later, dripping wet through, back to the original scene, which had now calmed down from earlier. Now there is nothing like lying down in a cold river bed, breathing through a straw to sober you up, so God did we feel stupid as we squelched our way back down the street.

As far as I was concerned, that was the end of it, other than waking up with a world class hangover. For Mark, it was only just starting though. He had only been in the Police himself a short time, so the next morning he came within a whisker of being drummed out of the force. He escaped with the biggest bollocking of his life for his involvement in the previous nights disturbance and had to keep a very low profile for the next year.

In 1983 we managed to get tickets for the England v Denmark game at Wembley. This was to be a virtual decider as to who would qualify for the European Championship finals in France the following year.

It was a game that England needed to win, as they already trailed Denmark and only the group winner qualified. We had five tickets, but Graham had to drop out, so the spare ticket was happily snapped up by a mate that I worked with called Chris. We took the day off work and left at about 9 o'clock in the morning, for an evening kick off.

I do need to emphasise here that I am not and never have been a big drinker. I could quite happily stop after two pints and be nicely merry for hours. My brothers and mates however, had the capability to keep on going and going and there was always the pressure to keep up with the drinking or face the ridicule if you couldn't. Nowadays I couldn't care less and will drink to sensible levels, but as a young and weak willed man I did my best to keep up.

After a few years of this I got to the stage where I just about managed to keep up and cope reasonably well. To Chris though, this was a whole new ball game.

We started off in the pubs round Wembley at a steady pace and by mid afternoon were nicely sloshed and had already been asked to leave one pub, when a rowdy game of Shove Ha'Penny went wrong (a game played on a large table, using coins for the players and a ball, with full pints of lager as the goals) and the table inevitably got turned over during the action, spilling beer everywhere.

We eventually settled into a pub near the ground by evening, where the atmosphere was building wonderfully. I don't know what it was, but one of us suddenly realised that we hadn't seen Chris for sometime, so we went to look for him. The first place we went was the car park and sure enough we found him there. The car had all four doors wide open and the hatch back door up. It looked like a bomb had been detonated inside and Chris was the victim.

I honestly thought he was dead.

I knew he was diabetic and seemed to remember him supposedly not allowed to drink too much, so when I saw him sprawled across the back seat, with his head hanging out of the door and a big pool of sick on the floor, I thought he was a gonner.

Fortunately one of us had enough First Aid knowledge to know to pour a pint of lager over his face, to revive him.........and it worked!

With Chris back from the dead, we made sure he was reasonably OK before going back to the pub.

Chris didn't recover enough to see the match until well into the second half, by which time England were already trailing 1-0 and sliding out of yet another Championship.

The '86 World Cup in Mexico came and went with the usual gang drinking in front of the TV, cheering our heads off and always having someone throwing up in the neighbours garden later. Inevitably this was followed by defeat and usually by some injustice. In this case, that little, fat, cheating, b****rd Maradonna, with his hand of God

When England qualified for the European Championships in Germany in 1988, we inevitably talked about going over, as we always had for every tournament, without ever making it. This time it was different though.

One of our wonderful Friday nights out, ended up with Robert, Steve and myself deciding that we would go this time (This was nothing new, as we did it every time). What was different was the fact that I actually applied for tickets. It was only a couple of weeks away, so I wasn't sure we would get any, but amazingly enough, three tickets arrived on the following Friday. Robert was on holiday with his wife at the time and I don't think he even remembered saying he would go.

At 8.30 the following morning, I was rudely awaken from sleeping my hangover off by Steve at the front door. It took a little while to quite get my head round why he was here and I can remember on the way into the City centre, still not being quite sure of it all.

Apparently, we had decided that there would be a huge rush of people that morning, trying to book ferries across to mainland Europe for the England games, so off we went bright and early, well at least early.

We booked the ferry using Roberts company car as our official vehicle and all was set.

All except Robert that was, as he didn't know we were going, so we decided to send him a letter telling him of the plans!

When he got back from his holiday, there would have been a nice note waiting for him, telling him he had two days to get ready to go. This gave him a bit of a problem, with his wife and his employer.

He ended up telling his boss that his Dad had been taken ill in the South of France and that he needed special dispensation to drive over and pick him up and amazingly they went for it.

I'm not sure what he told his wife, but it worked (eventually) and we were all set. I am sure that myself and Steve got blamed for it, but come the 16th June 1988, we were ready to go.

We did have a major disappointment along the way though, as we applied for tickets for the third game against the Soviet Union (that's Russia to you kids), thinking this would be the big deciding game. As it was England failed to get a single point from the first two games and so by the time we were due to leave, we were already knocked out.

This was a major blow, but undeterred we set off.

We were due out on the midnight ferry from Dover to Ostend, so with lots of time in hand we stopped near Gillingham for a few beers. This trip was undoubtedly one of the highlights of my life and it was as if we all knew it was going to be fun, as the banter on the way down was great. We were like giddy schoolboys on our first trip from home. We left Gillingham for Dover and arrived in plenty of time. We had consumed enough beer to be buzzing, so we really didn't need the extra cans of lager that Robert rustled up from somewhere as we waited, but drink them we did.

We were nicely merry by the time we boarded the ferry and headed straight for the front of the ship, where there was a bar and disco. Generally it was quiet and most people were settling down for the night, trying to get some rest before arriving in Belgium, early the next morning. I can remember there being a bit of an atmosphere, to start with. There was a table with four 'Rugby type' lads. There was also a

203

large party of Americans, about the same age as us and I can remember the Rugby types, slagging us off, rather loudly to the Americans, saying we were football hooligans. The trouble in Germany over the preceding days had been whipped into a frenzy by the media, so football fans were not exactly held in high esteem by the general public.

We didn't care to be honest. We knew we weren't hooligans and were absolutely flying by now. Usually when most people drink, they reach a level of 'merriment". That point when you are happy and still reasonably coherent, before descending into various stages. Some people get silly, some aggressive, some sleepy, some ill, but that peak of happiness doesn't usually last too long, before the others take over. That night we peaked early and never came down. I don't think I've ever had that again.

I can't remember how or why, but gradually, people started coming over to where we were sat and enjoyed the atmosphere that we were creating. We called for the disco to be put on and after a little arguing that most people wanted to sleep, we succeeded. The next few hours were electric. The Americans drifted away from the rugby guys to us and it was one continuous party. The beer kept on flowing and it seemed like everyone was up dancing and singing. There was one particular guy who thought he was pretty tough. He was with the Americans, but they all seemed to be in awe of him. He resembled Billy Idol in his punk days and he had a real attitude. We got warned a few times not to mess with him as he had a reputation of being a bad ass, but that just seemed to make it more of a challenge to us.

He had big black boots on with shiny metal plates across the shin that was supposed to make him look menacing. The first time he came over in response to some of the comments we had made about him, there was a collective gasp as the Yanks thought it was going to kick off. I asked him why he had his shin pads on the outside of his boots, to which he replied 'To kick ass"

"Yeah, but why have you got your shin pads on the outside of your boots ?' I asked again. He seemed perplexed by the question and our apparent lack of fear. He obviously didn't understand the football context of shinpads, which just made it funnier. The 'stand off' continued for a while and every time he was confrontational we just asked why he had his shinpads on the outside of his boots, which just made us wet ourselves laughing.

I don't know whether he thought we were too risky to take on because we were barking mad or what, but he eventually backed off and

204

let himself be won over by the exuberance that surrounded us. What made it funnier was the fact that none of the Americans seemed used to drinking, so the huge quantities of Stella that were being consumed made them all VERY drunk! We were absolutely buzzing all night. There was one kid who had a 'Virginia' University sweat shirt on. He kept telling us his name was Mark, or whatever it was, but we just continued calling him Virginia. He seemed a little annoyed at first, but we weren't going to change and with the mixture of our best Yorkshire accents, he did as he was told. "Narthen Virginia, getbeerin yertaht get", until everyone was calling him Virginia. I don't know what it was that night, but we were just taking the piss out of everyone and I don't think anyone knew how to handle us, so they went along with it.

The night continued as a wild party. Everyone was up and people kept coming up to us, telling us what a great night it was thanks to us and buying us beer. There were no real incidents, nothing mad or crazy happened, but I didn't want that night to end.

It was fantastic.

When it was announced that the ferry was docking at Ostend, we all said our goodbyes, including Billy Idol, who admitted that he thought we were 'alright' in his eyes (I'm sure he lost a bit of his reputation that night, though).

It was only as we descended (when I say descended, I mean fell down) the stairs to the car decks, that we realised that we hadn't the slightest clue where the hell we had left the car. By this time, I'm sure that everybody else was sat in their cars, waiting to go, whilst we were still in a heap trying to get down the stairs. One of us decided that we should at least try and look on one of the decks for our car, so we opened the door and literally fell through it and onto this car. By an unbelievable coincidence it was Robert's car. I don't know how many cars these things carry, but there were literally hundreds and by sheer fluke, we fell onto ours.

To say that we shouldn't have been driving is a ridiculous understatement. We could barely walk, let alone drive.

Having said that, Robert has always had the ability to drive when drunk.

It's not big. It's not clever. In fact, it is plain stupid, so don't try it at home, but that's just what happened.

We knew that we would have trouble, trying to drive in the state that we were in and would have a bigger problem being allowed through passport control and into the country. We therefore decided on a cunning plan to try our hardest to sit up and be sensible and once through, we would park up and sleep it off.

That was the plan anyway.

Instead we got a serious attack of the giggles as we queued to get out. The closer to passport control we got, the worse the giggles became. Eventually we edged forward until it was our turn to present our passports.

At that point the urge to giggle was just too great and we were crying with laughter as we were processed. How the hell the passport checking man let us through I will never know. The guy should have been sacked on the spot!

Once in Belgium, we tried to find somewhere quiet to park. For some reason we couldn't quite agree where would be a good place to stop, so when we were near a quiet cul de sac of modern houses, I decided to get out.

It was one of those daft arguments, not a serious one, so I thought I'd make the point of 'here will do', got my pillow and laid down in the street. The hilarious and predictable thing for them to do now was to drive off and leave me, which of course they did.

I wasn't worried, in fact, I was still very drunk and very tired, so simply stayed there and waited for them to come back. I was obviously so unworried about it, that I quickly fell into a deep sleep. What I didn't know was that, they really had driven off, not just round the corner, but off for a five minute drive, to "try and make me panic." So much so that, being also very drunk, they couldn't find where the hell they had left me!

In the meantime I had drifted into a deep and contented sleep. Imagine my confusion when about half an hour later, I was woken by a car horn sounding and a bloke yelling at me in Flemish or French or something.

You know how sometimes when you wake up suddenly and can't remember where you are or how you got there.

Well times that by a thousand!

I was woken up sleeping in the middle of the road in Belgium, with an irate driver telling me in some unknown language to get out of the bloody way! I guess I must have thought that I was still asleep and this was all part of the dream, because it sure as hell didn't make sense.

Using some caution, I moved to the pavement and settled down to try and figure it out, before again falling to sleep. Fortunately for me Robert and Steve had stumbled back to where I was and found me, deciding it would be funny to wake me up with a kick in the balls.

I think we then did actually have a rest before getting something to eat and pressing on in a more sober state. I don't know what miracle cure they put in Belgian croissants, but I can't remember having a hang over, just buzzing again.

Robert had an Alfa Romeo as his new company car, so we had a great cruising motor to travel in. We took loads of cassette tapes with us and had a wonderful mixture of music on all the way. Our plan was to drive to Luxembourg first, avoiding any potential riots that we had read were taking place constantly in Germany and then press on to Frankfurt for the match. We even discussed whether it was worth going to the game at all, with England being eliminated already, but I was really keen to still go, so we decided to stick to the original plan.

By late morning the hangovers were starting to hit, so we pulled into a small sleepy town on the Belgium / Luxembourg border. Robert was doing all the driving and was struggling most with his hangover, so he was the one that went into a pharmacy that we had found.

Now, all of us are OK at French, but none of us are good, so we would pool our thoughts together on what we needed to say, before we opened our mouths. On this occasion Rob, was sure he had it covered and went for it, declining our advice. Bearing in mind we all looked pretty ghastly, being unshaven, smelly and a little green by now, we entered the shop.

Myself and Steve had already started with the giggles again when we walked in and the Chemist must have thought that three deranged foreign vagrants had entered his shop, as he looked slightly unnerved by our presence.

I think Rob was attempting to say that he had a headache, but what he said actually translated as "I have a duck on my head". After repeating this and getting nowhere, he tried again, but this time it came out as "I am sick in the head." Me and Steve were wetting ourselves laughing!

The pharmacist was really looking worried now as Robert continued to repeat his instructions, but even louder and more assertive. He never actually asked for anything, he just told the guy that he was sick in the head and had a duck on his head, over and over again. Steve and myself were now unable to breath with laughter and were rolling around on the floor, holding our stomachs.

I would be amazed if he didn't ring up the nearest lunatic asylum, to see if they had any missing inmates as soon as we left.

Robert gave up eventually and we decided to drive on and go for the hair of the dog cure instead.

We arrived in Luxembourg, mid afternoon and found a lovely square in the City, surrounded by bars and started to partake in a few beers. We had a great afternoon, before heading back to our hotel.

Our 'Hotel' was Roberts Alfa. We packed everything into it and slept in it at night as well, so when we went back to change, we changed in the street.

We had Bruce Springsteen's 'Born to run' album playing as we got ready to hit the town. We shaved, washed and cleaned our teeth, all done while stripped down to our underpants, as Luxembourg's rush hour traffic drove past us.

I don't know why, but we got quite a lot of odd looks.

Maybe they hadn't heard 'Born to Run' before.

That done we were ready to go.

Except that Robert took a disliking to mine and Steve's choice of attire.

We both had Wednesday shirts on and Robert wasn't having it. It wasn't because we were wearing Wednesday shirts, him being a blade, I could understand that, but at the time Robert had a real bee in his bonnet about being English and wasn't going out with us looking like archetypal English football fans.

Eventually we relented and changed, although we wouldn't comply to his continental idea that draping a jumper over your shoulders and tying the sleeves together at the front made you look French. We did take the piss out of him for a while, before he eventually wore the jumper normally.

I can't remember much more about that night, except that we drunk a lot and had a good night, until we ended up in a Chinese restaurant, late at night. Our behaviour was pretty good to be honest. It was a table full of English journalists nearby that were the embarrassment. They were pretty loud and when talking about the hooligan problem in Germany, wanted everyone in the restaurant to hear their views.

They had no idea that we were there or were listening, but were making comments that all football fans were scum and laughing about being able to write what they wanted.

I presume that there was a mixture of journalists and wives / girlfriends on the table and they all thought it was hilarious. I was furious and had to be stopped a few times from going over and giving them what for.

When we did finish though we paid and as we left, we all went over and gave them a right mouthful. I think they were stunned and they just sat there open mouthed, knowing that everything we said about them was true.

We wandered back to our car hotel in the early morning and slept for a few hours.

When I did wake, I must have been having flashbacks from 24 hours earlier, because I woke with a start. For some reason, I had been dreaming that someone had kidnapped Robert and he was in great danger and despite him being sat only three feet away, I couldn't see him. Well I could, but in my befuddled state, it wasn't Robert, if that makes sense!

I was in a right old panic in my half drunken/half asleep state and couldn't understand why the other two weren't concerned. The more confused they looked at me, the more I shouted "Where's Robert!". As confused as I was by it all, it must have been equally puzzling for them, to be woken from their comas with me shouting "Where's Robert!" at them. Slowly my brain kicked into gear and Robert materialised in front of me, with a "What the f**k are you going on about" expression!

As I had woke everyone up nice and early, we set off into Germany and stopped at a very pleasant hotel / bar.

At 9 o'clock in the morning Steve and Rob had lager for breakfast. Being the lightweight that I am, I declined and had wine.

The drive through the Mosel valley was gorgeous and we arrived in Frankfurt in good time. We stopped in a nice bar by the river on a gorgeous sunny day.

I remember breaking the arm off my sunglasses before we left, but couldn't afford any new ones, so took them anyway, thinking that Johnny Foreigner would think it was the cool new style. I bet they thought I was a cheapskate, but at the time I was sure I was a trendsetter and Germans would be breaking an arm off their sunglasses, to keep up with the latest trend.

Far from the mass brawls that we had expected, our time in Frankfurt was great. Everyone was mixing happily, drinking and singing and having a good time.

The game itself was a bit of a disaster, losing 3-1 to the Russians. The stadium was a large bowl shape and during the game a Mexican wave was started. It progressed all the way round the stadium, until it got to the English. Instead of joining in, it got met with a load of V signs and abuse. Every time the wave came round, the same response happened and the rest of the stadium booed and jeered.

We don't help ourselves much at times do we ?

After the game Rob was still bothered about being English, so we drove over the border to near by Thionville, in France, which, for the record, none of us liked.

We had a problem the next morning, in that our petrol was dangerously low and as it was Sunday, nothing seemed open.

Robert had wandered off, before me and Steve woke, to try and find a petrol station, so when I woke and he really had gone this time, I was quite within my rights to start shouting again. But based on my two previous mornings experience, I simply took it as being another dream and went back to sleep.

We did eventually find fuel, just as the engine sucked up the last fumes of an empty tank and threatened to die on us, so off we went again.

By lunchtime, we seemed to have made good ground and had plenty of time to spare before our ferry later that evening, so when a beautiful little roadside hotel beckoned us, we stopped for a little light refreshment.

By now we were totally fluent in "Trois bieres si vous plait ," so we sat down in the warm afternoon sunshine to enjoy some bieres francais. We drank our first beers and ordered another "trois bieres si vous plait!". This time the cute little waitress said something back in French, but none of us had a clue what she said, so we just smiled and said "Oui, merci, trois bieres". She shook her head but more came and every time we ordered more, she would jabber away at us and then another more senior waitress would come and say something, but we just carried on smiling, even adding " un autre" (another) to the "trois bieres" for good measure. They stood there looking exasperated and talking between themselves, before giving that Gallic shrug and trois more bieres appeared. It was only when a rather large and posh wedding party arrived that we realised that they had probably been trying to get rid of the three rather scruffy football fans. But again we were buzzing, we were having such a good time, we didn't even try to understand them.

We were courteous enough not to get on the wedding photos and I'm sure we didn't spoil their day.

The trois bieres just kept coming, until we needed the loo. Me and Steve staggered to the toilet and were happily relieving our bladders when two rather elegantly dressed ladies walked in. We looked at each other in horror, both thinking exactly the same thing. "We are that pissed, that we are weeing in the ladies! Aaaaarrrgggh!" but when they were totally unphased by us being there, the penny dropped that we were in France and mixed toilets are the way things are there and we burst out laughing.

That afternoon was wonderful and we could have stayed there all day. In fact, we almost did. We totally forgot about the time, or the amount of money we had. Very, very fortunately for us we realised we had just over an hour to get to Ostend for our ferry, in time and hastily called for the bill.

We were all having such a good laugh (and were so pissed) that none of us even considered whether we would have enough money to pay. Equally as lucky was the fact that when we all emptied our pockets we literally had a few centimes to spare after we had paid.

We just made it back in time to get the ferry and arrived home absolutely knackered early the next morning. How Robert used to drink and drive the way he did remains a mystery, but I'm glad we can all safely look back on fantastic memories and think how stupid we were.

It is nice to see England fans eventually losing the reputation for aggro and that the national team is now supported in such great numbers with hardly any trouble. Unfortunately our European friends are about twenty years behind in terms of following football and still think that aggro is prevalent here. The reputation of England fans goes back to the seventies when they were undoubtedly the most fearsome in the world. This was simply a reflection of how the game was in the country at the time. As a result fans were more organised and passionate about the trouble so the reputation became rightly deserved.

The problem for the last ten years or so is that English fans have moved on. I am not saying that it doesn't happen anymore, it is just that as a rule English don't go looking for trouble. The European fans haven't caught up with the times and their hooligans still see it as a chance to match their hooligans against the notorious English.

A lovely non football example of this happened recently to my brother Mark.

He had gone on a trip to France with the lads, which was an excuse for a boozy weekend away. They had been out all afternoon and evening and just him and another bloke were slowly walking their way back to the hotel, when they realised that they were being shadowed by six or seven local youths. Eventually the youths caught right up with them and one of them asked them if they were English and which football team did they support.

It was obvious that they were in trouble, although most of the abuse they were getting was in French. It was apparent though that only one guy spoke English, as he seemed to be translating to the others what was being said, so they used some wonderful psychology on him.

Mark said to his mate "You know what's coming here don't you."

"Oh yeah. I know we are going to get a kicking, but let's make sure that we take one of them down with us"

"OK, lets get that gobby bas**rd in the white coat that's doing all the talking."

"Right, when they start, we will both go for him and give him a right hammering. At least we will have the satisfaction of totally taking him out."

On hearing this the translator in the white coat obviously had second thoughts, because there was a brief exchange of heated words in French, before the gang turned in the opposite direction and left them to it.

Maybe if our players and coaching staff of the national game had the same tactical awareness and passion and commitment of the fans we might have a better track record on the pitch.

Since winning the World Cup in 1966, there have been twenty one major International competitions and we have only made the last four on two occasions (inevitably losing on both occasions). For the richest league in the world that's not very good really is it and our latest crop of millionaire primadonnas can only finish third in a qualifying group for the 2008 European Championships.

Why on earth has nothing been done about this?

This is England. The mother of the game, with the richest and supposedly best league in the world, yet we can only deliver mediocrity at national level.

What the hell is happening?

CHAPTER 10

Why Watford?

A bit of a strange one this really. Before I started to think about this book in any detail, I would never have envisaged dedicating a whole chapter (albeit a small one) to Watford. There is no real connection between the clubs, no rivalry, nothing really. Yet when I started to 'research' this project I was surprised to find how many little incidents had occurred at a game with Watford.

So here it is my Watford chapter………..

Watford's ground has always seemed to be changing, like they never quite knew what to do with it, so as a result I have been on all four sides of the ground at different times. My first trip was to see a Terry Curran debut, when we were stood on the East side corner. I have also sat in the New Rous stand, but most events seemed to be when the away fans were on the Rookery end.

One trip was either early in the season, or late in the season, because it was a warm sunny day. I can't remember the season or even the score now, but I remember us taking a big following and that our little group were in two cars. One guy, who was a friend of my brothers, came down that day. He was a really nice lad called Mick, but wasn't a regular with us at games.

We were in Graham's car that day and Mick was in the same car as myself.

I was sat in the front and he was in the back.

We had the usual banter going south and had a few cans of beer on the journey, before stopping on the outskirts of Watford for a few drinks. By the time we set off for the game it is fair to say that we were in good spirits. I can remember being stuck in heavy traffic in Watford, as we headed towards the ground. I think it was a combination of football traffic and shoppers, as we were in an area heavily populated with shops. As we were hardly moving, Mick was stood up leaning out of the sun roof, greeting passers by as we slowly edged forward. Then without a word to anyone, he suddenly pulled his shirt off, followed quickly by trousers and pants and jumped out of the sunroof!

One of the first things I knew about it was seeing a pair of feet slide down the windscreen, followed by a hairy arse!

He was off. He vaulted over the other car in front, onto the roof and down the bonnet, then streaked up the high street!

We were killing ourselves laughing, as he suddenly came back into view, jumped in the car, just as we set off again and sat down as if it was totally normal.

The game itself is now an unknown quantity. I think we won or got a creditable draw, because we were all in a good mood as we left. Anyone who knows that end of the ground (or at least how it was, because I don't know if it has changed) will know that as you leave the ground you turn to the left and are faced with the back of a row of terraced houses. As a result you then turn a sharp 90 degrees to the right and carry on to make your way back to the street. Now I don't know if this was a regular occurrence at Watford or not, but on this occasion the exiting crowd was tightly packed in and so making the right turn at the bottom of the gardens was becoming difficult, with the crowd pressure from behind to go straight on becoming more intense.

Eventually something had to give and it did.

The garden fence gave way and the crowd surged forward, unable to make the right turn. I was lucky in that I was just behind this situation and only got pushed as far as the geraniums at the back. The garden filled up very quickly though and it must have been an awesome sight for the owners of the houses, who were watching through their upstairs windows.

"Mabel, the Jones's garden is full of Sheffield Wednesday supporters again."

It was totally unintentional and there was no malice intended, but the destruction must have been intense. Can you imagine the owners coming home later that evening, after an afternoons shopping and looking out of the back window. All their neighbour's gardens looking immaculate, whilst their garden, in isolation, had been flattened by a herd of stampeding wild elephants.

The funny thing was that those unfortunate enough to be pushed into the garden had no choice but to stay there, milling around aimlessly, until the crowds had all gone past, to enable them to get out. (It also makes me laugh thinking about if the owners were actually at home. Imagine sat watching the results on TV and turning round to see two hundred people with their faces squashed against your patio window.)

I can remember there been a few scuffles after that too, nothing serious, but when we got back to the car, Mick had gone missing. We waited for a while, but he didn't turn up.

No mobiles in those days, so there was no way of getting in touch with him. We waited and waited, before deciding that there was nothing we could do and set off home.

We later found that he had been arrested. I'd like to think for leading an attack on rival fans in nothing but his underpants, but this was never confirmed.

Mick was arrested and spent the night in the cells, so didn't get home until the following day. After a discussion with his wife, it was probably decided that he shouldn't come with us to any more away games.

Another funny incident was following a 4-0 defeat.

The incident happened on the M1, long after the game had finished. Graham had taken his car that day, which was a 3.0 litre Ford Capri and boy could it move.

There was a car full of Watford fans travelling up the M1 also after the game and as was expected, they made '4-0' and 'wan**r' gestures as they passed.

It was a mistake.

They only wanted to go one short junction up the Motorway and they must have felt pretty safe in their car, laughing and gesturing as they indicated to pull off the Motorway. Graham had other ideas however and swiftly undertook them to block off their exit and keeping them on the Motorway. Although maybe a little surprised by this action, it didn't seem to bother our Watford friends too much and if anything they gestured more.

As the next junction approached, they once more indicated to leave the M1, only for Graham to again position his car between them and the exit.

The same happened again at the next junction, where this time the driver put his foot right down to get some space in front of us to enable him to pull off. However he had nowhere near enough power to match the Capri's 3 litres and so with some pretty risky driving Graham flew up the inside and shepherded them back onto the Motorway!

This carried on for some time, with every attempt being blocked. Sometimes it was scary and down right dangerous, but with every junction that came and went our friends were physically shrinking.

No more the gestures and abuse, now it was avoiding all forms of eye contact except to exchange anxious glances between each other, as they tried to figure out what best to do.

It was eventually Junction 21, near Leicester when they successfully managed to get off the Motorway and probably seventy miles further North than they anticipated, but I am sure they must have been relieved as hell, to get off and see the Capri continuing north.

They must have been seriously worried that they would be brought all the way back to Sheffield.

Another odd exchange happened at a home game with Watford at the end of the 1978-79 season. Wednesday ended that season, strangely enough, with five consecutive home games and the first of those was against table topping Watford.

It just seemed a normal home game for us, as we drove along Penistone Road, heading to The Gate pub, as usual, but as we got near the Owlerton Speedway stadium, we saw an odd site. There were several cars that had been turned over. I mean physically turned over, on their roofs!

It was no surprise to see that all the upended vehicles were from Watford. I still don't know what went off to this day, for such action to take place, but the incident is also reported in Dougie and Eddy Brimson's book (which if I remember right is called 'Everywhere we go.')

Watford anticipated bringing a large following up that day, but they report that most fans turned back saying it was too dangerous. We didn't know what had provoked such a reaction, but it even continued inside the ground. We were in the North Stand as usual, but the Leppings Lane end, which was normally where away fans would stand, was taken by Wednesday hooligans. The small group of Watford fans that had made it

216

to the ground were also in the North Stand and although safe from physical attack, were subject to a constant bombardment of any object that could be thrown at them.

It seems so strange nowadays, looking back at this situation, that it was allowed to happen.

Hoolies were throwing anything they could at these Watford fans, with the Police standing by and watching, making no attempt to stop it, or move them somewhere safe.

There is no history between the clubs and we never did find out what that was all about.

Another eventful trip was back down at Vicarage Road on Boxing Day 1987. If I remember rightly it was an early kick off for some reason, which gave the game a slightly odd feel to it.

It was quite an important game as both sides were seriously struggling at the bottom, so going a goal down within 39 seconds was not an ideal start.

We had a strange visitor with us that day too. Mark had been to Gambia on holiday earlier in the year and got friendly with one of the locals. I don't have a clue how to spell his name, but it was something like Mumadi.

Mark had invited him over to England and was rather surprised when he decided to come over at Christmas.

It was his first visit outside Africa, so Lord knows what he must have made of it all, when he got dragged down to Watford for a game of football. The first half was quite eventful, because after going 1-0 down, we responded well and by 20 minutes were 3-1 up.

I can still see his look of total bewilderment, as he stood stationary, open mouthed, watching us all scream, dance and hug each other as each goal went in.

I don't think he could quite fathom it all out.

The rest of the game passed without incident, other than a solo attempt at the Watford fans by one guy.

We were on the Rookery end again, which in those days was split down the middle to separate rival fans, with a no mans land between the two fences. For some reason this Wednesdayite thought he would lead a solo raid on the Watford fans and climbed the wall at the back of the terrace.

The way it was constructed from memory, was a brick wall, to about six foot and then a vertical corrugated metal panel above it, leading up to the roof. This meant there was a thin ledge, along the top of the brick wall, which you could carefully edge your way across, should you be mad enough to want to get across the divide.

This was exactly what he did.

I don't know whether he was very drunk, gullible or did it for a bet, but this guy found himself, slowly edging his way across from the Wednesday side towards the Watford fans about ten yards away. This obviously caused some attention, as he was egged on by the away fans and goaded over by the home fans. I mean, it was absolute madness. God knows what he was going to do when he got across at them. One against about 1,500 are not good odds.

I think the closer he got to them, the more he realised this was not such a good idea, so when the Police came and ushered him down with two or three yards to go, I think he happily took the arrest. Our Gambian chum was even more mystified by this action when we explained that the soloist would have been pulled apart, limb from limb, had he dropped into the Watford fans.

We happily left with a win and retired to the nearest public house for a few hours liquid refreshment, to try and explain the intricacies of English football and society.

I think he was glad to go back home a few days later.

CHAPTER 11

Hospitality Boxes

I don't know what it is about hospitality boxes, but there always seems to be something happens when I visit one. In my working life I have been quite fortunate to have lots of invites to sporting events, both as a buyer and in sales. I guess it is probably something to do with the effect that huge quantities of free beer has on people. "Entertaining" customers has many different forms, but my experience has nearly always been that of total abuse of company money for all concerned.

As much as the stories in this section are football related, of course it didn't have to be football to have the company credit card hammered. Cricket was always one of my favourite days out. As usual, not many customers ever came with us and those that did were usually hand picked as being up for a good old jolly with the lads. Cricket is an absolutely fantastic day out (particularly if the weather is good) that I would recommend to any football fan. The western terrace at Headingley was our preferred choice. It seems that half the crowd come in fancy dress, so the atmosphere is already in party mode. As much as it always starts off quite civilised, an all day drinking session inevitably results in a mass of people in a drunken state and getting up to all sorts of pranks. There is a real camaraderie about cricket fans with absolutely none of the rivalry and hostility that you find at football. I only ever really went to International matches, so you don't generally get two large rival groups, but even where that happens the banter is pretty good.

I was quite lucky in a lot of ways, because virtually everywhere I worked, I ended up with a pretty good bunch of lads (I say 'lads' in a non sexist way, it is just that there weren't any girls in the teams.)

On one occasion I had moved from one site to another which was based in Stoke. My former colleagues decided that they would have their next sales meeting therefore at Stoke, so we could meet up.

Holding sales meetings at different sites was common practice, as it gave us the excuse to have a night out on the company's money, all in the name of team building. It also livened up the inevitably dull monthly meetings too.

Having said that, we would also find our own way of livening things up.

One thing we did was to set up secret little challenges such as having to get certain words into your presentation. Every month you had to give a fifteen minute presentation on what was happening with key accounts, which was tedious to say the least. To liven it up we would give each other a word such as "Brass rubbings" or "Porcupine" and you had to some how get this word into your presentation. Of course it was kept secret between two or three of us and the Directors and managers present would wonder what the hell you were on about, when you suddenly digressed to mention "cheesecake" for no apparent reason, but it made us giggle (quietly.)

At one company we had a game called "Buzzword Bingo", where we would prepare a bingo card for each of us, but instead of numbers we had buzzwords or phrases, such as "Teamwork", "Singing from the same hymn sheet" or "I've got a window in my diary…". As these phrases inevitably came out during the meeting, you crossed them off your sheet, just like Bingo. When you had got them all, you had to shout "Is that the fire bell?" (which was ridiculous, as the fire bell was that loud it ripped your ears off). The beauty about such stupid games was the fact that the Directors and depart*mental* heads had no idea what was happening and comments such as "You are all behaving like school children" simply made it more fun.

To keep the Stoke trip 'real', the visit would include a site tour and when they visited Stoke, I volunteered to take the guys round the factory when they finished their meeting.

By three o'clock they decided they had had enough and left for the hotel and I was asked to join them there, instead of doing a 'stupid bloody factory tour'. I had to decline because I had so much work to do and eventually left at 5.30.

When I got to the hotel, they were all absolutely pissed and just consuming their third bottle of Champagne (it was one of the lads birthday) with no intention of stopping drinking.

We had a few more before heading into one of the 'Stoke' towns for more beer and an excellent curry (I say excellent, because it tasted superb. The owners were obviously not impressed with our rather loud behaviour though and the fact that we set fire to the table cloth. I presume that they took revenge in the ingredients as the next day, without exception, every single one of us were stuck to the toilet for about four hours!)

It just so happened that there was a Gentleman's Club very close to the hotel (strange how that always seemed to happen), so we finished the night in a lap dancing club. How the hell they got their expenses signed off I will never know, but that was a typical night on the company.

This was a common example of how company money was spent, just on a normal night out and I am sure I could write a whole book on this subject alone.

In 1984 I worked as a buyer for a local company called Crosby Kitchens. Crosby will be in Wednesday history as the first company to sponsor the blue and white shirts. We even had a visit from the team to the factory and got to meet the likes of John Pearson, Tony Cunningham and Peter Eustace which was great.

I spent five happy years there and there were some real characters. One of the great things about CK was table tennis. The staff canteen had two tables and it became the ritual to play for half an hour straight after lunch. This in itself caused some biological issues, as running around straight after a heavy cooked lunch gave me digestive problems. This manifested itself in particularly bad wind for the next hour or so and I must admit that even I found the smells pretty revolting. It got so bad that it became customary for my boss to disappear out of the office that we shared for the first hour after lunch. This was actually quite a bonus though as he could be quite a miserable git! I think my disgusting farts was one of the main reasons that we later got moved to separate offices on the executive floor. Double bonus!

I absolutely loved the table tennis sessions as I love all racquet sports, but I didn't get off to the best of starts with the game. For anyone that hasn't played TT, there is quite a technique to hitting the ball and it

221

can take a bit of getting used to. When I had played before, the bats that I had used were the ones that were rock hard plywood with nobbly bits on the bat face. The ones used at work were covered with a more professional rubber that could impart huge amounts of spin to the little ping pong ball. Consequently any new starters who were up for playing got absolutely slaughtered. The amount of 'chop' to give backspin was so great that unless you read the spin and countered it by giving your own spin, the ball would simply fall off your bat. No matter how hard I tried to hit the ball up, I simply couldn't get it over the net. I only weighed about 6 stone at the time (I'm a fat b*stard now at a whopping 7 stone) so my inability to get the ball over the net lead to all sorts of mickey taking. "Come on John, it's only a ping pong ball for Gods sake! Haven't you got the bloody strength to hit it over the net!" Of course everyone were killing themselves laughing at me, whereas I was getting frustrated and furious. There was one guy called Mel, who was superb at chopping the ball and made me look like a complete and utter idiot. He was a real great character, so his piss taking was something else and he revelled in my humiliation. God how I hated that guy for the first week! Of course, after a weeks suffering I eventually worked out how to play it and quickly improved.

Fortunately there was soon another sucker that joined us and this time I was mercilessly joining in, enjoying the fact that it was some other poor sod that was suffering.

We had some great games, because we were all pretty good. We even had a young lady joined our ranks, but she could play anyway, so never went through the humiliation that us other TT novices did. She had real technique and could smash like a pro. I mean she put everything into it, great footwork, full body action, everything. She had a terrific figure too, so was always popular with us when she played. One particular day though, she attracted a massive crowd. She was wearing a wrap over skirt, which was fine until she hit her first smash. The wrap in the skirt parted as her leg position stretched the skirt open and revealed her long leg. This was nice enough, but that day she was wearing stockings, so every smash resulted in a flash of her stocking tops and every now and then a strap of suspender. Now the factory was probably 99% male, so word seemed to pass round very quickly and we soon had people queuing up outside to watch us play. Every shot was matched with 'Ooooohs' and 'Aahhhhhs' and every winner cheered. People were coming over to see what all the fuss was and why this game of TT was attracting such a crowd. The canteen became packed.

We had a rule that the winning pair stayed on, so she spent all lunch break playing, as no one opposing her could concentrate enough on their shots. I still don't know whether she was aware of what she was showing, but she carried on regardless.

Oh how I love table tennis.

One of my first experiences of corporate hospitality was in September 1984 at Liverpool.

Wednesday had finally arrived back in the First Division after a 14 year absence and were doing quite nicely. We had been to Anfield the previous season for a league cup quarter final replay. There were 12,000 Owls there that night and despite being thumped 3-0, every one who was there would remember a resounding "We'll be back" chant that went on for ages at the end.

Well, sure enough a few months later we were indeed back. Instead of going with my usual mob I was invited by a shipping company, based in Liverpool, to go with them, so me and a good friend of mine, who was a sad Liverpool fan took up their offer.

We met in the City centre and were sufficiently fed and watered before being driven to the ground. We weren't actually in an executive box, instead we had centre stand seats and a pretty good view of the game and the masses of Wednesdayites over to our left.

Now at the time, Liverpool were reigning European Champions, having beaten Roma in the final in Rome some 4 months earlier, so I steeled myself beforehand that in all likelihood I was going to take some stick and Wednesday would be heavily beaten.

I was pleasantly surprised with how we started and when after only 8 minutes, Bruce Grobelaar made a hash of a clearance and Imre Varadi hit a 30 yard shot into an empty goal, I was bleeding ecstatic.

I leaped up screaming my head off and became very conscious of the fact that although the thousands of Wednesdayites to my left were going mad, and that there seemed to be loads in the stand opposite, I was the only one in the entire stand where I was, that was cheering.

I got stacks of abuse, but nothing too severe as there were still 82 minutes left and everyone knew (myself included) that this was just a glitch and Liverpool would go on to win.

That's the way it went and Wednesday became pegged back into their own 18 yard box as the shots rained down. We were saved by the woodwork a few times, some bad finishing and some desperate defending, but amazingly at half time we were sill hanging on at 1-0.

The second half continued in a similar vein to the first, with the woodwork helping us out and then in the 68th minute a break by Brian Marwood down the right wing and another fumble by Grobelaar left Gary Shelton with the ball at his feet 6 yards out in front of the Kop.

Even in my slightly inebriated state, I swear time stopped still for a second, before Shelts thumped it in for 2-0.

I went absolutely mental, but it is a funny thing celebrating an important goal on your own. Normally we would all be in a big heap, hugging each other and falling down rows of seats, but on your own, you become very aware of your solitary shouts.

The abuse that I got was pretty severe this time.

A whole heap of four letter words were thrown down at me. I can even remember a fat lady in her 60's wrapped in about five red scarves, telling me to sit my "fat f***ing Yorkshire arse down" (which I thought was a compliment, because no one had ever told me I had a fat arse before) but I was far too gone to care by now and continued screaming and yelling my head off like a deranged lunatic.

It's not that I was brave or hard, I was simply too ecstatic to care.

Some scouse pillock carried on mouthing off at me, so I stood up and tried to justify that I had watched Wednesday for 15 years, all in the bottom divisions and here we were winning 2-0 at the home of the reigning European Champions and of course I was happy! But I don't think anyone heard, because I got shouted down with abuse and all sorts of threats.

The guy that brought us looked pretty pissed off too, because, one, his team were losing and, two, he looked as though he would have to justify to his boss, how he had allowed a major customer to get beaten up!

He tried to get me to leave before the end, but I was having none of it and happily stayed and applauded the lads off the pitch.

How I didn't get smacked that day I don't know. But it was bloody fantastic!

My next experience was almost a year to the day later. We got invited down to an executive box at Tottenham the following season and this time my boss came with me. It was a lot safer being behind glass but it still ended up with conflict.

The production manager where I worked, was called "Clarkey" (maybe something to do with his surname being Clarke) and he was a Spurs fan. So with the obvious banter flying around before the game, he made sure that he ventured south for the match also.

As the ground began to fill up, we noticed with delight, that by a bizarre coincidence, Clarkey happened to be sat about ten rows directly in front of the box that we were in.

We had quite a few beers by kick off, so when Lee Chapman scored with a diving header after 20 minutes, we were up banging on the glass trying to get Clarkey's attention and making 1-0 gestures.

Unfortunately the lead only lasted 10 minutes before a certain Chris Waddle equalised. Inevitably, we got the same reaction from all the Spurs fans around us, who obviously didn't realise that we were only gesturing at our chum in the crowd. They thought we were giving it large to everyone, so they made sure they let us know what they all thought.

The game was run by Waddle that day, ably supported by Ossie Ardiles and Glenn Hoddle and the goals kept pouring in.

Every time Spurs scored the glass would get a thumping and gestures of 2-1, 3-1, 4-1 and 5-1 from everyone in range.

Even the punters in the neighbouring boxes were having a go!

Ah well, you can't win them all.

I had another good trip to White Hart Lane a number of years later as well. This time it wasn't to see Wednesday. The company that I worked for at the time had a box there and I took a load of Sunderland fans down, who were customers.

I was careful to only invite the 'lads' down though, so it meant we could have a good time too, instead of 'working' and having to be a 'host'.

I arranged to meet a colleague, Andrew, in London at Kings Cross station, so we could get across to White Hart Lane together.

He had just started seeing one of the girls in the office, so we met up early, in able to have a few drinks and hear the gory details of his new relationship, before our customers turned up.

We got to the ground in plenty of time and started to abuse the company expense account. It was so good, that I really didn't want the customers to arrive, as we were having such a good laugh.

I'm not a good drinker anyway, so having a few at lunchtime is pretty lethal for me. There is nothing like a good lunchtime session though and so by the time our Mackem friends arrived, we were pretty pissed. We of course did the decent thing and stopped our personal chat, to mix with our guests.

I think three of them worked at our clients site but the other three I had never met before (totally against company guidelines of course, as we were only supposed to entertain, important decision makers), but they were all good lads and the drinking continued at a pace, with loads of wine and beer being consumed. It turned out to be quite fun, especially as Wednesday won 2-0 away at Bradford   (which I was following on the TV at the back of the room). In fact, it's a good job they did, as my cheering kept waking Andrew, who had fallen asleep, face pressed against the glass window at the front of the box, during the second half, much to everyone's amusement.

The game ended with a victory to Spurs and we left reasonably early, to get our train home, while our Wearsiders headed for a night out in Luton (don't ask.)

The train tickets we had, meant that we had to be on our return train by about 7 o'clock, otherwise we had to pay again, so we made sure we left in time. Now coming to North London seemed pretty easy. We got a tube part of the way and then had to get a local train to the ground, so going back would be easy, yes?

Wrong!

We stood on the platform chatting away, getting a few odd looks as our northern accents would leave Spurs ears to think we were obviously Sunderland fans, but I can't say we were bothered a great deal.

Anyway along comes the train, heading in the opposite direction, to the one we arrived on, so on we got, sat down and continued our chat. It was only after 15 minutes or so, that we realised this was supposed to be a 5 minute journey and we hadn't even seen a station. The train then came to a halt and we were stopped for another 10 minutes in the middle of nowhere. By now we were getting a little unsure of where we were supposed to be heading. The two lads opposite us seemed completely off their heads, so we didn't get any sort of rational answer that we could understand. We therefore asked another guy stood near by, who told us he was Norwegian and didn't understand us, followed by the next who was Greek and another who was, well to be honest I don't know, I gave up by then. That's London for you, full of bloody foreigners!

It was clear though, that we were on totally the wrong train, when we eventually pulled into a station, like Walthamstow, or somewhere obscure. We got off and took our chances and eventually found a tube

226

station. I was getting a little bit anxious by now, because I certainly didn't have anything like the £70 or £80 I thought I would need to get home, if I missed the last train and I just felt too old to be having to hide in the loo from the ticket collector!

I had 12 minutes before my train was due to leave and we hadn't a bloody clue where we were and not in a great state to think as rationally as we should. By pure luck, there was a direct tube to Kings Cross and I arrived, by a lot of good fortune and some damn fine sprinting, just as the train was about to leave. Andrew believed he had a few minutes to spare, so opted to buy his new girlfriend some sexy underwear to take home.

It was a bad decision, as he missed his train and had to stump up the £70 (or at least the company did) to get home.

He did tell me later though that she looked great in split crotch panties and matching peep hole bra!

That same year I was invited up to a customer's box at Newcastle. They were playing Bayer Leverkusen in the second round of group matches of the Champions League, so I thought it should be a good one.

It was a strange old night all round really.

I got there in plenty of time, so thought I'd get parked up easy enough. Wrong!

In rip off Britain, you don't get anything for free and unless I coughed up a minimum of £5 I wasn't parking anywhere. Reluctantly, I found a car park, only to realise that I didn't have enough change for the ticket machine. Strange occurrence number one was asking a Scottish guy if he could change me a £10 note, to which he said no, but would give me £5 in coins anyway.

I was flabbergasted! I thought Scots were like Yorkshiremen with the generosity taken out, but this guy just gave me five £1 coins. Feeling a bit confused still, I walked back to my car and was aware of an attractive young lady heading towards me. I assumed she was going to ask me for some change for the car also, but instead asked if I was going to the game. I said yes, and she told me that she had driven down from some place near Edinburgh and she came to nearly every home game. I was still waiting to be asked for change, but she didn't. Now I was getting seriously confused! In fact she was getting very friendly and asked me where in the ground I was sat, as it would be nice to meet up inside. I told her I was in the executive box, but she was happy to walk up to the ground with me anyway. We were chatting away and she was being very flirty.

As we got to the main stand, I made my excuses to leave, to which she asked what I was doing afterwards, as she was staying overnight and maybe we could meet up for a drink afterwards.

She was quite an attractive lady, so I looked around to see if there was a hidden camera crew filming and Jeremy Beadle was around somewhere in disguise, but no. I said that I didn't know what time I would be out and she said she would wait in the car park for a while after the game.

I was still confused, as I simply don't get this blatantly chatted up, especially not by such an attractive woman as this!

This was a strange old evening.

I made my way to the glass front of the stand and waited at the bottom of the lifts, where I had arranged to meet my hosts and who should be stood there but our old friend David Pleat. He was obviously waiting to be picked up by someone as well (carefully resists the temptation to deliver the obvious punchline!)

Now for anyone not close to SWFC, David Pleat is widely acknowledged by the fans as the manager responsible for the start of clubs decline, so when our eyes met a few yards apart, I couldn't help but blurt out "David Pleat!". He smiled and nodded, as if to say, 'Yes that's right I'm a celebrity, you will want my autograph', but instead I found myself instantly saying "You're the idiot responsible for wrecking Sheffield Wednesday."

His face was an absolute picture! Fortunately for me, the person he was meeting walked up at that moment and shepherded him away, but as he went he turned back and looked at me, totally perplexed, trying to work out why as Director of football at Tottenham, attending a European game in Newcastle, a total stranger walked up to him and accused him of wrecking Sheffield Wednesday!

I'm glad he was ushered away at that time as I don't know what the hell I would have said next. We would probably have stood there in an embarrassing silence for 5 minutes, but I'm glad I said it all the same. I can't stand the bloke. He talks such utter nonsense.

As for the game, I am always hearing about how wonderful these Geordie fans are, so thought the atmosphere would be electric for a big European game, especially as they were so close to making the quarter finals. They won the game 3-1, with Alan Shearer scoring a hat trick, but the atmosphere was very poor.

I ended up sitting in the main stand, due to a cock up with the arrangements and I just kept thinking that they don't appreciate what they have got.

The only time they sang was after a goal and then it went back to being quiet.

After the game, I stayed to hear Alan Shearer's speech in the sponsors lounge, but had to leave part way through, as I knew the car park would close soon and I didn't fancy being stuck there all night. (No I did honestly. That woman never entered my head)

Being a legend up there, everyone hung on to every word he said, so when I got up and walked out, Shearer looked at me as I walked past and said, "was it something I said?" which got a big laugh from his admirers. I almost told him he would be better at Wednesday, but thought it best to bite my lip and so smiled and left.

I walked back to the car, wondering if my admirer was there still, but she had obviously left after pulling some fat Geordie bloke!

One of the companies that I worked for had an executive box at Old Trafford, so I got to see quite a bit of Man United in the 1990's (as long as it didn't coincide with a Wednesday game.)

Most of the matches that I went to were European games, so I saw some great games, but usually not beyond the quarter final stage. Once it got to the semi finals of the Champions League, it was funny how the box got commandeered by some high ranking member of the board. We had the same 'host' for most of the season, so we built up a good rapport with her. She would welcome us, sort out drinks and serve the food and because it all went on to the company bill, she would get a very generous tip too.

At the start of one season, we got to know the new 'host' and during one of the games, she told us about the last game of the previous season, where a colleague of hers had worked our box.

Man United needed to win their last game to secure the title, so the box got taken by a very senior person. The box seated eight, but apparently there was only two people turned up for this game, which the host was surprised at, with it being such a major game. Apparently the host had been given a very, very, generous tip, well before the game had even started and soon it dawned on her that she was expected to provide more than just the usual service. Allegedly she wasn't that type of girl and declined the request, although we later heard that someone from outside the club did indeed provide the required service, if you know what I mean.

Certainly nothing like that ever happened, when we had the box. (No, it didn't. It really didn't. What are you like!)

Of course the one league game that I was interested in attending at Old Trafford, was when Wednesday played there. I ended up going two Saturdays running as it happened. Barnsley made a very brief visit to the Premiership, so I took a customer, who was a Barnsley supporter, to see a 7-0 thrashing. The fixture list deemed that Wednesday (who were in the relegation zone) visited the following Saturday, so I can't say that we expected anything from the game, but it was a chance to see the match and enjoy some hospitality.

The box was ridiculously abused at the time, so who ever wanted the box could have it. Of course, you were supposed to take customers with you and to a large extent they were invited, but it was mostly the more 'matey' types, where you could have a good laugh, rather than the important 'decision makers.'

For the Wednesday game there were no customers whatsoever. It was me, my brothers and my friends.

We got there nice and early and went straight in the ground. I had a polo shirt on with a Wednesday logo and showed the eight passes to the 'bouncer' on the door to let us in. Melv was the second one in and as we walked up the stairs to the box, he told me that the 'bouncer' had called me a w*nker after I had gone in (because of the SWFC shirt, before anybody comments!)

I asked if he was sure and Mel said that it was definitely aimed at me.

Now having the might of a corporate hospitality box behind you, makes a huge difference to a verbal confrontation with an 18 stone muscle bound Neanderthal.

I wouldn't even dream of picking a fight with such a thug, but both he and I knew that corporate hospitality carries a lot of weight, so I wasted no time in charging back down the stairs to confront him.

"Have you got something to say to me?" I asked him, instantly interrupting the next group of entrants and stopping them in their tracks (They must have thought I was right hard, or more likely a total lunatic, wanting to pick a fight with Goliath here.)

"I'm not sure what you mean Sir" he politely replied.

He did. He knew exactly what I meant and both of us knew who had the upper hand.

I'm sure he just wanted me to go, but I was having none of it.

"You called me a w*inker, in front of clients, as we were coming in. One of them told me."

"No I didn't."

"Yes you did."

"No I didn't."

"Yes you did."

It went on.

"Look can we just get in please," one of the punters held up asked.

"No," I told him firmly. (I was enjoying this!)

Eventually someone in authority came over to see what the problem was.

I was getting carried away now!

"I don't expect MY company to shell out £30,000 for an executive box and be called a w*nker in front of clients by some moron in a bow tie, as I come in."

The senior guy couldn't apologise enough, despite Thug boy still denying it.

He apologised profusely and told me that he would be dealt with later.

Satisfied I had made my point, I went back up to the box, where everyone else was, feeling pretty pleased with myself (No. No-one bothered to come down with me to confront the bouncer. They just wanted free beer.)

Man United were top of the league and reigning Champions, so as expected the game was pretty one sided, but I don't think anyone minded too much. The 'free' wine and beer was being consumed in huge quantities, which helped numb everyone to the drubbing on the field.

If you have never been in an executive box, the rules are that you cannot consume alcohol once the game has started, so the common trick is to pour your beer into a cup and saucer, so to the outside world, it looks as though you are drinking tea like it is going out of fashion and boy did we drink some tea that day!

231

Wednesday were 6-0 down, when we eventually pulled a goal back, to great jocular celebrations and banging on the glass window at the 53,000 Man United fans.

Normally this sort of behaviour would bring quite a hostile reaction from those in the ground near to the box, but at 6-1 up, they all seemed to see the funny side of us singing "You're not singing anymore."

I saw 14 goals in those 2 games, 13 for Man United, but the important thing for us (and it was totally worth the 6-1 beating) was that it signified the last game in charge for David Pleat, who was duly sacked the next day.

During that same season, I went to the Man U v Nottingham Forest game and did actually take customers. Not just customers, but important ones at that.

They were late getting to the game, because of traffic, whereas my boss, Peter, got there particularly early and with nothing else to do, started to drink the contents of the wine cellar.

Now Peter, liked a drink anyway, so given a good two hour start on everyone else, he was pretty pissed by the time our guests arrived.

We had our meal as soon as they arrived, but were still sat eating as the game kicked off, with Forest scoring in the first minute or so. No one jumped up or cheered because no one saw it. One of the Forest folk spotted it on the TV that shows the game in the box and they all sort of commented 'Oh good we've scored' and 'What a pity that we didn't actually see it'. For the next ten minutes or so they were pulling Peter's leg about the score (for he was a Man U fan), but soon United equalised and he jumped up cheering his head off. I think they forgave him, as he was clearly quite tipsy, but when a couple of minutes later Man U scored again, they clearly weren't prepared for "Two f***ing one, get in there you Nottingham ba****ads!"

Even I was horrified!

Now Peter was quite a character and could get away with quite a lot, but he had way over stepped the mark this time. You can get away with it with some people, but these guys were serious suits! The big difference also, was that these guys weren't even proper football fans and didn't understand how you can get so carried away with it. For Peter to be in their faces swearing his head off was totally incomprehensible to them.

232

I was seriously worried that I would end up losing a £1 million plus account and it took a lot of wine in tea cups, before they eventually saw the funny side of it.

If I had to choose my best Executive box trip, it would have to be Crystal Palace for the 1991 -92 seasons.

Our good friend Borman was living in London where he ran a pub. He won some form of Brewery competition and the prize was an executive box for any London team of his choosing. Wednesday had had a cracking season and as it drew towards the end, were still in the running to win the League title (although I don't think any of us thought that was the case.)

Our sights had been firmly placed on the top three, as that would mean qualification for the UEFA Cup and the glory of a long awaited European trip. Having achieved one of my ambitions of playing at Wembley in a Cup Final in the previous season, qualifying for Europe was my final fan ambition.

The run in left it pretty much a two horse race between us and Arsenal for that third place. With just eight games to go, we were 10 points clear of arse and the main threat we believed would come from fourth placed Liverpool. It wasn't even as if we were going to go on one of the crazy runs where we throw it away, it was just that arse didn't lose any of their last seventeen games, so when we visited Southampton with just four games to go, the gap had closed to three points with goal difference (as usual) heavily against us. In fact it got so important that I can remember for the only time that I know of in history, that a Sheffield United goal was wildly cheered by Wednesdayites. We were drawing 0-0 at the Dell at the time while arse were playing at our piggy friends. The half time scores were read out and "Sheffield United 1 Arsenal 0" was greeted with enormous cheers.

We went on to win that game 1-0 courtesy of a David Hirst goal, whilst arse drew 1-1 with the pigs, which opened the gap up by a further two points.

A 2-0 home win against Norwich the following week, meant that we needed two points to be mathematically certain of qualifying for Europe, or hope that arse would drop points.

The further worrying thing for us was that our last game of the season was against Liverpool, so we really didn't want to have to go into that game needing anything. As a result the Palace game became vital and guess which game Mr. Borman had requested for his prize?

Oh Yes!

Although we hadn't seen Borm for a few years (I'm sure he left because of the stick he used to get) he invited us all down and we rendezvoused at his pub. It was very early, but the beer went down anyway.

I was driving home later, so of course stayed sober. The same can't be said for the rest of them.

The guy who was our 'host' said it was the first time anybody had drunk the box dry and he had to go and re stock the box bar.

It was a great afternoon....... Just. Because we came mightily close to being thrown out after severely winding the Palace fans up, below us on the Whitehorse Lane terrace. It was all just good banter to us, but some of their fans were taking it a bit too serious, so when a rather fat lad in a stupid coat started mouthing off at us, it started to get a bit more personal.

It resulted in a visit by the officials to warn us about our conduct, but when the game actually got under way, it all got back to normal and the focus was on the game.

Paul Williams gave us a 1-0 lead and at half time arse were only drawing at Chelsea.

It was looking good.

It was looking even better with ten minutes to go, when the TV in the box told us that Chelsea had gone 1-0 up also.

We are going nuts, but as we know, football is a funny old game and in the 87th minute, not only do arse equalise, but so do Palace.

Bloody hell Wednesday. Only we can do this.

Those last few minutes drag by forever.

First the whistle goes at Selhurst Park and we have secured a point. It is now all down to the Chelsea arse game.

God this is agony!

It takes forever, but finally.....Chelsea 1 Arsenal......1 and the box erupts. It's like we have won it ourselves. We are screaming and hugging each other in a big heap. Beer is being sprayed everywhere, in the absence of Champagne and there are tears too.

I bloody hate football sometimes. No most of the time, but it is times like this that make it so special.

The feeling is impossible to explain other than sheer f*****g joy!

It got silly after that. Who would we play? Real Madrid? Barcelona? Ajax? Benfica? (as it happened it was Spora Luxembourg. Spora who? Yes, exactly!)

The song that had been sung on the terraces for the last few weeks (a little hopeful at first and then the nearer we got, a lot more cautious) was now booming out.

"And our friends are all aboard, Jim McCalliog and David Ford,

Then along came David Hirst, Roland Nilsson and Paul Warhurst,

We're all going on a European tour, A European tour, A European tour."

We must have stayed in the box a good half an hour after that just singing and laughing and, yes even more drinking.

This was amazing!

We eventually left the box and headed out. The team was just leaving to get on the coach, so we had a brief chat with them and congratulated them. The thing is they all looked disappointed. They genuinely believed the late Palace goal had robbed them of a chance of the title, as that is what they were aiming for.

Strangely, we never realised that.

Europe was damn mighty fine to us and we were on top of the world.

Borm had his cousin down for the game too. She was actually a Unitedite, but he invited her anyway. I think she was about 14 if I remember rightly and she had been helping herself to alcohol un-noticed. As a result she was pretty pissed too and Borm was struggling to keep her under control.

No one really noticed when she told Borm she needed the toilet (and we are talking No 2's here) and said she could not wait any longer.

Without any hesitation, she climbed over a wall and did a poo in their front garden. No word of a lie.

We were horrified.

Eventually we got back to the car and drove across London to Borm's pub.

It was brilliant. There was only Mark, Kev Lancs and myself in our car, but we were rocking! Unusually, we had a cassette tape on of all the early Diana Ross and The Supremes stuff, and we were singing our bloody heads off. Fantastic!

CHAPTER 12

Final Word

OK now the serious bit.

Well, I guess the first thing I would like to say, is how much I have enjoyed putting this together. Researching into this book has brought back such great memories. I have loved revisiting my life and it has brought back memories of so many people and little events that happened, sometimes not connected with football, that have made me realise how lucky I am to have had such a good life so far.

The scary thing is that it all goes by so frighteningly quick and events that seemed so fresh in my memory are now scarily twenty or thirty years old! How the hell has that happened then?

It seems strange when I think ahead of the day when I die (a bit bloody morbid! - Ed) and I won't be there. All the thousands of games that I have lived through, sweating, screaming, agonising and yet one day there will come a time when Wednesday are playing and I won't be there. It will all just carry on as normal and hardly anyone will even notice my empty seat. Sad really, but that's life ands we should maybe try and remember sometimes that it is just a game, regardless of what Bill Shankly said.

I guess looking back it puts a lot of the individual games into perspective, in that what seems such a massively important thing at the time probably won't even be remembered in a few years.

Don't get me wrong I still leap up and scream abuse at the referee for yet another incompetent decision, but when you look back over the years there are so many games that I don't even remember anymore.

Life flies by so quick. When you are twenty you think you will stay like that forever, but things in life change so slowly that it creeps up on you without you even realising.

So, whatever team you support, enjoy your time as much as you possibly can and savour those happy moments (unless you are a blade or l**ds!) (or any of the SOF) (oh, and you can probably add Man City to that because since Sheikh Yabouti has bought them, I am sure they will become as bad.)

So has football got better or worse over the years?

Well, in my humble opinion it has got worse. On the positive side, the stadiums are generally a hell of a lot better and the violence that happened up and down the country week after week has reduced dramatically.

But that is about all I can think of that has improved.

I have never considered myself as working class, but I think that the game has moved away from this massive group of people and as a result is has lost something.

I recently went to Millmoor to see Wednesday play a League Cup game at Rotherham and it really brought it home to me that the game has lost so much.

I remember the number of times that I had been squashed into that ground. I have stood on all four sides over the years and although Millmoor has never been a good ground. (It has always been a 'Fourth Division ground'), it was always absolutely heaving when we played there. The atmosphere was always fantastic and I have such wonderful memories of encounters there. A tight little ground where the fans would be breathing down players necks. It was always a fantastic place to go.

Yet in 2007 it seemed a shadow of the place. The ground itself doesn't seem to have changed much, bar for seats where standing used to be and a half finished new stand along the side. Yet the atmosphere was nothing. There was no 'electricity,' No passion. No real noise. No buzz. When the goals were scored, yes there were cheers, but it didn't seem to mean the same to everyone.

Maybe I am just getting older, but it has definitely lost something in my opinion.

Attendances would probably contradict all this, as they have steadily increased over the years, but this is not scientific research. It is just my opinion.

There is still passion there, but now it seems to be reserved for the games that have more meaning.

I live in West Yorkshire, so have come to develop quite a dislike for L**ds.

Not exactly surprising as no one in Sheffield likes L**ds (no one in the country likes L**ds!- Ed), but to put it in perspective, 99.5% of hatred is for the pigs, with the remaining 0.5% reserved for L**ds.

When Wednesday played there towards the end of the 2006-2007 season, I obviously went to Elland Road.

It was a great day, meting up with the lads and having quite a few beers in a pub packed with Wednesdayites before the game and then Wednesday cruising to an easy win. Wednesday hadn't been in good form before the game, so it was with great joy that Chris Brunt lobbed their keeper from about 35 yards to put us 2 - 0 up. In fact I was so pleased I took my shirt off and threw it!

I had never had any desire to celebrate any goal in such a fashion until this moment, so God knows why I did! Fortunately the people around me were so scared by the sight of me topless, that they demanded the return of the shirt, pronto!

That was a good afternoon. Wednesday had sold their allocation of 6,000 (something that L**ds never do when they come to Hillsborough. Just over 2,000 came to Hillsborough that same season, a mere five games after their Premiership play off final defeat to Watford)) and totally enjoyed taking the piss out of a silent Elland Road for 89 minutes (I didn't enjoy injury time too much though as we managed to convert a 3-0 lead with one minute remaining to 3-2 and hanging on with only 10 men at full time.)

But it was nice to see that the passion is still there.

Talking about L**ds has brought me nicely onto my soap box for the last time too. Isn't it criminal when there is so much money floating around in the game, that clubs are still on the verge of going out of business.

L**ds escaped their recent brush with administration and continue to exist. I know they were rightly punished for this, as were Rotherham, Bournemouth etc but there is something wrong about wiping out your debts for the sake of a few points. Personally I am proud that Wednesday have soldiered on with the debt we have. I would hate to give up the "1867" and all the history that goes with it. Yes I know Sheffield Wednesday would still keep playing as Sheffield Wednesday 2010 or whatever, but that 1867 is very much part of what being Wednesday is all about.

Other clubs like Scarborough weren't so lucky. They went out of business owing 'just' £2.5 million. Why on earth did this happen, when there is obscene amounts of money in the Premier League

There are so many clubs in major financial difficulties including a lot of 'bigger' clubs.

They say that even the bottom club in the Premiership will earn over £50 million for one season. Even my poor maths makes that way over £1 billion slopping around in the Premiership.

Why don't the FA take some of this money and distribute it to the lower leagues?

I am not saying that clubs shouldn't be accountable for their own situations, but something must be done to safeguard the future of the game.

With the amount of foreign players coming here just for the money, I seriously wonder about the future of the English national team.

There is talk about creating a two tier Premier League, which in a lot of ways makes sense. I would bring Rangers and Celtic down to join as this would bring a lot more interest to the dull SOF that dominate and the PL2 would also be a lot more competitive and interesting. The whole thing makes so much sense that it surely won't happen.

The thing that makes me so angry about the Premier League situation is that no one seems to be in control of what is happening. The SOF just keep getting more and more of the money and the gap keeps widening, making it more and more boring. Really, what is the point of it all?

As I said before I think it would be better all round if they formed a European League and we got rid of these plastic TV clubs and surely this will happen. The SOF will keep on getting greedier and will chase the money wherever it is. Let them bloody well go and freshen up our stale leagues

It would also be good to revamp the League cup too and combine it with the Scottish equivalent. The competition could be regionalised until, say the Quarter finals and then the remaining English and Scottish teams could be drawn together. This would bring a whole new vitality to what has now become an unloved competition.

A SOFless British cup and Premiership would give a new vibrance and see the silverware spread out again.

239

My club seems to keep going through its usual ups and downs, downs and more downs again, but then that's what football fans know happens.

At least we seem to have got our club back, following some very turbulent times.

When the Chairman calls fans "cretins and scum" and the club starts suing its own fans, you know things aren't right to say the least. There were even rumours that the SWFC board had been infiltrated by blades under the stewardship of ex chairman, Dave Allen. The club was going backwards, with our best players being sold, the squad being drastically cut to the bones, fans sued and abused and the biggest single hike in match day prices in the clubs history, following a last day escape from the third division. Attendances obviously plummeted and the club appeared in total disarray. I think nearly all fans would agree that this was one of the lowest points in the clubs proud history. Forget someone breaking in to the ground and painting the goal posts blue and white, taking over your rivals boardroom would be the ultimate coupe de gras!

Fortunately for us we have had a mini revolution in the board room in 2008-09 and relationships between club and supporters have been restored to what they should always be.

It is funny actually that during that spell of discord, Wednesday were linked with a multi million pound buy out. If I am honest I was very excited at first. The thought of years of struggle being behind us and with a reported £50million per season being poured into the club, it would inevitably lead to us being part of the "big five," Cup glory, European adventures, etc. etc., but you know what, it also scared me.

Because with all that success comes the inevitable woodwork fans and glory hunters and the thought that I would lose "my" club. Sure it would be great fun storming the Championship and hurtling up the league but at what price?

I am sorry, I just can't put my finger on what it is, but the real Sheffield Wednesday would get lost in the money men's takeover and I'm really not sure I want that. I love my trips to Hillsborough, sharing the experience with real die hard supporters that have Wednesday in their blood. I don't want a new 70,000 seater stadium to accommodate all the new plastic fans. I don't want to be a Chelsea or Liverpool that has a team full of foreign mercenaries and w***er type fans from all over the country.

As it transpired there was no multi million pound Abramovic type buy out. We got our takeover with two honest guys in Nick Parker and

Lee Strafford, who I believe have Wednesday in their hearts, their feet firmly on the ground and with good business sense will ultimately take the club back to where it should be, without selling its soul.

Sadly what happens off the pitch has become more important than what happens on the pitch, as this ultimately dictates what happens to your club.

You only need to look at what happened to us, L**ds, Southampton etc to see that.

Conversely, look at crappy little clubs such as Bolton, Fulham and Wigan that have established themselves in the Premiership by getting things right off the field.

Football is always changing and so things that I have put in here will soon be out of date and make me look stupid. Lets all hope that it is the bit about England not winning anything.

Come on Mr. Capello!

Are fans treated any better now than in the Seventies?

Well, maybe so in that facilities are much better, but most clubs still take advantage of the loyalty of supporters, in a way that other industries wouldn't dare to.

I have a friend who is a genuine Man United supporter and has had a season ticket at Old Trafford for about twenty years. He is now getting to the stage where it is becoming a serious financial problem for him to keep going to games. His season ticket is now over £900 and he also *HAS* to pay for tickets for all domestic and European home games, as part of the conditions for his season ticket. This is way too much and football is slowly losing its established customer base.

Police attitude to supporters has improved a lot too, but a recent incident at a game at Grimsby in 2004 summed a lot up.

Someone I know of was with a group of known Wednesday hooligans in a pub before the game. The Police were keeping a close eye on them, so when this lad wanted to leave to go and put a bet on for the Grand National, he was stopped from leaving. He was quite an intelligent lad, so when he reasoned with the police man that his refusal to let him leave, infringed on his human rights, he was told;

"You are a football supporter. You have no rights. Now get back in the f***ing pub before I arrest you."

Sadly this still sums up the attitude towards most fans.

So after all the heartache, all the agro, all the money involved in watching our teams, why do we do it?

241

Certainly at times I have seriously questioned it. There is part of me that wishes I wasn't tied to this club, that I could just stop going and not care. But I can't. I hate walking down Penistone Road at five o'clock on a Saturday (that wouldn't be a problem in the Premier League as no bugger kicks off at three o'clock on a Saturday anymore!) after another defeat and everything in the world seems wrong, yet I still go back. And that is because when they win, no matter how poor they have played, how fortunate to get the result, it makes everything in the world fantastic.

It is like a drug.

At one time I had travelled to 81 of the 92 league grounds to see Wednesday play, but now it is hard to say how many I have been to. Clubs like Halifax, York and Oxford are no longer in the league. Whereas clubs like Scunthorpe, Arsenal or Walsall are no longer at the same ground, so how do you count those?

I guess the 92 club will be elusive to me now.

In my time watching Wednesday I have ventured all over the country. I have done daft things like go to Aldershot, Bournemouth, Brighton and Cheltenham for night matches. We once went to Torquay on a Friday night for a pre season friendly. We still laugh about the gate man that night.

One of the lads used to show his Police card at the gate and they would let him in without paying. I don't know why, but it works at most grounds up and down the country. Better than American Express.

The gateman asked if me and Steve were in the Police too, so we said yes, but had forgot our cards. He begrudgingly let us in without paying with the words "and next time you must show your cards." How we laughed. "Next time!" As if mighty Premier League Sheffield Wednesday would ever play Fourth Division Torquay again!

But, you know what, just a few years later we had tumbled down the division and the Gulls got promoted so were playing them in the League.

As Greavsie would say, "it's a funny old game!"

There have been so many people that have come and joined our travelling band of followers and have all subsequently moved on but every one of them have brought their own personality and contributed to the great adventure.

I thank every one of them for making it the most amazing time.

As for me, well I have still got a season ticket in the North Stand and I still love going.

I had a spell when David Pleat took over, when I lost my passion for the game and strangely it took relegation to the Third Division (now called First Division) to get that pride and desire back.

I still get the old butterflies in the stomach before a game, when it is time to set off, with a mixture of hope and dread. I love the ritual of having a couple of pints in The Travellers before the game and so many times, that is the best part of the afternoon. We have had many a good afternoon ruined by going to the match, rather than stopping in the pub, but we will keep going, in the hope of that win which will make everything in the world right.

And when Wednesday are hanging on to a one goal lead with just minutes left and my nerves are in shreds, I will still turn round to Mark and say, "you know what, I bloody well hate football."

John would love to hear from you with any comments good or bad.

We would love to do an IHF 2 so if you have any weird or funny stories you want to share please contact us and we will get back to you as soon as we can.

www.peakpublish.com

New Titles From Peak Platform

 ## Jumping Fish - Fiction

Boji the Dolphin
by
Robert Alan-Havers
In Search of Independence

Dead Head
by
Chris F Coley
The book that OFSTED
will want to ban

It's Just Not Village Cricket
by
Philip Algar

**Selected Short Stories by
Bolwar Mahamad Kunhi**
Translated work by award-winning
Indian Writer

 ## Peakpublish - Non-fiction

peakpublish

India Calls
by
Sudhindra Mokhasi
True Call Centre Stories

Just Call Me Daisy
by
Lyndsey Bradley
Breast-feeding
Mothers' Stories

Playing for England
by
John Hemmingham
The England Supporters

**Coaldust to
Stardust**
by
Jackie Toaduff
Billy Elliot Pales in
comparison

The Best of France
by
Trevor Snow
8 Self-drive
Themed Tours

**344 A story of the
Pretoria Pit Disaster**
by
Andrea Jane Finney

Visit Peakplatform.com for more information